AT THE SIGN OF THE CUPID & LION

MEMOIRS OF A NAPOLEONIC OFFICER

By JEAN-BAPTISTE BARRÈS

Edited, with an introduction, by his grandson, MAURICE BARRÈS

8vo. Cloth. Printed jacket. $4.00

New light on Napoleon is always interesting. Recently Maurice Barrès, the famous French novelist, unearthed some remarkable manuscripts of one of his ancestors who enlisted in the Guard under the Consulate, was at Eylau, Austerlitz and Leipsic, and in the terrible retreat after that last disastrous battle. He was then promoted officer and transferred to the line. He gives a stirring account of the 1830 revolution in Paris, where he was stationed at the time.

M. Barrès prepared the manuscript for the press and contributed a preface; it is here printed for the first time in English, providing new thrills for the ever-growing number of readers of Napoleonic literature.

LINCOLN MAC VEAGH
THE DIAL PRESS
152 W. 13th St.   New York

MEMOIRS OF A NAPOLEONIC OFFICER

MEMOIRS OF A NAPOLEONIC OFFICER JEAN-BAPTISTE BARRÈS

Edited, and with an Introduction, by his Grandson
MAURICE BARRÈS

Translated by BERNARD MIALL

LINCOLN MAC VEAGH
THE DIAL PRESS
NEW YORK · MCMXXV

CONTENTS

	PAGE
MY GRANDFATHER (PREFACE BY MAURICE BARRÈS)	9
THE ABBÉ PIERRE-MAURICE BARRÈS	25
THE EMPIRE	29
MY ADMISSION TO THE SKIRMISHERS OF THE GUARD	30
ARRIVAL IN PARIS	32
THE CORONATION OF THE EMPEROR	38
THE PRESENTATION OF THE EAGLES	40
AN EVENING AT THE PALAIS-ROYAL	41
DEPARTURE FOR ITALY	42
I DECIDE TO KEEP A DIARY	43
WE RETURN TO FRANCE	52
PARIS	53
LEAVING PARIS FOR THE GERMAN CAMPAIGN	55
OUR ENTRY INTO GERMANY	58
AUSTERLITZ	74
SEVEN MONTHS AT RUEIL	81
WAR AGAINST PRUSSIA	83
JENA	86
THE EMPEROR ENTERS BERLIN	89
GOING TO MEET THE RUSSIANS	93
EYLAU	98
THE EMPEROR TASTES MY BREAD	106

PAGE

HEILSBERG 107

FRIEDLAND 109

TILSIT 111

BACK TO FRANCE 115

TRIUMPHAL ENTRY OF THE GUARD INTO PARIS 119

I AM APPOINTED SUB-LIEUTENANT 123

NINETEEN MONTHS IN FRANCE 126

SPAIN AND PORTUGAL 134

CAMPAIGNS OF 1813 AND 1814 159

I RECEIVE THE LEGION OF HONOUR 164

THE TWO BATTLES OF BAUTZEN 164

DRESDEN 173

THE DISASTER OF LEIPZIC 180

SIEGE OF MAYENCE 197

THE FIRST RESTORATION 202

THE RETURN TO FRANCE 202

THE HUNDRED DAYS 208

THE SECOND RESTORATION 212

THE WHITE TERROR 214

BARRÈS IS PUT ON HALF-PAY 220

AT THE ARCHBISHOP OF BORDEAUX' 225

FROM SAINT-OMER TO NANCY. THE DANCES OF SAINT-MIHIEL 228

AT NANCY 229

MY MARRIAGE 230

CHARLES X 234

A SESSION OF THE FRENCH ACADEMY 238

IN THE PLAINE DE GRENELLE 240

THE REVOLUTION OF 1830 246

THE ORDINANCES OF JULY 246

CONTENTS

PAGE

THE THREE GLORIOUS DAYS :—27TH JULY 247

28TH JULY 251

29TH JULY 259

ADHESION TO THE NEW GOVERNMENT 267

THE JULY MONARCHY 275

THE ROYAL FAMILY 276

REVIEW OF THE NATIONAL GUARD 277

THE DUC D'AUMALE AT EIGHT YEARS OF AGE 279

STROLLS IN PARIS 280

AT THE DUC DE DOUDEAUVILLE'S 284

FROM METZ TO WISSEMBOURG 286

SCHOLASTIC DIFFICULTIES IN ALSACE 289

ALSACE ACCLAIMS THE CITIZEN-KING 291

INSURRECTIONS AT STRASBOURG AND LYONS 296

THE CHOLERA OF 1832 298

A DAY OF REVOLUTION 299

LIFE AT STRASBOURG 301

AFTER THIRTY YEARS' SERVICE 303

INDEX 311

MY GRANDFATHER

THREE manuscript-books in stiff covers, obtained from " Wiener, papetier, Rue des Dominicains, 53, à Nanci," their many pages covered with an easy and legible script, already much faded with the years : such are the volumes into which my grandfather Barrès, officer of the Grand Army, having retired to Charmes-sur-Moselle, carefully transcribed the dozens of little note-books, tattered and soiled, which he had carried about with him, in his haversack, for twenty years, over half the highways of Europe. " Itinerary " is the precise title which he gave these records : " Itinerary and recollections of a soldier who became a superior officer (Barrès, Jean-Baptiste Auguste), born at Blesle (Haute-Loire) on the 25th July, 1784 ; or succinct picture of the days of march and sojourn in towns and villages, in garrison or on passage, in camps and cantonments, in France and also Germany, Poland, Prussia, Italy, Spain and Portugal, from my entry into the service on the 27th June, 1804, to the 6th June, 1835, the date of my admission to retirement on half-pay."

I have always seen them, those greenish exercise-books, the colour of the uniform of the Chasseurs of the Guard ; the colour, too, of the laurels of Apollo which I admired eight years ago in the vale of Daphne, near Syrian Antioch. When I was a child my father showed them to me ; and when a big lad I was given them to read. If the truth must be told, I used to bend over them with more good-will than pleasure. I felt that I had, there in my hands, something for which my father entertained a pious affection, and that at his death I should receive it as his most precious legacy; something that belonged to him, my sister and myself, and to no one else. But in those days I went no farther; I did not feel my profound kinship with my grandfather. Only time can teach us to discern the foundations of our being. Now this recognition is complete; I do not distinguish between myself and those who preceded me in the family, and assuredly their last moments are nearer to me than many of the days and years that I myself have lived, which inspire me only with the most fastidious indifference.

This Sunday morning, the first morning of my annual visit to Charmes, I have just been taking the walk beside the Moselle that my father and my grandfather used to take. The fresh youth of the landscape was dazzling; its silent background tragic. Beside the river the shouts of children were scaring the fish; the birds were singing with none to hearken; the bells of the village were ringing furiously, scattering at random their age-long summons. I finished my morning by going to the cemetery to hold converse with my kinsfolk.

The inscriptions on their tombs remind me that my grandfather died at sixty-four, and all my people died at about that age; they warn me that it is time for me to set my affairs in order. " How comfortable we shall be there ! " that delightful madman Jules Soury used sensibly to say, when he went to Montparnasse to visit his mother's tomb. But this profound repose reveals its smiling countenance only to those who have completely fulfilled their task and carried out their programme. Now I begin to feel that time is hurrying me a little.

I should like before I die to give an idea of all the images with which I have been most pre-occupied. To what does this instinct correspond ? It is the most general thing in the world. It is, I think, the result of a sort of piety, which impels us to declare our gratitude to the most beautiful things we have known in the course of our life. We want to define ourselves, to pay our debts, to sing our song of thanskgiving. In truth, a doubtful explanation ; but we have, here, a very vague impulse of veneration, a sort of hymn that we murmur on the brink of the grave. I have always planned to make for myself, under the title " What I owe," a brief list of the obligations which I have contracted, in the course of my life, toward persons and circumstances. If I am an artist, a poet, I have but played the music that lay in the hearts of my forbears and in the countryside whose air I breathed even before my birth. All that I know of my father and my mother confirms this conviction. What are my books ? I have written a little of Spain and of Asia ; I have laboured to defend the French spirit against the influence of Germany ; I have praised Lorraine. Well, I have seen my father brood, enchanted, all his life, over the images which he brought back from a journey made about 1850 to Algeria, Tunis and Malta. My veneration for the army, for the genius of the Emperor, and for military glory seem to prolong the emotions that my grandfather felt, and the dazzling memories that remained to him, amidst all the hardships of a soldier's life, from certain mornings in Spain and Portugal. His experiences are the taproot that has nourished my books with a sap whose latent romanticism was reabsorbed beforehand by his robust sense of life. Lastly, if I have spoken much, it may be overmuch (or so my best friends have sometimes laughingly told me), of the things that I have seen under the skies of Charmes, I was following the example of my great-grandfather Barrès (the father of the writer of these *Memoirs*), who published a monograph on the canton in which he too lived.[1] Of all the ideas to which I have devoted myself none is more rooted in me than the sense of my dependence on my family and my countryside. I have my own life, truly, but it is bounded by my four

---

[1] *Description topographique du ci-devant canton de Blesle*, au Puy, an IX.

seasons and attached to a collectivity that is stronger than I.

These are my dreams in the cemetery, beside my parents' tomb. A few tall poplars adorn this field of repose, and I watch them shivering in the wind. In the distant country-side the same gust of wind sets moving the woods of the hillsides and the orchards of plum-trees. Each one of us is like a leaf of one of those trees. We are eager to win an increase of sap and of light, and then, of a sudden, comes detachment and death.

I am publishing the *Memoirs* of J.-B. Barrès so that they may serve as the preface to and the elucidation of all that I have written. A young man is torn away, uprooted, by the shocks of the Revolution, from a little town in which his forbears have lived, to their knowledge, for five hundred years. He roams the world, gathering memories of things that must have impressed him all the more in that he belonged to a sedentary race, and then, in the end, he returned to strike root once more in the heart of a Lorraine family and a little town just like his own family and his native town. Such was my grand-father ; such the origin of that handful of ideas and feelings to which I am so monotonously faithful.

*   *   *   *   *

Born at Blesle, in Auvergne, in 1784, my grandfather J.-B. Barrès sleeps at Charmes, in Lorraine, under a slab of the Vosges sandstone, with the date 1849. This is the only displacement that I know of which my family has accomplished since the fifteenth century. From father to son we have desired to " see the light, live, and die in the same house," in this little town of Blesle, where, as notaries and physicians, we go back to a Pierre Barrès, a document of whose, dated 1489, is now in the possession of the learned and scholarly Paul le Blanc. Before the day of this Pierre Barrès we were at Saint-Fleur, where another Pierre-Maurice Barrès played his part in the Hundred Years' War, and, far back in the centuries, we came from that old " Barrès country," the *pagus Barrensis* of the Merovingian castularies, which are sprinkled with such names as Murrat-de-Barrès, Lacapelle-Barrès, Mur de Barrès, Lacroix Barrès, and from which we probably took our name.[1] This secular refuge, this stronghold of the central table-land, my grandfather exchanged for a refuge no less ancient when he took his place at the hearth of a Lorraine family as sedentary as his own. Yes; " in the days when the French did not like one another," when my youthful comrades of the *Revue blanche* requested Herr, the famous librarian of the École Normale, to draw up in their name, against me, a bull of excommunication, they had sufficient intuition to scorn me as the typical product of the small French town. I am happy in being just that.

I did not know my grandfather ; he died thirteen years before I was born ; but many aged persons have spoken to me of him, in Charmes, who remember his friendly but rather severe and ceremonious manner.

In those days our little eastern towns were full of the veteran officers of the Grand Army. At Charmes, at the same period, I had another ancestor, my mother's grandfather, who likewise had served in the wars of the Empire, but left no memoirs. It was with such men that Erckmann-Chatrian used to talk. I am sure that in order to write their *Conscrit de 1813* the two Lorrainer novelists must have had at their disposal documents like that which I am publishing. They would only have needed to take the first few pages of J.-B. Barrès' diary, telling of him on the march, as a young volunteer, from de Puy to Paris, his

---

[1] *Les Ancêtres auvergnats de Maurice Barrès*, by Ulysse Rouchon, publ. Champion ; *Bulletin historique et scientifique de l'Auvergne*, 1907, Nos. 7 and 8 : Address by M. Marcellin Boudet on the reception of M. Maurice Barrès into the Académie of Clermont-Ferrand ; the " Origines auvergnates de Maurice Barrès," in *Paris-Auvergne*, 4th February, 1906.

first sight of General Bonaparte in the courtyard of the Louvre, his installation in the barracks of Rueil, to add a masterpiece to their national series.

For these pensioners of the Grand Army the people of Lorraine had a great regard. They adopted them without reservations. Born at Charmes of a father who was born there, surrounded by the kinsfolk of my mother and grandmother, who belonged from time immemorial to this little town, I never suspected during my childhood that there was a bond between me and another territory, nor do I find that my grandfather, when a widower, thought of returning to his father's countryside. He had made his wife's home his own, and when once he had completed his *Itinerary* he began to write, in succession, a history of the province of Auvergne and a history of the duchy of Lorraine.

He was a man who had more education than instruction, but a very keen and curious mind. I spent my early years as a reader in turning over the leaves of his books and those that he bought for his little boy, his only son, my father. I was formed by their Walter Scotts and Fennimore Coopers. Formerly I thought his *Itinerary* was lacking in literary merit. That is no longer my opinion. My grandfather tells with perfect clearness what he has seen, and sometimes says delightful things. One might think that his attention was wholly confined to the cares of service and the horizon of the march and halting-place, but here and there a different note reveals the fact that there were other things in his mind. I like his gaiety when, as a young soldier of twenty years, on the eve of the battle of Jena, chance quartered his squad in a girls' school : " The birds had flown, leaving their feathers : their pianos, guitars, part of their wearing apparel, charming sketches, some engravings and books. . . ." I like the memory he preserves of a moment in Germany, on the morrow of the terrible days of Leipzic :

" I saw in the village of Ober-Thomaswald, for the only time in my life, *a kind of rose-tree whose wood and leafage smelt of roses*, like the flower itself, which was very lovely." And it pleases me that as an old man he should have retained in his Charmes transcription the ingenuous trait he had recorded in his Friedland note-book, the weakness for appearances characteristic of every young Frenchman : " Our fur bonnets had become hideous and repulsive. They were replaced. I had the good fortune to light on *a bearskin that was as fine as those of the officers !* " And his sensibility is not that of the imagination, but the more profound and nobler sensibility of the heart. At Lutzen he writes : " Our young con-scripts behaved very well. Not one of them left the ranks, and there were some there who had been left in the rear because they were sick, but who came to take their places in the ranks. One of our buglers, a boy of sixteen, was of their number. He had a thigh carried away by a bullet and died at the rear of the company. *These poor children, when they were wounded so that they could not march, came to me to ask leave to fall out of the company to get their wounds attended to.* This was an abnegation of life, a submission to their superior, which touched me even more deeply than it astonished."

*　　*　　*　　*　　*

I will call a halt. It is not my business to analyse this *Itinerary*, since the essential portions are in these pages, to be read. It is the memorial of a whole life. I am compelled to omit a multitude of daily entries, but I leave sufficient to enable the reader to accompany J.-B. Barrès on his chief route-marches and his campaigns. We may witness the cheerful departure of the young man when he leaves his father's roof, at the age when the curiosity is keenest ; we shall enter with interest into the many glimpses that a Chasseur of the Imperial Guard must

necessarily have had of the great man, of whom he was
privileged, moreover, on several occasions to receive the
directly spoken words ; we shall hear him tell of his
battles and his fatigues ; we shall come to know his
profound sense of duty and honour, a sense whose expression
is in no wise lyrical or theatrical ; but how definite it is,
and how real ! In 1815 we shall see him on half-pay.
The arrogance of the émigrés on their return, and the
affronts which some of them were foolish enough to lavish
on men whose nobility and virtue had won titles as fine
as those of the Crusaders, are depicted by my grandfather
with a multitude of little touches, such as it did not enter
into Balzac's programme to amass, but which are worthy
of that great historian of manners, and which point to
the very great difficulties which a monarchical restoration
would encounter in France. The king returned in 1815
with his title and prestige secure ; he represented the
authority of which all felt the need. But what useful
purpose was served by this host of nobles, reduced to
reconquering, one by one, by their pride and their knowledge of the world, the rank which they no longer occupied
outside their imaginings ?   The ruler is the man of whom
all have need, and he is a ruler in proportion as others
feel themselves incapable of replacing him.   J.-B. Barrès
helps us to understand that the Frenchmen of 1815 did
not in the least know what to do with their dukes, mar-
quises, counts and viscounts, and that it was precisely
this perplexity which led the latter to behave with a
pride that was intolerable, committing actions of which,
I fancy, they would never have dreamed in an environment
of unanimous acceptance and real activity. The revolution
of 1830 was less a rebellion of France against her king than
of every Frenchman against a returned aristocrat.

Finally, we read of my grandfather's marriage ; then
of his retirement and his settling down in the midst of
his wife's family ; and then we come to his last words,

his philosophy of life, and the moral of the tale. He was a soldier of the Grand Army ; one of those great and simple men who are the eternal treasure of our race.

He is an example of the kind of men whom the small towns of France were producing at the close of the eighteenth century. We could not possess a more reliable and efficient instrument for the tasks of a great civilization. While fashionable society, Paris, and Versailles had lost their inward equilibrium, what a fine type of man our provinces were still producing !—a type whose physical and moral energies are always ready to expend themselves with a controlled energy. No uneasiness, no hesitation, no weariness, no " sickness of the age," but an abundant store of quiet strength. No one who had not read these pages would have thought it possible to live a life so varied, so full of danger, so near the greatest genius of the age, and yet to retain this exactitude of mind, sensible and severe, and perfectly harmonious.

It was not that Barrès was immune to the Emperor's power of charming men and sweeping them off their feet. Read his account of the scene which he witnessed on the eve of Austerlitz, when, in the bivouac where his men were sleeping, Napoleon suddenly appeared out of the night, holding in his hand a letter : " One of us took up a handful of straw and lit it to enable him to read it. From our bivouac he went to another. The soldiers followed him with blazing torches, shouting ' Long live the Emperor ! ' These cries of love and enthusiasm spread in all directions like an electric flash ; all the soldiers, non-commissioned officers and officers provided themselves with improvised torches, so that for leagues, from our front to our rear, there was a general blaze, which must have dazzled the Emperor." That was what my grandfather saw : the genius enveloped in the blaze of love and enthusiasm. And on the following day, when, with his comrades of the Guards, Barrès climbed the heights of the plateau to enter into battle with the cry of " Vive l'Empereur ! " the Emperor himself addressed them. " After making a sign to us with his hand that he wished to speak to us, he said, in a clear, vibrating voice which thrilled us through : ' Chasseurs, my Horse Guards have just routed the Russian Imperial Guard. Colonels, flags, guns, all have been captured. Nothing could resist their intrepid valour. You will imitate them.' He passed on immediately to give the same news to the other battalions." Such minutes set their seal on a whole race. But this boy of twenty, this soldier of the Imperial Guard, comes into contact with this multiplier of enthusiasm without allowing himself to be in any way perturbed. He depicts for us scenes that are the starting-point of a whole romanticism, and stores up their memory, without a single theatrical word, in the sanctuary of his heart. All are stirred to the depths of their being, but even in their first amazement they do not break down their native reserve ; the lyrical harvest will be for a later season ; all through the nineteenth century these unparalleled moments will return like phantoms to arouse the sons of heroes and prevent them from sleeping. What a mystic food ! What rich treasures, and how justly proportioned ! What a preparation for radiant heat and brilliance ! Of what a sacrament did our fathers partake !

Thus was romanticism born (which I, for my poor part, have endeavoured to judge and elucidate, without ever ceasing to respect its originative ardours), or here at least were its first preliminaries. It is a remarkable fact that my grandfather and his brothers in arms, while they brought into the world the essential elements of this fever, themselves betrayed no symptom of it. Stendhal has said the great thing : Napoleon set all this youth to work. . . . Action absorbed it to the point of suppressing all nostalgia. In the perils and hideous fatigues of war the soldier of the *épopée* may sometimes turn about, with

pained astonishment, if an insult is offered to his heroes ;
but as a general thing these noble men lived side by side
through the same dream, in the high satisfaction of being
the conquerors, crowned with laurels. They turned away
from every-day reality, that often appeared in so dismal
a light, to intoxicate themselves with the sense of honour.
They had their lofty conception of themselves, the resound-
ing testimony to their glory in the Emperor's bulletins,
and the admiration of all when they returned to Paris
and their families. Melancholy and isolation, those
indispensable conditions of romanticism, made their
appearance only after Waterloo and under the Restoration,
when, having become " the brigands of the Loire," and
half-pay soldiers, they endured with amazement humilia-
tions which they knew they had not deserved. After 1815
the soldiers of the Grand Army were profoundly troubled
by the feeling that they had not received their due, and
that they were cruelly out of tune with society, and it
was then that things assumed, for them, a new and a
tragic rhythm. They were acquainted with moral isolation. Great memories ; a humiliated, solitary heart ; by
this time romanticism had acquired its two chiefest motives.
But before its blossoms could appear time had yet to do
its work and distance give rise to mirage.

These noble soldiers of the Grand Army, these great
peasants, if I see them rightly, were spirits of circum-
scribed enthusiasms. There is not a word of a " life
beyond " in the memoirs of my grandfather ; no religious
pre-occupation. Had the Imperial Guard chaplains ?
I do not know, having read these pages. It would seem
that Baron Larrey, the celebrated surgeon, had to suffice
for the dying needs of these heroes. These initiators of
mighty dreams are prodigiously rooted in the actual. My
grandfather's desire for advancement is eminently sensible.
Advancement is the reward of seniority, of wounds, of
the opportunities of distinction that war may afford and

protectors favour. It was later that men's dynamic energies, unchained, were oriented upon this epoch, a time when all merits, it was imagined, received from thc Master an immense and immediate reward. The lucid Stendhal himself, in his life of a functionary of the Empire, shows us none but material and short-sighted desires for success in his career ; he wanted an income of four thousand livres and every woman he encountered. This is not the scheme of a great life. He is entirely absorbed by his petty, comfortable sensualities, the pleasures of garrison life, the interest and the tedium of his changes of residence. We are far from the days when his Julien Sorel, deprived of a social setting and launched into the infinity of desire, was to see in the *Memorial de Sainte-Hélène* a book of inspiration, a breviary of energy. De Vigny still speaks with repugnance of a feeling that had grown up about Napoleon, which he styles fanaticism : the idea that all would go well if one were faithful to the chief ; that one would then be favoured with rank, decorations, gifts and titles. Senancour compares the Emperor to an Asiatic conqueror who holds that all things and persons should be in their appointed place : horses, battle-cars, warriors, priests, and so forth. For the actors of the incomparable epic only reality counted ; and if any thrill of a deeper emotion was felt, it was only in danger confronted, in discipline accepted, in the accomplishment of the daily task. Twenty years later it was another matter. About 1827 the mirage was already formed ; the past was becoming a source of inspiration. Prestige was an established fact. The sun of romanticism had risen in the heavens of the imagination, with its real effective power and all its drawbacks.

The sons of his warriors did not at once deify their Cæsar. At their first glance they were rather a trifle scandalized. The intermediate period had been so cruel ; France was bled white, and the Allies imposed upon her

a law which she seemed to have forgotten.   See how long
it was before Victor Hugo began to regard in a romantic
light the services to the State of his father!   First of all
he evoked images of his mother.   He proposed to re-erect
the statue of Henri IV;   he celebrated Quiberon and La
Vendée.   His father had captured Fra Diavolo, had been
aide de camp to King Joseph in Spain, had progressed in
a cloud of glory through Prussia and Austria;   but the
young poet was more ready to be influenced by his brother-
in-law, M. Foucher, a mere functionary, an *embusqué*,
head clerk in the Ministry of War.   He did not see what
the men of *Après la bataille* and *Le Cimetière d'Eylau* had
to offer him until General Hugo lent him his *Memoirs*
and invited him to go and have a talk with him at Blois.
Then indeed he was fired, and with him all his generation.
As for the actual combatants, it would seem that the
love of action and a primitive positivism held them back
to the very end from any kind of transfiguration.

May these explanations throw a little light on the
spiritual origins of the generations with whom we have
made the journey through life, and enable us to forecast
the mysterious influence that may be exerted in ten years'
time, on the French genius, by the Great War which we
have lately witnessed!   Ferments whose leaven is not
yet active are at work for our sons in the filled-in trenches.

*   *   *   *   *

I am publishing these *Memoirs* at the age when my
grandfather completed the work of transcribing them in
their final form.   I have corrected the proofs instead of
re-copying them.   It was at Charmes, a century ago, that
he completed his *Itinerary,* and within the same horizon
I am beginning the story of my life, its intellectual itinerary.
I am editing his notes of the stages of his life, written in
the dawn of the nineteenth century, in order to set them
as a preface before all that I have accomplished.   But I

have not done this because I am closely preoccupied with
myself; I am sated with myself, and have ceased to be
interested in my own modes of feeling, which have inconve-
nienced and imprisoned me for sixty years; I wish rather
to publish a document that belongs to the life of the nation.
Memoirs of this nature constitute a corner-stone of the
national House of Life.   Considering them at a century's
distance, I am stirred, when I perceive how completely in
accord was this modest soldier with so many noble minds
that to him remained unknown; whom he was not
destined to encounter, yet who thought as he did; living,
all unwittingly, within touch of one another.   When I
read what my grandfather tells us of the day of consecration when he helped to line the streets as the Emperor
went by, I think of what André-Marie Ampère wrote that
same evening, after watching the Imperial procession.
The sight of a standard that hung in tatters, rent in the
wars, and the " cold hands, painful, to-day, for those who
are under arms," [1] are the things that impress themselves
on this great thinker, this fine genius, with his noble
sensibility.   He has a thought, the thought of one unknown for another to him unknown, for my grandfather;
and I, a hundred years later, feel an impulse of affection
for André-Marie Ampère and his son Jean-Jacques.   It
is thus that the conception of the motherland takes shape
in one's heart.

Again, such memoirs are an excellent aid to the under-
standing of what a French family really is; to following
the curve of the national spirit and discerning the true
political pattern of France.   What, essentially, do we
see in these pages?   I repeat: a child of the central
table-land, wrested by the turmoil of the Revolution from
the soil of which he had been for centuries a part, in which

---

[1] The passages cited in this Introduction are not always identical with
the corresponding passages in the text, as they are not in every instance
drawn from the same version of the Diary.—Tr.

his forbears had struck root, ever since the days of Roman Gaul; who for long years was a defender of France one and indivisible, until the tide of events led him to settle on the very confines of the country he had served; in that Lorraine where he founded a family.

It is my hope that this book, if time permits, will be elucidated by others which will serve to complete it. In the memoirs of my childhood I shall have occasion to comment on some letters of my mother's and father's in my possession which tell how the Prussians came to Charmes in 1870, and remained until the indemnity of five thousand million francs was paid. It may be that my son will one day, like so many of his comrades, write of his four years of the Great War, which he completed in a mounted battalion of Chasseurs, in the Vosges.

Of such publications, at once glorious and commonplace, there is no French family but can furnish the like, giving plain and tangible evidence of the eternal peril to which France is exposed and the necessity of maintaining our ancient ideal of honour.

MAURICE BARRÈS.

CHARMES,
   17th August, 1922.

THE ABBÉ PIERRE-MAURICE BARRÈS

THERE are several references in these *Memoirs*, from their very outset, to my grandfather's elder brother, my great-uncle Pierre-Maurice Barrès. His was an interesting and a complex personality, of which M. Ulysse Rouchon, not long ago, drew an attractive picture in *Les Débats* :

" Pierre-Maurice Barrès, born at Blesle on the 22nd September, 1766, was one of the last licentiates of the old Sorbonne. He began his priestly studies in the great seminary of Saint-Fleur, and there received the minor orders. Under the constitutional episcopate of his compatriot Delcher, the curé of Brioude, elected, on the 28th February, 1791, Bishop of Haute-Loire, the young cleric, then raised to the diaconate, went to Le Puy, took the oath, and was entrusted, together with the Franciscan brother, Teyssier, and Bonnafox, curé of Lempdes, with the reorganization of the great seminary, abandoned by the nonjuring Sulpicians.

" Circumstances interrupted his term at the great seminary at the end of the year 1792, at which time the management was confided to the vicars episcopal. He then relinquished the habit of the ecclesiastic, and on the organization of the École Centrale of Le Puy he was inducted, at his own request, by a municipal decree of the 3rd Frimaire of the year V, into the chair of Belles-Lettres.

" Barrès was one of the most distinguished and devoted professors of this new college. We find him on the 10th Germinal of the year VII presiding over certain exercises

in eloquence and speaking of the value and the characteristics of true liberty ; and on the 2nd Floréal of the
year VII celebrating the centenary of the death of Racine.

" On the 15th Fructidor of the year XII the masters
and pupils of the École Centrale dispersed ; but Pierre
Barrès had already, five years earlier, been advanced to
a higher office.   At the time of the creation of the prefec-
tures he was appointed, by a decree of the 15th Floréal
of the year VIII, secretary-general of the department of
Haute-Loire.

" For sixteen years the ex-professor was a valued
member of the administration, and without exaggeration
we may say that he bore almost unaided the whole weight
of the department's affairs.   Endowed with a rare activity,
he neglected neither the duties of his office, nor the
pleasures of life, nor social relations.   The most delicate
missions were often confided to him.   In 1812 he went
to Paris in support of the city of Le Puy's right to a *lycée* ;
in 1816 he was sent to Lyons to defend the interests of
the department against the Austrians.   His skilful intervention in the matter of the settlement of the indemnities
due to the troops of occupation won him the cross of the
Legion of Honour.   Having thus reached an eminent
position in his own part of the country, Barrès might
legitimately have cherished higher ambitions, but as the
result of one of those crises of the conscience which are
the appanage of the elect, the ex-cleric, on returning to
Le Puy, presently resigned his office.

" The news caused great astonishment in the district,
and gave rise to much comment ; but already the ex-
secretary-general was at Bordeaux, with his friend Cartal,
the superior of the great seminary.   Eighteen months after
his retirement Mgr. d'Aviau ordained him priest, appointed
him vicar of the parish of Saint-Michel, and, at the same
time, assistant-professor of Moral Philosophy in the
faculty of Theology.   These functions drew attention to

Pierre Barrès, who became grand vicar on the 1st April, 1819.

" A most popular preacher, a celebrated spiritual director, the Abbé was for some years confessor to the Duchesse d'Angoulême. He was no less appreciated as a correspondent, according to the late lamented Canon Pailhès ; and his letters, which were bequeathed, with all his papers, to the Grand Seminaire, should merit a special publication, which would be an event of interest.

" On the 29th April, 1838, he died at Bordeaux, and was buried in the crypt of the primatial church of Saint-André."

Thus the learned scholar, M. Ulysse Rouchon. I may add that we find the name of Pierre-Maurice Barrès in the history of Mme. Fourès, the pretty lady who was Bonaparte's mistress in Egypt.

The Abbé Pailhès, well known for his valuable works on Chateaubriand and Mme. de Chateaubriand, wrote to me saying that he wished to draw my great-uncle's portrait and publish his correspondence. According to him, Pierre Barrès was a profound thinker. I do not know whether he has elucidated the mystery of his life and the enigma of his conversion.

M. B.

MEMOIRS OF A NAPOLEONIC OFFICER

(JEAN-BAPTISTE BARRÈS)

THE EMPIRE

A CONSULAR decree of the 21st March, 1804 (30th Ventôse of the year XII), created a corps of Skirmishers (*vélites*) to form part of the Consular Guard and to be attached to the Chasseurs and Grenadiers à Pied of that crack regiment. Two battalions, each of 800 men, were to be formed, one at Écouen, under the name of *chasseurs vélites*, and one at Fontainebleau, under that of *grenadiers vélites*. In order to gain admission thereto it was necessary to be possessed of some education, to belong to a respectable family, to be at least 5 ft. 2 in. in height, at least twenty years of age, and to pay 200 francs mess-money. The prospects of promotion were not especially attractive, but those acquainted with the mind of the then Government, the warlike propensities of the head of the State, and the First Consul's desire to rally round him men of all opinions, and to make sure of the attachment of all the influential families, believed that under this new name, borrowed from the ancient Romans, he was designing to set up a forcing-house for officers.

In the early part of April my elder brother, secretary-general of the Prefecture of the Department of Haute-Loire, who died, in 1837, vicar-general of the see of

Bordeaux, approached the family and proposed to my father that I should be entered in this privileged corps, of which he had great hopes for the future. The idea of seeing Paris, of learning something of France and perhaps foreign countries, made me at once accept the proposal put before me, without very solemnly considering the serious responsibilities I was about to incur. However, on maturer reflection I was readily able to confirm my spontaneous decision, in spite of all my parents' efforts to dissuade me from entering on a career so arduous and so dangerous.

My Admission to the Skirmishers of the Guard.

On the 18th May (28th Floréal), the day on which Napoleon Bonaparte, First Consul, was proclaimed and saluted as Emperor of the French, the Minister for War, Alexandre Berthier, signed the papers of enrolment in the Skirmishers of the twenty-five young men of the department who had applied for admission.

On the 20th June I repaired to Le Puy to receive my *lettre de service* and present myself for inspection. My departure was fixed for the 25th. I left Le Puy the day before in order to see my worthy parents and I remained with them until the 27th. The last moments were painful to my excellent and beloved mother. My father, less demonstrative and more reasonable, displayed more firmness or placidity, lest I should too keenly regret my departure. The tears in all eyes, the sadness depicted on all the faces that surrounded me, moved me profoundly and took away all my courage. Having paid my debt to nature, I set off at a gallop to hide my tears.

A few hours later I was at Issoire, where I joined my travelling companions, my future comrades in barracks. I at once placed myself at the orders of the first superior given me by my new career. This was a lieutenant of the 21st Regiment of Light Infantry, a Corsican by birth, one of the veterans of the Egyptian expedition, highly original, and although possessed of little education, an excellent fellow. His name was Paravagna. It was no light affair to take to Paris twenty-five young fellows, all pretty independent, having as yet not the least sense of the duties imposed on us by our position as recruits, or of subordination. He was seconded by a sergeant to whom no one paid any attention.

On the 27th of June we came to Issoire. On the 28th, at Clermont, we were taken to the house of the sub-inspector of reviews, in order to be presented to him. He counted us from his window, to our great displeasure, and thereby drew from us some exceedingly sarcastic remarks.

On the 30th we made a halt at Riom, the 1st of July at Saint-Pourçain and the 2nd at Moulins. Before reaching this town we were overwhelmed by a frightful storm, which alarmed us by the mass of water it hurled against us, quite ruining our modest baggage. We did not leave Moulins until the 4th, to sleep at Saint-Pierre-le-Moutiers.

The rather high expenses of these short daily marches impelled us to hire carriages to take us more quickly to Paris. The lieutenant for a long while opposed this; he threatened to have us arrested by the gendarmerie if we took the liberty of starting without his permission. We laughed at him and his threats. However, after long discussion the matter was arranged, we paying for him and the sergeant. The latter lost by the arrangement the munition bread, which was surrendered to him, and M. Paravagna some of the good dinners to which he was treated. Concessions having been made on either side, we got into our carriages, that is, into *pataches*, four in each, and set forth, very well satisfied, although jolted about, wetted to the skin and feeling as though every bone in our bodies were broken in these barbarous vehicles,

which are suspended on springs.   We passed successively
through Pougues, Charité-sur-Loire, Prouilly, Cosne,
Briare and Montargis.

On the 6th July we came in the evening to Nemours,
and there we slept.   This was very necessary, for our
bodies were bruised all over.   During this journey of forty
leagues by post-chaise I had an accident which might
well have called a halt to my military career at the outset.
Having climbed a hill on foot, I tried to get into the
patache without stopping it.   Misled by a hanging curtain
between the crupper of the horse and the front of the
vehicle, I rested my hand on it and fell between the two,
tumbling heavily on the road.   By good fortune none of
my limbs came in the track of the wheels.   I escaped with
a few bruises and the pleasantries of my comrades.

On the 7th July, at Nemours, we took our places on
good stage coaches, and set out early in the morning.
At Fontainebleau a brief halt gave us time to see the
château and to watch the Grenadier Skirmishers, who
had already arrived, at their drill.   These were the delights
awaiting us, toward which we were posting almost at a
gallop.

ARRIVAL IN PARIS.

On the 7th July, 1804, at four o'clock in the afternoon,
we entered Paris by the Rue du Faubourg-Saint-Victor,
where we alighted.   Once on the pavement, we each
took a portmanteau and made our way to the Rue Grenelle-
Saint-Honoré, where we had been told to go to a hotel.
The arrival of twenty-five sturdy young fellows, fatigued
by their walk through Paris with their packs on their
backs and hunger in their stomachs, and consequently
in a very bad temper, terrified the landlord, who declined
the honour of entertaining so many young budding heroes.
Hard put to it to discover a house large enough to lodge

us all, for the lieutenant would not allow us to separate, we were conducted to several different addresses. Finally we found shelter in the Hôtel du Lyon, Rue Batave, near the Tuileries.

And so I was in Paris, of which I had dreamed for so many years! It would be impossible to describe the pleasure I felt when I entered the capital of France, that great and superb city, the home of the fine arts, good manners and good taste : all that I saw in those first moments struck me with admiration and astonishment. During the few days that I remained there I found it hard to define my feelings and fully to realize the impressions made upon me by the sight of so many monuments, so many masterpieces, and the immense activity that absorbed me. I was often in a sort of stupor, as though dazed.

This sort of sleep-walking came to an end only when I found myself able to define and compare, when my senses had grown accustomed to appreciate so many marvels. How delightful my sensations were! One would have to emerge, as I did, from an ugly little town, for the first time deserting the paternal roof, having as yet seen nothing truly fine and beautiful, in order to understand all my delight, all my happiness.

8th July (19 *Messidor*).—Our lieutenant, very eager to be rid of us and to complete his troublesome commission, led us very early in the morning to the Military College, to enter us in the Imperial Guard. Having had our descriptions recorded and heights taken we were distributed among the two corps of Skirmishers, each according to his stature ; thirteen were admitted to the Grenadiers and seven, of whom I was one, to the Chasseurs. We then separated with keen regret, all the more painful as during the journey an intimacy had been established which nothing had impaired. As for the lieutenant, he

3

could not help displaying a satisfaction which was not flattering to us.

We were given leave to return to Paris and there do as we liked, without being compelled to attend roll-call, until the afternoon of the following day.

On our return to the École Militaire we went by way of the Tuileries in the hope of seeing the Emperor, who was to review the Guard in the court of the château and in the Place Carrousel. I was fairly well placed for the sight of this fine spectacle, and was able at ease to consider this mighty man, who had overcome anarchy, having vanquished the enemies of France, and replaced by order the deplorable and bloody doings of the Revolution.

I found myself for the first time lodged in a barracks. I found nothing very attractive in this new life ; but as I had known for a long time that as a soldier I should have to surrender a great part of my liberty and of the comfort of family life, I did not trouble myself about it overmuch.

I was given my uniform as the day went on, and equipped with the underclothing and the footwear that I should require. I was given a blue uniform coat, the lining and piping being scarlet, buttoned across the breast with buttons bearing the Consular fasces (those with the eagle were not yet struck) with the legend : *Garde Consulaire* ; a pair of breeches and a waistcoat of white tricot, rather thick and warm ; a three-cornered hat with yellow cording ; epaulettes of green woollen cloth and red tabs ; musket, cartridge-pouch, sabre, etc. We were instructed to let our hair grow in order to make a pigtail and to sell such of our belongings as had not been taken from us. Finally, we were allowed, as a favour, to go to the play, if we so desired, until the time of our departure for Écouen.

I remained in Paris until the 12th July inclusive. During these five days, having a fair amount of liberty, I visited all the monuments and sights of the city.

13th *July*.—Leaving Paris in the detachment, knapsack on back, musket on shoulder, for the garrison appointed for the Chasseur Skirmishers, where the battalion was being organized, I was placed in the 4th company, commanded by Captain Larrousse. The name of the battalion commander was Desnoyers. There were five companies in the battalion, each at that time numbering thirty-six men, but increased in strength daily by the arrival of Skirmishers coming from all parts of France. My number on the roll of the corps was 234.

Our pay was 23 sous 1 centime per diem. Nine sous we gave to the mess, 4 went to the fund to provide underclothing and shoes, and the other 10 were given us every ten days (every decade) as pocket-money. The fare was good and the pay enough to provide all absolute necessaries, but deductions were often made which were not always very scrupulously accounted for, and of which we dared not complain, for the sergeant-majors were all-powerful in the companies.

The magnificent château of Écouen, which, after Austerlitz, was to become a school for the daughters of members of the Legion of Honour, had been made ready as the quarters of our battalion of Skirmishers.

Two days after we arrived there, that is, on Monday, the 15th July, I was greatly surprised to see, in the buttonholes of the officers and some of the non-commissioned officers, a handsome decoration suspended by a red ribbon of watered silk. I learned that this order was that of the Legion of Honour, of which the first distribution had been made the previous day by the Emperor Napoleon in person, in the Temple of Mars, at the Invalides.

17th *July*.—The Emperor passed through Écouen ; he was going to Boulogne, to give crosses to the troops encamped on the French coast, who formed the army intended to descend upon England. We lined the hedge

along the height before descending into the town. The
Emperor did not stop to inspect us, which wounded
our self-respect as conscripts.

The months of July, August, September and October
were passed in drilling, cleaning our arms and kits and
going on full-dress parades, and learning how to perform
our duties under all sorts of circumstances. Before the
end of September we were perfect in our drill and already
seemed like old soldiers. The battalion at this date
already exceeded 700 in strength, and more recruits
were arriving daily. But I was at this stage attacked
by an ophthalmia which caused me much pain and ill-
health, and in Vendémiaire I had to spend a month in the
Gros-Caillou hospital to re-establish my health.

15th August.—On this the Emperor's birthday I was
in Paris with several comrades, without leave. We
started on foot, at eleven o'clock, after roll-call and the
morning parade ; having reached Saint-Denis, we took a
carriage which conveyed us to the gate of that name.
What with following the boulevard until we came to the
site of the fête, taking part in a few games, paying one
or two calls, dining at the Palais-Royal, taking coffee in
company with ladies, returning to Écouen, travelling
back twenty-five miles in the same fashion and arriving
in time for the evening roll-call, ten hours were devoted to
this fantastic escapade. A few were punished, others
fell sick ; I was neither one nor the other, thanks to my
health and the good-will of the sergeant of the week,
who delayed a little in handing in the roll-call, hoping
that I should return before the time of grace had expired.

On Sundays, after parade, we explored our surroundings,
which are very interesting, and very lively, in the summer,
or we went to the patron saints' days at Montmorency,
Villiers-le-Bel, Sarcelles, Gonesse, Saint-Denis, Saint-Ouen,

etc. These fêtes, which were thronged with people and very gay, pleased me greatly and refreshed me after the fatigue of the week.

The time passed quickly, as it was fully employed; I thought little of my native countryside or the home of my childhood, because I had found myself in this situation of my own free will and without constraint. However, one Sunday, early in the morning, strolling, rather dolefully, alone with my thoughts, along the loveliest paths through the woods, I heard suddenly somewhat excited voices at a distance of a few paces. I turned in that direction, and before I could reach the spot from which the voices came I was aroused from my abstraction by the sound of a shot, followed by another. I ran forward, greatly excited, saw one of our officers covered with blood and beside him the assistant surgeon of the battalion, M. Maugras, and an officer who was holding him up, while two others were hurrying on horseback in the direction of Paris. It was plain to me that I was the witness of a duel à mort. Such, I heard, were the conditions of the duel. This painful incident made a great impression on me.

One evening—it was the 11th November—while we were celebrating the fête of St. Martin, which is the fête of the infantry soldiers, a new recruit to the Skirmishers entered the banqueting-hall, knapsack on back, carrying the order of incorporation in the company in his hand. To hasten up to him, help him to rid himself of his military impedimenta and find him a place at table was the affair of a moment. As he was sitting beside me and as I learned that he was from Auvergne, I asked the sergeant-major, who had been invited to the mess, to give him to me as my bed-fellow, mine being in hospital. This request was granted, to my great satisfaction. This choice was all the more agreeable to me in that the young man was perfectly well-bred, and my compatriot, and in every respect his distinction of manner was displayed. (This young man, whose name was Tournilhac, and who came from the neighbourhood of Thiers, was a captain in the Russian campaign, in which he had two fingers frost-bitten, which did not prevent him, when, on the heights of Kovno, the treasure of the Grande Armée was abandoned, from taking great handfuls of gold from the staved-in casks and rejoining the remnants of his regiment. He then came to the help of all his comrades by generously giving them all the money they needed to cross Prussia and reach the banks of the Oder. He would not take service again under the Restoration.)

27th November.—We were warned several days beforehand that we should be on duty at the coronation of the Emperor Napoleon and that we must hold ourselves ready to set out. For this great ceremony we had to receive our dress uniforms with the eagle buttons, our enormous bearskin bonnets, which covered our small beardless faces, and other articles of uniform which had not yet been given us.

Quartered at the École Militaire, we Skirmishers were distributed among the messes of the old Chasseurs, as though rationed out, with orders to find room in beds which already had two occupants, who could very well have dispensed with this importunate augmentation. We had to resign ourselves to sleeping three in a bed, and to live in rooms where we could not move about, so crowded were they. This seemed to promise us a pleasant time !

The Coronation of the Emperor.

2nd December (15 *Frimaire, year XIII*).—Hardly had the day dawned when we were drawn up on the Pont-Neuf, waiting to receive orders as to the place we were to occupy. The company lined the roadway in the Rue

Notre-Dame. As we should be compelled to stand still on the frozen ground in the bitter cold, under a cloudy sky, this meant a day of fatigue and privation. However, when the constituted authorities began to arrive, when the Legislative Corps, the Tribunate, the Senate, the Council of State, the Court of Cassation, the Court of Exchequer, etc., began to pass in procession, we were pleased to be so well placed, to have nothing in front to deprive us of the fascinating scene displayed before us. And when the rich carriage of the Pope arrived, drawn by eight magnificent horses, preceded by his chaplain, mounted on a mule ; when the Paris staff, with Prince Murat at its head, preceded and followed by an immense column of cavalry of all arms, appeared ; when, finally, the magnificent imperial procession revealed itself in all its splendour, we forgot the cold and fatigue in our admiration of this resplendent pomp.

The procession having entered the church, we were allowed to walk about in order to get warm again. Finding myself near one of the doors of the vast basilica in which so astonishing a ceremony was being performed I entered, following the Prince Eugène. Once inside I could scarce have made my way forward had not a friend of mine, of the Skirmishers, whose company was on duty in the church, made it possible for me to get into a lofty grandstand. I obtained a good place without much difficulty, because the people thought I had been sent thither on duty. Thence I was able to see at least two-thirds of the ceremony, which was all that the most fertile imagination could depict in its beauty, its pomp, and its remarkable character. One must have seen it in order to form any idea of it. The recollection of it will remain engraven in my memory as long as I live. Before the end of the Mass I withdrew to resume my place.

At night we returned to our quarters, and having eaten our supper I went to see the brilliant illumination

of the Tuileries and the surrounding monuments. The
day was well occupied, but it also offered the imagination
many striking memories.

THE PRESENTATION OF THE EAGLES. [1]

6th December.—As on the previous occasion of our
taking duty, we rose before daybreak in order to march
to the Champ de Mars, where we were drawn up by
eight o'clock, to receive our eagles and surround the
throne with all the splendour which troops lend to these
ceremonies. Great preparations had been made to give
this new consecration all the pomp and majesty which so
impressive a solemnity demands. As well as ourselves,
the other regiments of the Guard, the troops of the Paris
garrison and those that had arrived to take part in the
coronation, the deputations from the National Guards of
France, and from all the departments of the Army and
Navy, were drawn up in battle array. The Champ de
Mars, extensive though it be, could not contain all those
that had been convoked or had come of their own accord
to receive and swear fealty to the flag that was on this
great day to be presented to them.

After the presentation of the eagles to the leader of
each body of troops and the taking of the oath, the march
past commenced. It was a very lengthy business, and
was not completed until nightfall. We were the last
to leave the field. If the weather had favoured this
solemn majesty it would have been beautiful indeed ; but
the thaw, the rain and the cold had chilled, if not the
enthusiasm and devotion of the Army for its glorious chief,
at least its legs and arms. We were standing in mud up
to our knees, especially opposite the immense and magnificent staging where stood the Emperor, surrounded
by his Court and the whole General Staff of the Army.

---

[1] The staff bearing the flag or " colours " was topped by a gilt eagle
with folded wings.—TR.

I saw amidst this armed immensity the sergeant of
the 96th regiment of the line who carried, in a little
silver urn fastened upon his breast, the heart of the first
Grenadier of France, the valiant La Tour d'Auvergne, to
die on the field of honour.

An Evening at the Palais-Royal.

A few days after our return to Écouen I went again
to Paris with my new friend Tournilhac, to bid farewell
to some of my compatriots and to see if I could raise some
money from one of them. Having made a very light
breakfast, for which I paid with the last money I had
left, we parted, each going his way on his own business,
to get the money he hoped to obtain. We agreed that
neither would accept any invitation, and that we should
meet at five o'clock precisely under the wooden arcade
of the Palais-Royal.

I was punctual at the place of meeting, my stomach
being as empty as my purse. I waited for a long while,
a very long while, but saw nothing of him whom I secretly
called my rescuer. My position was critical. Without
money, without food, without refuge, I was trembling
with anxiety and cold, for the weather was very inclement.
I feared that my giddy-pated comrade, set before an
appetizing table near a good fire, might have forgotten
me. My reflections were extremely dismal. But at last
he came, as poor as myself but more resolute. " Come
and see a captain of Hussars I know. He's a good fellow,
an excellent soldier, kept at home by the gout ; he'll be
delighted to give dinner to two starving heroes."

And in truth we received a cordial and whole-hearted
welcome. After an excellent dinner, given and consumed in a generous spirit, near a warm fire, my friend,
quite unembarrassed, said : " That's not all, captain.
You must let me have a hundred sous to go to the play

and pay for a bed in a hotel." The captain, like the well-bred man he was, gave us the coin and hoped we should enjoy ourselves. I was astonished by his almost paternal entertainment of us, and the delight which this excellent man experienced in obliging two young rascals.

After leaving the Vaudeville we spent more of our sous at the Café Anglais, but still had enough money left to pay for a bed ; but it was past midnight, the hotels were closed, and once more we found ourselves in the streets. Tired, shivering with cold, we took refuge in a guard-house, where they were good enough to take us in. I promised myself solemnly that I would never again, if I could help it, find myself in such a position.

DEPARTURE FOR ITALY.

15th January, 1805.—On the 14th January, 1805, the order came to take all the men fit for service who were at the school of the batallion and form them into two detachments which were to be despatched to Paris. I was placed in the first.

We did not know for what expedition we were intended, but we knew we should not return again to the Écouen garrison, where we had had such a grilling—I don't mean that we were harshly handled, for the discipline there was easy—but we had done such a lot of drills there !

We were prodigiously burdened, and to aggravate our embarrassment we carried on our knapsacks, bound to them by cords, our monstrous fur bonnets, enclosed in cardboard cases like a lady's muff-box. On the march we were caught in the rain ; the soaked cardboard was reduced to pulp ; presently, to our disgust, our bonnets fell in the mud. Imagine soldiers having to carry such hideous things in their hands or under their arms ! We looked a regular band of gipsies.

At last we reached the École Militaire, soaked to the

skin and absolutely worn out by the weight of our packs, the badness of the roads and the difficulties of our march. The better to restore us we were made to sleep three in a bed and received orders to prepare ourselves to be reviewed by the Emperor on the following day.

After a most painful night we got under arms at day-break to march to the garden of the Tuileries. There each company of Chasseurs (the old soldiers) was augmented by a portion of the 1st detachment of Skirmishers ; they were ranked according to their stature, and we were told that henceforth we were incorporated in these companies. I found myself in the second company of the second battalion. Introduced into the ranks of these moustachio'd veterans, all of whom boasted at least one chevron, we looked like young girls beside these swarthy, mostly hard-bitten faces, full of jealous resentment at having been given such youthful comrades. This operation completed, we marched into the court of the château, where the Emperor reviewed that part of the Guard under orders for Italy. Its ranks having been organized, we marched off and returned to the École Militaire to make ready for our departure on the morrow.

I Decide to keep a Diary.

17th January.—Before our departure Marshal Soult reviewed us in the Champ de Mars. Sleet was falling, which was very disagreeable. The review being completed of that portion of the Guard which was going to Italy, composed of one regiment of Grenadiers and Chasseurs à pied, one regiment of Grenadiers and Chasseurs à cheval, one legion of special gendarmerie, and the Mamelukes, we marched off on our way to Essonnes, where we slept. Late in leaving, we were late in arriving ; I was cruelly fatigued, on account of the length of the march, the bad condition of the roads, the weight of my knapsack, and, above all, because I was not accustomed to marching. Before the billets were distributed each Skirmisher was paired with an old Chasseur. At first sight, and judging by the gruff tone of my companion, I did not congratulate myself on the award of chance.

It was on this day (while chatting with a Skirmisher friend of the prodigious events which we had witnessed during the ten months of our service, and of how glad we were that we were going to see that beautiful country of Italy, so celebrated in history, above all since the immortal campaigns of 1796, 1797 and 1800) that the idea occurred to me to make notes of all the interesting things I should see during this journey, and to record the date of my arrival in various towns, whether great or small—in a word, to keep a diary of my wanderings. My friend was of the same way of thinking, and told me that he would do the same.

I have always kept this diary with regularity, entering almost every day, in a manuscript book devoted to this purpose, observations whose recollection I thought I ought to preserve, without troubling my head as to the unimportance of the periods or the facts recorded, or the manner in which they were represented, or the little interest which this almost daily labour might offer. It was for myself that I did it ; it mattered to me then very little whether it was good or bad, trivial or interesting. The essential thing was to persevere and to keep it up. I continued to do so, painstakingly, despite many hindrances.

If I am now re-writing it, this is in order to unite the many manuscript books of which this journal is composed, books which are soiled and torn, with many illegible pages, owing to the numerous journeys and removals which they have suffered. I am copying it also in order to restore to my memory the many records which it contains. In busying myself over this lengthy task I shall discover a means of so employing my days and my long winter evenings that they will seem to me less tedious. As I go out but little and live almost alone, this will be a remedy against idleness and the bitter reflections of melancholy old age.

I am not introducing any change of importance into its original text. As I wrote it, of evenings, on my travels or in garrison, or at night in bivouac, so it will be in its new form. If my son one day runs through this diary, he will realize that I lacked neither constancy in my determination to keep it nor patience in making a fair copy, a very tiresome and laborious task for an aged man with little skill in writing. . . .

18th January.—On setting out from Essonnes, we put our knapsacks on the carriages, keeping only our bearskins, which we carried slung over our shoulders. They were enclosed in cases of ticking, which were given us the day before our departure. In order to affix these to our knapsacks we were advised to obtain straps, without any particular length or colour being specified, so that there was a regular medley. We were responsible for the costs of transport, which were to be 20 centimes a day. Each company had its cart, and we were free to remove our knapsacks on arriving at our destination.

21st January.—Sens.—We stayed a few days. On reaching our quarters my bedfellow told me gruffly that I must before all clean my musket, my shoes, etc. I told him to mind his own business : I was not taking any orders. A quarrel ensued which was to reach its issue the following day, when a Skirmisher came in with his comrade and proposed that we should keep together on the march and live together. Their intervention assuaged our mutual irritation and the proposal was accepted. That same evening we met together, for supper, and have up to the present continued to do so, whether at the halt which is habitually made half-way to our destination, or at the latter, where dinner is prepared wherever is most convenient. As a rule we live well, spending no more than our pay.

This Skirmisher's name is Journais. Having become a captain, he was taken prisoner in Spain and taken to England. The tedium of his captivity drove him to suicide.

26th January.—Since leaving Paris I have formed a habit of going to a café to read a political journal, in order to keep *au courant* with the news of the day. Thus I learned at Avallon that we are on the way to Milan to be present at the coronation of Napoleon as King of Italy.

3rd February.—In the morning, at Mâcon, before the regiment marched, I asked and obtained permission to embark on the barge going to Villefranche. I arrived before the regiment, although it was already late. A cold day, snowy ; it was better sailing on the Saône rather than stumping through the mud.

5th February.—At Lyons.—The young Prince Eugène Beauharnais, son-in-law of the Emperor, commandant-in-chief of the whole Guard, reviewed us on the Place de Bellecour, still littered with the ruins made by the hammer of the Revolution. In the full uniform of a mounted Chasseur of the Guard, he wore a wide flame-coloured sash across one shoulder, to which was attached an enormous gold cross. This new rank or dignity was created quite recently, under the style of the Grand Cross of the Legion of Honour. . . .

On the 13th February, on leaving Lyons, I was wearing new shoes, that blistered me cruelly. Compelled to fall behind, I arrived long after the regiment, harassed with fatigue, with my feet in a deplorable state, at Bourgoin.

Before reaching Pont-Beauvoisin, on the 14th, we passed

through the small town of Latour-Dupin. I stopped to buy a pair of shoes, being no longer able to march in those I had on my feet.

16th February.—To Chambéry.—Before entering the town a Skirmisher, Baratier, a native of the place, treated all the soldiers of the regiment to wine and light pastries. Open casks filled with wine had been placed at intervals along the route, with peasants in attendance, to hand us glasses filled with wine as we marched past, and also the above-mentioned pastries. We were allowed to slacken our pace, so as to have time to eat and drink.

24th February.—Crossing Mont Cenis.—The road, which was difficult, and barely visible through the snow, was so slippery that every hundred yards or so, when we were descending the steep slope leading to the Novalesa, I fell flat on my back. Fortunately my knapsack served as a buffer, for without it I believe I should have broken my bones a hundred times over before reaching the bottom of this long and awkward descent. These frequent falls took place because my shoes had no heels, the soles being flat and smooth as glass. We found the cold pretty sharp as soon as we left our quarters, but when we had passed the hamlet of Ramasso and had reached the extreme heights it became excessively severe. I saw, in passing, the Hospice du Mont-Cenis, but I had only a rapid, imperfect glimpse, on account of the fog and the quickness of our march. Less than an hour after passing this inhabited spot we were approaching the clear skies of Italy. We left behind us the frosts and storms and began to breathe the warm air of that country, which we were eager to see, thinking ourselves fortunate to behold it.

The company was detached at Bussolino, a small town a league beyond Suza on the Turin highway. My bedfellow and I slept in a stable with an ass and a goat. In the morning I washed and whitened the band of my bonnet, in order to pass the captain's inspection. When I went to get it and fix it on my full-uniform headgear I found the goat was eating it, and had already swallowed more than half of it. I recovered it almost whole, but so soiled and damaged that it earned me two days in the guardhouse. After leaving Lyons we had the privilege of carrying our knapsacks, but I was by then broken to marching.

27th February.—To Turin.—We stayed there till the 2nd March inclusive. On the evening of our arrival town and country were covered in deep snow, so that in both the roads were impracticable. Despite the continuance of the snow, and although it was anything but agreeable out of doors, I could not deprive myself of the pleasure of visiting every quarter of the city, and all the public buildings, and making myself acquainted with all the sights of this fine and beautiful city. I saw almost all there was to be seen.

During these three days' rest our captain, M. Bigarré, received a despatch to the effect that he was promoted major in the 4th Regiment of the Line, commanded by Prince Joseph Bonaparte. As his Imperial Highness was never at the head of his regiment, Major Bigarré could regard himself as Colonel of the 4th line regiment. Before leaving us he gave all the officers a dress plume of heron's feathers and a big dinner. This was a courteous and distinguished fashion of making his farewell.

9th March.—To Abbiategrasso.—It was here that the French were overcome in 1524, which cost the Chevalier Bayard his life.

10th March.—Milan saw the end of our journey and our exertions. I was in excellent health, very glad to enjoy a little rest, and to find myself in the capital of wealthy Lombardy, quartered in the citadel of Milan. On our arrival the officers, non-commissioned officers and men of the Royal Italian Guard came to invite us to dinner that very day. We Chasseurs went to the barracks of the Italian Chasseurs, where we found a number of tables in a great courtyard, very well provided for a soldier's banquet. The banquet given by the cadets was a gay and very brilliant affair, owing to the great number of highly distinguished personages who were present as spectators. They wished to enjoy the pleasant sight of the frank harmony which prevailed there, and of this joyous and magnificent gathering, which was to cement the alliance between the two nations.

(A few days before we returned to France we reciprocated the polite attentions of the Royal Guard. The banquet was held in the courtyards of the citadel, with less pomp but equal cordiality.)

8th May.—Two months after our arrival the Emperor Napoleon made his solemn entry into the capital of his new kingdom. This was a magnificent affair. The infantry lined the streets when he went by on horseback, in the midst of the guard of honour, in brilliant uniforms, sent thither from all the towns of the kingdom. Two divisions of cavalry and one of Cuirassiers preceded and followed, comprising all the general and staff officers of the French Army in Italy. I saw at the head of the troops the commander-in-chief of this army, the conqueror of Fleurus, Marshal Jourdan, as well as a large number of generals who, although young, had performed notable exploits of arms.

26th May.—The coronation had not the brilliance of the ceremony in Paris, but was none the less very fine. We lined the streets along two different routes as the

Emperor went by : when he was proceeding to the cathedral of San' Ambrogio to set the Iron Crown on his head and when he returned to the palace after the ceremony. The coronation took place in the morning, in the city cathedral. The troops remained massed around the cathedral, the Emperor having gone thither on foot from his palace by a graceful gallery built expressly for the purpose. The chief purpose of the evening ceremony was to reveal him to the people in all the pomp of royal majesty. With the Emperor were the Empress, the Princes Joseph and Louis Napoleon, Prince Murat, Prince Eugène, several marshals and generals, the ministers of the kingdom, the prominent officials and the personages of the two Courts, who preceded, followed or surrounded the carriages of the procession. This impressive ceremony was favoured, and its brilliance augmented, by magnificent weather.

There was then a succession of brilliant fêtes ; I saw Garnerin rise into the air ; chariot-races gave one some idea of the famous Olympiads ; an immense set-piece of fireworks covered the whole top of the façade of the citadel on the side overlooking the city. Of the illuminations, that of the dome of the cathedral surpassed the rest in its brilliance and the immense number of lights ; games of all sorts took place in the great public place, which is planted with trees and surrounded with magnificent palaces. I saw there the plan of the battle of Marengo, at a given hour of the day, in relief and on a large scale ; all the corps of the two armies were shown in the positions which they occupied at the stage of the action represented by the model. These brilliant fêtes lasted several days and attracted great numbers.

3rd June.—This morning the general was beaten in the courtyards of the citadel, long before the proper time, or the beating of reveille. To dress and arm and form ranks was the work of a moment. We made for the

Piazza d'Esplanada, where Napoleon was waiting. After we had been drilling for some time he ordered us to load our muskets as for firing practice. It was found that we had only ball cartridges ; however, this did not matter ; we tore them open at the end containing the bullet. The manœuvres commenced ; all sorts of firing exercises were executed before the thousands of persons who had flocked thither to see this early spectacle, which took place in front of the principal houses of the city. Well, despite the haste of the whole affair, there was not a single accident ; not a soldier there forgot to carry out the order given to tear the cartridges open at the end containing the bullet. This shows the confidence of the Emperor in the devotion of his guard, the coolness and address of its men, for the Emperor was often in the line of fire inspecting the execution of the various movements.

During the early part of June the Doge of Genoa, Geromino Durazzo, came to assure the Emperor of the desire of the Senate and the people of Genoa to see the Ligurian Republic incorporated in the French Empire. I was one of the guard of honour sent to meet them. But this fallen sovereign refused the honour and dismissed the guard on the spot. He had three francs given to each of us and a diamond ring to the officer in command.

The ninety-two days which I spent at Milan I employed in inspecting the town and its monuments. I often went to the Brera library, to spend a few hours there. I went once to the great theatre of La Scala, which is said to be one of the finest in Italy. I used to go every day to a café to read the *Journal de l'Empire*, and to a reading-room to read the romances then in fashion. Several times I went to see the Abbé Depradt, a compatriot and a friend of my father's, the Emperor's almoner, at the convent of Santa Maria. (In after days he was an ingrate

to his benefactor.) I used often, with others of the Skirmishers, to explore the neighbourhood of Milan, where the
excellent methods of cultivation and the vigorous vegetation are worthy of all admiration. During these walks
I saw many beautiful landscapes, and a particularly
beautiful one is that in which the celebrated echo repeats
itself as often as forty times. It is in the courtyard of
La Simonetta that this remarkable natural phenomena
is to be heard. On these walks, which were often of considerable length, we used to seek refreshment in one of
the many taverns which we came across ; but we never
managed to get anything better than hard-boiled eggs,
salad, and a rough wine.

Our military service and our drill at Milan were by
no means fatiguing. An increase of pay and a few other
advantages contributed to the charm of our sojourn
there. For my own part, I left the city with great regret.
Flesh food, however, was dear, and offered little variety ;
and while I shall never forget the happy times I had there,
neither shall I forget that for three months our supper
was always of rice, which ended by making this farinaceous
food intolerable to me.

Finally, after a number of parades and reviews, before
either the Emperor or his marshals, we left Milan on the
22 Prairial (11th June) to return to Paris.

WE RETURN TO FRANCE.

13th June.—We crossed the Lesina, in boats, where
it leaves Lake Maggiore. I greatly regretted that I could
not visit the Borromean Islands, and above all Isola Bella ;
the distance was not very great, but the necessity of drying
my kit, which had been soaked with rain during almost the
whole of the march, prevented my going thither. The
shores of the lake are wonderful for their fresh beauty and
picturesque landscapes. It is an enchanting countryside.

15th June.—At Duomo d'Ossola, a small town at the foot of the Alps, we were quartered in a church, which we entered wet to the skin ; there was no fire at which to dry ourselves and nowhere to hang up our clothes. In such circumstances a soldier's life is indeed wretched.

17th June.—At Simplon, a village half-way up the mountain, they spoke German. On this day we passed through three different regions In the plain it was summer ; the people were gathering the harvest ; that was in the morning. Before we reached shelter, towards noon, the fresh green turf, covered with primroses, violets and narcissi, offered us a picture of spring, the more actual in that the air was mild and fragrant. In the village we were surrounded by hoar-frost and cold, harsh vistas that reminded us almost—except for the snow—of the pass of Mont Cenis. It looked as though we were close to the glaciers. I tried, with a comrade, to reach them, but after marching over an hour in the direction of the nearest one we gave up the attempt, for it seemed to recede farther and farther as we advanced.

27th June.—To Coulanges, a little town in the department of Léman.—It was a year to-day that I bade farewell to my people. We celebrated this day with all the respect that such a date, so remarkable in the life of a young man, inspires in anyone who feels the highest veneration for the authors of his days. The four of us together respectfully performed this pious duty.

PARIS.[1]

We reached Paris on the 18th July, thankful to rest after a long march, made very rapidly in the greatest

[1] While these recollections were appearing in the *Revue des Deux Mondes*, I found one of the manuscript-books containing the first versions

heat. A sojourn in the capital, with every possible desire to make its acquaintance ! I was wild with delight to have such a chance !

The public buildings, the libraries, the museums, great and small, and sometimes the play : these were my favourite sources of amusement. I also attended a few public lectures ; but despite the superficial ideas that I acquired, my mind would never settle down to listen to these academic professors. I would fain have had the whole of my time at my disposal, to see everything, hear everything and get to know something of everything. Our service was onerous ; the frequent and rigorous roll-calls would hardly allow me to go where I should have wished ; however, I was content with my lot. I was hoping it would continue when the sound of the trumpet shattered the scaffolding of my intentions.

We received orders to repair to the camp at Boulogne, to make part of the army intended to be thrown upon the English coast.

When we had received the necessary kit for embarkation, and had been reviewed several times over—and these reviews were more exhausting than a day's march, on account of their length and their minute detail—we found ourselves at last, our knapsacks on our backs, outside the wall of the École Militaire, waiting only for General Soulès to turn to the right-about and say " Vive la gloire ! " But nothing of the kind occurred. A special

written on the spot, during the campaign of 1805. I found it with a mass of letters in a drawer, rather difficult to open, of the desk at which J.-B. Barrès doubtless used to write. There was no longer time to use these notes for the *Revue,* so in place of doing so I have used them here instead of the later version.

My two texts are pretty much alike, but the earlier is more ingenuous and less cheerful. About 1840 J.-B. Barrès suppressed or lightened the sufferings and disillusions of the young man of 1805. It is curious to see how the latter, touched by a ray of sunlight, recovered his enthusiasm and his varied and abounding curiosity. Unfortunately this orginal text runs only from the 29 Messidor, year VIII, to the 28 Brumaire of the same year.—M. B.

courier arrived from Boulogne, bearing an order from the Emperor. We turn to the left-about and returned to our quarters with the injunction to remain there and hold ourselves in readiness for another destination.

Then followed a fortnight of parades, reviews and manœuvres. One might have thought that our leaders had decided to plague us into longing to go on a campaign! And this was what everyone was saying.

Finally the rumours of war with Austria gained credence, and instead of casting ourselves on the iron-bound coast when an intrepid army was delighting in the thought of crossing the Channel to attack, at close quarters, the country which the newspapers called *la perfide Albion*, we were despatched to the Rhine, whither so many glorious memories invoked the French Army. We had been forty-four days in Paris.

LEAVING PARIS FOR THE GERMAN CAMPAIGN.

31st August.—We left Paris quite content to go campaigning rather than march to Boulogne. I was especially so, for war was the one thing I wanted. I was young, full of health and courage, and I thought one could wish for nothing better than to fight against all possible odds; moreover, I was broken to marching; everything conspired to make me regard a campaign as a pleasant excursion, on which, even if one lost one's head, arms, or legs, one should at least find some diversion. I wanted, too, to see the country, the siege of a fortress, a battlefield. I reasoned, in those days, like a child. And at the moment of writing this, the boredom which is consuming me in cantonments (at Schönbrunn) and four months of marching about, months of fatigue and wretchedness, have proved to me that nothing is more hideous, more miserable, than war. And yet our sufferings in the Guard are not to be compared with those of the line.

Our road as far as Strasbourg was beautiful, but long. So that we should not come up against the columns that were marching down from Boulogne to Chalons-sur-Marne, we were marched through Provins, Langres, Vesoul and Colmar. The weather, but for a few days, was constantly fine. Everything conspired to make me find the beginning of campaigning pleasant. My desires too were in harmony, but my health refused to correspond with them; I had lost appetite, and was burning with fever; the fear of being left in some hospital gave me strength; I would not even resort to the carts. The variety of scene, the desire to go on, and a good constitution supported me, and I reached Strasbourg still intoxicated with glory. Several of my comrades, not more unwell than I was, stayed behind in the hospitals and there found their deaths. The old proverb about overcoming illness should above all be observed by soldiers. Woe to those who go into hospital on campaign! They are isolated and forgotten, and tedium slays them rather than their sickness.

Between Belfort and our destination the roads were covered with troops, and above all with forage-carts, which all the inhabitants of the Upper Rhine, the Vosges and La Meurthe had been forced to give, as requisition. After twenty-three days we arrived before Strasbourg. Before entering the city we paid certain attentions to our toilet. We donned our bearskin bonnets and our plumes, and the guard of honour came to meet us. We were quartered in the Feinck-Mack district of the town.

26th September.—The Emperor, having set out from Saint-Cloud on the 24th September (2 Vendémiaire) arrived in Strasbourg on the 26th. At the Saverne Gate a triumphal arch was erected, with inscriptions foretelling his victories. His entry was announced by salvoes of artillery and the ringing of bells. The guard of honour, resplendent in its youth and its uniforms, led the majestic procession. It was welcomed by exclamations a thousand times repeated. The inhabitants of Alsace flowed after it like a torrent. At night, in the midst of the illuminations, the spire of the cathedral was a pillar of fire floating in the air.

I was on guard at the Imperial Palace. I had the opportunity of seeing the presents and the curiosities that were given to the Emperor, notably a monstrous carp from the Rhine.

After the 20th, part of the troops from the Boulogne camp, those coming from the interior, and the Imperial Guard began to pour into Strasbourg through all the gates, taking what munitions they needed, and made for the Rhine, which they crossed at Kehl. They were finally organized on the right bank, while awaiting their marching orders. Men and horses were bivouacked in the streets; the waggons of the artillery and the heaps of stores and equipment choked them; there was such a muddle that one hardly knew where one was.

27th September.—We were now almost the only troops left in Strasbourg. Before leaving we had to wait for the Guard, which was to come from Boulogne. It arrived on the 27th September. It was a fête-day for everybody, thus to meet again after so long an absence; especially for the youngsters. The authorities at once set about amalgamating us. All the Skirmishers changed companies. I sincerely regretted mine, and entered the 9th of the 1st battalion of the 2nd regiment.

Each of us was issued fifty cartridges, four days' munitions, and campaigning utensils. I had the very great advantage of being the first selected to carry the stewpot of my squadron, as being the most junior in service.

OUR ENTRY INTO GERMANY.

29th September.—We left Strasbourg before daylight and were to assemble beyond Kehl. For the first time, at ten that morning, I beheld the Rhine, and I did not cross the majestic river without a secret feeling of contentment when I recalled to memory all the noble feats of arms which its banks had seen. Then warlike reminiscences made me long for a few glorious encounters in which I might satisfy my eager impatience.

The whole of the Guard having arrived, we marched away with Marshal Bessières at our head. Never had the Guard been so numerous. It was an immense column. The day was long and tiring, on account of the sun, the dust, and our munitions, which crushed us—me above all, with my heavy cauldron. If I had fallen I could not have risen again, so completely was I at the end of my strength. I could no longer march; I dragged myself along. When, at ten o'clock at night, we reached a village near Rastadt, I was so weary that I could neither eat nor sleep. I began to regret Paris.

{*1st October.*—We were under arms before daylight, sorely fatigued by the previous day. Before we marched a proclamation of the Emperor to the troops was read to us. It announced the opening of the campaign against the Austrians, who had invaded Bavaria; it announced also forced marches and privations of every kind; it was received with shouts of " Vive l'Empereur ! " We were also warned that there would no longer be any prolonged halts, or day's marches of regulated length as in France, and that we must therefore carry our victuals for the march. Further, we were forbidden to miss roll-call, to fall to the rear, etc.

That day we marched from dawn to sunset. We lay at night in a village three leagues from Ettlingen. (I

am not able, at the outset, to cite names correctly, as I
could not in those days understand the language very
well.) We were fed by the inhabitants, in accordance
with arrangements made in the houses of Baden, Wurtem-
berg and Bavaria. There was a village on the river Ems,
less than a league from Ensweihingen, in Suabia, where
all the inhabitants were assembled in the market-place
awaiting us, and when we arrived each peasant led off
as many soldiers as he could provide with lodging and
adequate food. From the crossing of the Rhine to the
Danube we had a great deal of fruit, which the troops
greatly enjoyed. The cool acidity of the apples assuaged
the burning thirst that consumed us. There was no wine
and little beer, and that poor.

On the 7th, at Nordlingen, in the night, the *night march*
of the regiment was sounded (a sort of tattoo or alarm
peculiar to each corps). The regiment was soon under
arms, knapsack on back. It was to leave at once for
Donawerth. This unseasonable alarm deprived us of
some hours' comfortable sleep, which we sorely needed.
But the military situation was rapidly developing, and
necessitated the assemblage of the troops at the seat of
war. There had been fighting on the 7th on the Tech,
for the possession of the bridge and the march upon
Augsburg. On the 8th we reached Donawerth. In the
evening we heard the guns ; it was the victory of Wer-
tingen, won by Marshals Lannes and Murat over the
Austrians under General Auttemberg.

On the 9th we crossed the Danube at Donawerth, by
the bridge, which the enemy had not had time to destroy
on retreating. At a short distance from the river, in the
vast fertile plain which we were crossing to reach Augsburg, the company lieutenant, with whom I used often
to talk, pointed out to me the place where a monument

had been erected to the valiant La Tour d'Auvergne, the first Grenadier of the Republic, killed by a lance-thrust at the battle of Neubourg, on the 27th June, 1800. As news of the occupation of Augsburg had not yet reached us, we were ordered to bivouac for an hour or so, to the misfortune of the neighbouring hop-growers, whose poles served to warm and dry us.

The 10th and 11th October we spent at Augsburg. During these two days, which were detestable owing to the amount of snow and rain that fell on them, the army, as we afterwards heard, completed its great wheeling movement round Ulm and finally cut off the enemy's retreat. The Emperor arrived on the 10th.

On the 12th we left Augsburg in the afternoon, and a few hours later were in darkness. We found it difficult to march on account of the mud, which was sticky and tenacious on this black, heavy soil. Already I was finding it difficult to drag my feet out of it when I had the misfortune of discovering that one of my trouser-straps was broken. As it was impossible to go on walking I stopped to put on another, but in the meantime the infantry were arriving, with the cavalry and the artillery of the Guard (my battalion formed part of the vanguard). I was forced to wait until all this mass of troops had gone by, in order not to be crushed, jostled, lost in this host, itself lost in the mud, which was horribly kneaded and tempered. This took a long time, there being so many troops. At last I threw myself headlong into a squadron of our own men. With them I reached our quarters and slept in a hovel that was given us for a guardroom.

On the following day, the 13th, at daybreak, I attempted to regain my company, but this was impossible ; it was too far ahead, and the road was too choked with troops.

I continued to march with the detachment I had found
the night before. The roads were even more impracticable,
owing to the enormous mass of snow that had been falling
all night long.

Having come to Guntzburg as the night was closing
in I asked and searched for my company. It was impossible to find it ; it was on the banks of the Danube. The
town was topsy-turvy, the houses full of dead men and
wounded, sick men and well, hurried, crowded together,
piled in heaps. Unable to find shelter anywhere, I took
refuge in the town hall, where I was so fortunate as to
find a corner near a well-heated stove, where I was able
to warm myself, dry my things, and find shelter from
the inclemency of the season. I resigned myself to my
dismal lot, although I was without food and without
comrades to cheer me, and surrounded by Austrian
soldiers who were wounded and even more wretched
than myself. Separated from my company, which was
my military family, I found myself in a truly deplorable
situation.

At daybreak I once more began my search for my companions in arms. I found them at last on the right bank
of the Danube, near the bridge, in a comfortable bivouac,
with abundance of food. Having accounted for my
absence, I received from all my friends the most gratifying
marks of friendship, particularly from an old Chasseur
from my own part of the country, who had been a Grenadier
in Egypt, and was wounded in the breach of Saint-Jean-
d'Acre ; he had been very uneasy at my absence. He
gave me part of his rations, which he had put aside for
me. From the way in which I did honour to the breakfast
he offered me he was able to judge of the privations I
had suffered during this miserable incident. Tears of joy
ran down his worn cheeks when he saw me eating with
such good appetite. Ah, it is a nasty thing to be lost
in the midst of an army on the march !

On the night of the 14th the company passed to the left bank of the Danube, to guard the head of the bridge which had been burned by the Austrians, but by which it was still possible to cross by means of a few planks.

For two hours I stood sentry on the edge of a ravine on the other side of which was an enemy sentry. We observed one another without firing, in order not to disturb the rest of that portion of the army that lay in the neighbourhood.

About midnight we re-crossed the Danube, and the whole of the infantry of the Guard ascended the right bank for about a league, in order to take up its position on a height, where we passed the remainder of the night, without fire and without shelter, in an Arctic wind.

Then, for the first time, I witnessed an example of the horrors of war. As the cold was very bitter some men were detached to fetch wood, in order to bivouac. The village whither they went for it was devastated in a moment; not content with taking the wood, they carried off the furniture, the farm implements, the linen and other movables. The officers became aware of this devastating torrent, but too late. Strict orders were given, condemning to death all soldiers who should be found with linen, portable property, etc. If this order had been executed throughout the whole campaign the whole Grand Army would have been shot. Several men did pay the death penalty.

This spectacle, new to me, wounded me to the heart. I shed tears over the fate of these poor villagers, who had in a moment lost all their possessions. But what I saw later caused me to regard them as still happy in their misfortune. As I was a novice in the military art, all that was contrary to the principles in which I had been trained surprised me; but I had time, afterwards, to become accustomed to such things, through satiety as much as of necessity. A Chasseur Skirmisher, having gone with the rest to the village to seek for wood, found a goose that had been killed. Being a novice, he carried it confidently back to camp, and was encountered by M. Grosse, the major in command of our regiment, who, having himself struck him a few blows with his stick, ordered that he was to remain a fortnight with the vanguard, and that the goose should be hung round his neck until it became putrid. In vain did the young man protest his innocence ; the sentence was carried out, more to set an example to others than to punish him.

All day we heard the sound of cannon and musketry in the direction of Ulm. This was the fine victory of Elchingen, won by the corps of Marshal Ney (the 6th Army Corps) after a stubbornly contested action.

15th October.—At daybreak the regiment set out from Guntzburg and went into action a little less than a league from the town, to guard a bridge over the Danube. Several guns had been placed in position to prevent the crossing in case the enemy should attempt to pass. Our company was the farthest forward and the first to sustain the shock. We spent the whole day under arms, waiting to see whether the enemy had any desire to trouble our security. I was in a position from which I could observe the success of our columns ; the sound of the guns was terrible all day long, as was that of the well-sustained musketry. Unused to the din, I was dazed by it, although I had no fear of hearing it closer at hand. On the contrary, I should have been glad if we had fought, in order to prove that even if one were new to such work one had as much love of glory as the veterans.

The enemy left us in peace, so part of the day we spent in making straw huts. All that was found in the village, whether of wood or of eatables, was removed. The same scenes of horror were enacted, but this time I was less sensible of them ; moreover, necessity demanded them. At night I was on guard the other side of the Danube, on sentry-go ten paces from the Austrians. Only a little canal separated me from the enemy sentry ; he left me in peace, and I did the same for him.

Hardly had I gone off duty, at midnight, when we were torn away from our lovely bivouacs and despatched farther on, through the darkest, coldest night imaginable, in order to be near the Emperor. In this new position we found nothing : no straw on which to lie, little wood for burning, and a north wind that was like a wind of Lapland. I passed a wretched night ; roasted on one side, frozen on the other. That was all the rest I got.

Anyone who asked nothing better than to amuse himself, to delight in a novel and pleasing sight, might have been gratified ; a number of immense lines of bivouacs, continuing as far as eye could reach, offered an enchanting spectacle ; thousands of fires were scattered along the wide horizon ; the bright, twinkling stars contrasted too greatly with our position, which was anything but dazzling. This was the first time I passed the night in bivouac ;| I did not find it very fascinating ; it is a dismal way of going to bed. Many a time since then I have stated my opinion that the best of bivouacs is not worth the most wretched of hovels.

16*th October.*—At the break of day we left our bivouac to march on Ulm. The day's march began very badly ; the roads were choked with mud and obstructed by the artillery. It was raining violently. We came to a wood, where we found a clearing by the roadside. We were so plagued by the artillery and cavalry that we were left there until they had gone by. Four hours later we were still there, under a torrential downpour, up to the knees in mud, having eaten nothing all day, all our limbs stiff with the cold. What was delaying the army in its march was the bridge at Elchingen, a quarter of a league distant, which had been cut by the enemy, and so ill repaired by us, on account of our haste, that it was feared every moment that it would break. An aide of Marshal Bessières came to fetch us out of this death-trap, giving orders to move us at once to Elchingen, to the Emperor's headquarters. Each followed the path that seemed to him best in order to get there as quickly as possible. When I had crossed the bridge I beheld, for the first time, a battlefield.

The spectacle froze me with horror, but the calling I had embraced was to make me forget all such feelings. The plain was covered with corpses, nearly all Austrians. In the village the streets, houses and gardens were all littered with the dead. Not a corner but was sprinkled with blood. We were billeted in the houses. I was not able to go to sleep at night for lack of space to lie on the plank floor. The houses were full of wounded men, without inhabitants, and were wrecked. I had nothing to eat all day ; I could not even dry my clothes, which were sodden with water. Four days later they were still not quite dry.

Such was the upshot of the 23rd, one of the cruellest days of the campaign. The Emperor had not taken off his boots for a week. But the movement of our army corps had so upset the enemy's plan of campaign that negotiations for capitulation were commenced; but we did not accept them.

17th October.—It was then that the Emperor gave the order to break through the defences in order to attempt an assault.

As soon as day broke every man did his best to get hold of some potatoes ; a few minutes later we were served with biscuits, which could not have come at a better time. The general was beaten, and in a moment we were drawn up in battle array above the village of

Elchingen. There we remained all day, to contain the enemy in case he should make a sortie in our direction. There was fighting all day long not far away, although we did not take part in the action. The din of the artillery breaching the defences of Ulm was so loud and so terrible one might have thought the whole world was being destroyed. At night, having gone in search of wood in the vicinity of our position, to warm ourselves a little, the darkness was so profound that I loaded a dead Austrian on my shoulders, having taken him for a log. This startled me terribly. We did not withdraw until nearly ten o'clock at night, having all the trouble in the world to extricate ourselves from the mud.

I was billeted in the superb abbey where the Emperor was lodged. In all the halls, chambers, corridors and cells fires were lit to cook our potatoes. It is impossible to imagine the beauty of this abbey.

The cannonade could still be heard until the night of the 17th, when it suddenly ceased. We learned shortly afterwards that General Mack, abandoning all hope of cutting his way out, had just capitulated, placing in the hands of the Emperor the whole of his army and the fortress he had not defended.

18th October.—We did not go out all day, which was a great comfort, enabling us both to rest and to clean our weapons, which were corroded with rust. During the night, in the midst of a terrible storm, the Danube overflowed and carried away the bodies that were still unburied. They must have learned in Vienna of the misfortunes of the Suabian army, for they floated down the river like the wreckage of a ship.

20th October.—The Emperor spent the whole day at Ulm, on a hill, to watch the march past of the Austrian army, which came out with the honours of war and piled its arms before him. The Emperor, surrounded by a portion of the Guard, sent for the Austrian generals and treated them with the greatest consideration. We then went to pass the night in Augsburg.

The Emperor came to Augsburg preceded by the infantry Grenadiers, who carried the ninety colours taken in this first campaign. This brilliant and martial entry produced in the inhabitants an amazement difficult to describe ; they could not persuade themselves that so great an army had been destroyed in such a few days.

At roll-call on the third day, in the company orders, the proclamation was read of the Emperor to the soldiers of the Grand Army, enumerating all the battles and the trophies which they had won in a fortnight, and announcing the approach of a second campaign against the Russians. An imperial decree, dated from Ulm, reckoned as a campaign the month of Vendémiaire, year XIV, independently of the present campaign.

24th October.—To Munich.—The regiment of the Chasseurs set out from Augsburg on the 23rd October, quite early in the morning, slept at Schwabhausen after a fatiguing march, and reached Munich at three o'clock in the afternoon of the 24th. The latter part of the road was magnificent. We made our entry in full uniform ; an immense crowd had gathered to see us pass. The inhabitants were apparently glad to see the Guard, and their protectors. They received us with the greatest rejoicings. Nowhere had we been treated so well. They kissed us in their delight at being freed from the molestations of the Austrians. They had decorated their houses with emblems expressing the joy they felt in receiving their saviour and their rescuers. Food was abundant ; poultry cost a mere nothing. The only thing that was dear was bread.

On our arrival I was sent to mount guard at the Imperial Palace. The Emperor arrived at nine o'clock at night. All the notables of the Court came to receive him. They were covered with decorations, orders and epaulettes. The Elector's Guard amused me more than anything I saw that night. Its bearing is grotesque ; its costume is very like that of the troops of the time of Henri IV ; it consists of fine, very tall men, all armed with a sabre and a pike.

For two hours I did nothing but present arms, so many great personages were admitted to offer their homage to the Emperor. I had never seen so many decorations of all kinds and all countries as passed before me during that exhausting guard. I believe I must have received the profound salute of all the princes, dukes and barons of reconquered and grateful Bavaria. Under these circumstances, a soldier of the Emperor, a warrior of the Grand Army, had some title to deserve the impressive salute that he was accorded.

25th October.—An almost complete prostration and a sleepless night made me long for a comfortable bed and a good twelve hours' rest. I lay down with such hopes, but about ten or eleven o'clock a discordant ringing of the house-bells rudely awakened the five or six of us who were quartered together. It was an adjutant-major of the regiment, who ordered us to repair with arms and equipment to a guard-house to which he directed us.

Having arrived there, with some others of the Chasseurs who had been told off in the same way, we were sent out on the Landshut road, a league from Munich, to guard the great park of the army. The night was profoundly dark ; the rain was falling in torrents ; it was such weather that at any other time one would not have turned a dog out of doors. In vain did I remark that I had just come off guard ; I was told that that would be taken into account

another time. There was nothing for it but to march
off, since duty and the service demanded it.

There we were, ten or twelve of us, wading in deep
mud, marching at hazard and regretting with all our hearts
the excellent sleeping accommodation we had had to
leave. On reaching our destination our comrades of the
1st corps (Marshal Bernadotte), whom we relieved, left
us an excellent hut of boards, furnished with good straw,
a bivouac fire that was burning quite fiercely, and plenty
of wood to feed it. This was at least some compensation
for our misfortune, and one we richly deserved, but unhappily this unexpected favour soon eluded us. Hardly
had we posted sentries at the points indicated, the rest
of the post taking possession of the hut that promised to
be so useful to us, when the fire blazed up so fiercely that
the men who had entered the shelter had all they could
do to get out of it without being attacked by the flames.
Our efforts to extinguish the fire were without result, and
in a few minutes all was destroyed. Unhappily we had
no time to remove all the muskets, knapsacks, and bearskin bonnets which were inside. The two missing muskets
were loaded, like all those of the men on duty at the
post, and once the fire had reached them they went off. I
was on sentry-go in the road ; a bullet struck my bonnet
above my head and passed right through it, without my
feeling it much. The lofty flames and the two shots raised
the alarm in all the posts round about. Everywhere there
were shouts of " To arms ! " The uneasiness was general,
as it was feared that an attack was being made to capture
the great park of artillery or blow it up.

When reconnaissances had been made and all were
informed of the cause of this sudden alarm all became
peaceful again, materially speaking, but the fear of punishment, and the unpleasantness of our vexatious position,
kept us on the alert during the rest of our guard.

Returning to Munich at two o'clock, we all, in a body,

reported the vexatious incident to the adjutant-major of the week, who, having received the general's orders, sent the sergeant and the corporal to the guard-house of the camp and the Chasseurs to their quarters until further orders. Thus ended a night full of anxiety and fatigue, which might have had very unpleasant consequences if the fire had reached the great park, which was rendered impossible by the torrential rain.

On the 26th my ill-health, and the fatigue and excitement of the previous day, deprived me of all desire to inspect the city of Munich.

On the 5th, 6th and 7th November, on the banks of the Danube, we were several times under arms, especially during the night, in order to watch over the safety of the Imperial headquarters, for a very large portion of the Russian Army was still occupying the left bank. The patrols along the bank, in this bitterly cold weather, and in a dense fog, were by no means amusing.

On the 8th November we moved to Strenburg, where we were quartered so thickly that more than half the men of the Guard had to bivouac. Despite the snow, which was falling in avalanches, the foragers of the companies (and there were many of them) found some excellent cellars of Hungarian wines. We drank of these to warm ourselves, to refresh ourselves, to dispel the tedium of being crammed and half-stifled in rooms when we could not move hand or foot; lastly, we drank so much that if we had had to fire our muskets that night we should not have been able to handle our cartridges. . . . A benevolent spectator of this gigantic orgy, drinking next to nothing, I marvelled, without being dazzled, at the surprising capacity of some of the men, which was truly Gargantuan.

On the following day, the 9th, during a long and fatiguing march, most of the men, being forced to lie down by the roadside, having no legs to follow their comrades, had sufficient proof that this wine was harmful rather than beneficial to the health.

During the day we passed the site of the terrible battle of Amstetten (5th November) between Oudinot's Grenadiers, combined with the cavalry of Prince Murat, and the Russians, and then came to the little town of that name. We had to cross several rivers, whose bridges, cut and hastily repaired, greatly delayed our progress.

On the 12th November, half-way between Saint-Poelten and Burkesdorf, we met the magistrates of Vienna, who came to implore the Emperor to spare their capital and their sovereign, and to offer him the keys of the city. The Emperor followed close behind us; he therefore passed through us with the Viennese. They then witnessed a scene which must have proved to them how the Emperor was loved by his troops.

We climbed a very steep slope and lined the road on either side. The 9th corps, which climbed the hill with us, gave way to the same impulse as the whole Guard. In a moment the cries of " Vive l'Empereur " ran all along the line, our caps and bonnets on the ends of our bayonets; the Emperor's carriages passed at a walk, so that the deputies had plenty of time to take in the plaudits which the Guard and the Army offered their sovereign. The Emperor was in one of the Court carriages; this was the first time he made use of them since leaving Paris.

After crossing the Rhine, every time His Majesty met us on the road we halted to give him military honours and salute him with our acclamations. All the corps of the army did the same unless otherwise ordered. Often, at these unpremeditated reviews, the Emperor complimented regiments which had distinguished themselves in a recent action, filled gaps by promotion, and distributed decorations. This was a fortuitous happening which was eagerly desired, and the desires of many were satisfied in this way.

13th November.—Less than half a league from Vienna, instead of continuing our route, we entered a village to our left, called Schönbrunn. This incident annoyed us greatly, for we had expected to be quartered in the city. One thing that did not at all please us was that from the middle of the village market-place we could see Vienna across the valley ; the mass of spires, belfries and towers formed a striking contrast with the countryside, which was covered with snow. On the same open place was the Imperial Palace which the Emperor had chosen for his residence.

We were quartered there for duty in the palace. Roused in the night, without being ordered on duty, I was compelled, with other comrades, no more anxious than myself to go trotting about at such hours, to patrol round the park, which meant an hour's march.

We were forbidden to go to Vienna without leave.

16th November.—The regiment was preparing for parade when the order for departure was received. This news was a thunderclap. We knew little of what was happening ; it was not until much later that we learned of the course of events. We could not imagine what was preventing the Emperor of Austria from making peace. We were marching into a new country, little known, offering few resources. The Russians, still fighting as they retreated, drew us perforce into the most frightful country, and this, above all, at a time of year unsuitable for marching. I confess frankly that this departure displeased me sorely ; which did not prevent my making the journey with the rest.

We left Schönbrunn at two o'clock and after half an

hour's march we entered Vienna. I passed through this city keenly desiring to become acquainted with it, but the time had not yet arrived. On leaving the city, half dead of cold, we could only run to prevent ourselves from freezing. We came to Stockerau at ten o'clock at night. The Emperor slept at Stockerau.

17th November.—Leaving at daybreak, we marched all day without a halt, as far as the Taya, which we had to cross at ten o'clock on a very dark night, by a yielding, swaying, very narrow plank. Our ranks, greatly depleted during the last few hours by the long and exhausting march, became even more so, as the least blunder resulted in a tumble into the water. Consequently those who found themselves on the farther side of the river were by no means numerous, and hardly sufficed for the service of the Imperial headquarters. Another cause which contributed to the large number of men who were left behind was the many cellars filled with Moravian wine which were met with along our route. It may be imagined that exhausted men, ill-fed and sleeping little, always on the march, took advantage of these rare and excellent opportunities to put new strength into their legs and seize a moment's bliss, but unfortunately abuse followed on the heels of beneficial use.[1]

---

[1] Here ends the original version, which, as the text indicates, was for the most part written at Schönbrunn in 1805. I can give only a portion of it, as of the whole *Itinerary*. We cannot, as I have explained, follow the Skirmishers day by day, in the rain and the mud, through their long days without food, through all the little incidents of their heroic endurance ; but what is here given will enable us to understand what was at work in the mind of Commandant Barrès, thirty-five years later, when he re-wrote the notes made in his twentieth year. His sufferings he thenceforth relegates to the background, and he takes pleasure rather in the curious things that he has seen and the great events in which he took part. For example, in this campaign of 1805 the sufferings of the Grand Army were necessary in order that Napoleon might outflank the enemy at a considerable distance along the valleys of the Main and the Neckar, and then, wheeling suddenly southward, descend the Danube from Wurzburg to Donawerth. This march, so onerous to J.-B. Barrès and his

AUSTERLITZ.

On the 30th November Barrès was in bivouac five miles from Brunn, to the left of the Olmutz road, on the slope of a low hill.

1st December.—In front of the position we occupied was a hillock covered with guns. The Emperor's bivouac lay between us and this hillock. Beyond it was a small plain sloping gently to a brook that ran from left to right. This plain, very long in the direction of the brook, was commanded by heights that took their rise on the other side of the brook and stretched from the woods on the left to the ponds and marshes on the right.

At night, by the light of the bivouac fires, a proclamation of the Emperor was read to us, announcing a great battle for the following day, the 2nd December. Shortly afterwards the Emperor came to our bivouac, to have a look at us or to read us a letter which had just been brought to him. A Chasseur took a handful of straw and lit it so that he might read it more readily. From this bivouac the Emperor went on to another. Men followed him with burning torches to light his path. As his inspection was prolonged and extended the number of torches increased ; soldiers followed him shouting " Vive l'Empereur." These cries of love and enthusiasm spread in all directions like an electric fire ; all the soldiers, non-commissioned officers and officers provided themselves with improvised torches, so that in less than a quarter of an hour the whole Guard, the united Grenadiers, the 5th corps, which was on our left, in front of us, and the 4th, to the right of us, as well

comrades, placed them between Ulm and Vienna, and cut off the retreat of the Austrians. Ulm being taken, Napoleon moved upon Vienna and drew the two emperors, the Russian and the Austrian, some seventy miles north of Vienna, to the battlefield of Austerlitz, which he himself had selected and reconnoitred ten days previously. What genius in the leader, what hardship for the troops ! In 1835 Barrès preferred to forget these hardships.—M. B.

as the 3rd, farther away and in front, and the 1st, which
was more than a mile to our rear, were doing the same.
It was a general conflagration, a movement of enthusiasm,
so sudden that the Emperor must have been dazzled by
it. It was magnificent, prodigious. Having watched it
for some time I returned to my bivouac, after searching
for it for a long while, all the lights having made me lose
my bearings. I am sure it was a mere chance that inspired
this torchlight procession and that the Emperor himself
had not expected it.

2nd December.—Long before daylight the reveille was
beaten in all the regiments; we stood to arms and
remained in battle formation until the reconnoitring parties
had returned. The morning was cold, the fog fairly thick;
there was complete silence throughout our ranks. This
extraordinary calm after so wild and uproarious a night
had in it something solemn, as of a majestic submission
to the decrees of God; it was the precursor of a violent,
deadly storm about to rise and lay empires low.

The Emperor, surrounded by his marshals and the
leading generals of his army, had taken up his position
on the hillock of which I have spoken, giving orders for
the disposition of his troops and waiting for the mist to
clear away before giving the signal to attack. The signal
was given, and very soon the whole of the immense line
of battle was in action.

Meanwhile the 1st corps, which was in the rear, moved
forward, passing to the right and the left of the little hill;
saluting, shouting " Vive l'Empereur ! " and waving their
headgear on the points of their bayonets, swords and
sabres, Marshal Bernadotte at their head, bearing his
hat aloft in the like manner, and all to the sound of drums
and music, and guns and a sharp musketry fire.

After the 1st corps had passed we began to move; we
formed the reserve; it consisted of twenty picked battalions,

eight being of the Imperial Guard, two of the Italian
Royal Guard, and ten of Grenadiers and light infantry
united. Behind us marched the cavalry of the Guard
and several battalions of Foot Dragoons. The picked
battalions were in close column formation, by divisions,
within deploying distance, having eighty pieces of artillery
in the intervals. This formidable reserve marched in line
of battle, in full uniform and bearskins, plumes flutter-
ing in the wind, the eagles and the standards to the fore,
pointing with a proud gaze the path to victory. In this
order we crossed the plain and scaled the heights with
shouts of " Vive l'Empereur ! " When we had reached
the plateau which the Russians had occupied a few minutes
earlier, the Emperor halted us in order to address us,
having signed to us with his hand that he wished to speak.
He said, in a clear, vibrating voice that thrilled us :
" Chasseurs, my Horse Guards have just routed the Russian
Imperial Guard. Colonels, flags, guns, all have been
taken. Nothing could resist their intrepid valour.
You will imitate them." He then departed immediately to say the same thing to the other battalions in
reserve.

The Russian Army was pierced in the centre and cut
in two. The left-hand portion, which was facing the
right wing of the French Army, encountered the corps of
Marshals Soult and Davoust ; the right-hand portion, the
corps of Bernadotte and Lannes. The reserve linked up
the four corps and kept separate what had been divided
by the able manœuvres of the commander-in-chief and the
valour of the troops. After a quarter of an hour's breath-
ing-space the infantry of the Guard changed its direction,
turning towards the right, to go to the support of the
4th corps, by marching along the high ground.

Coming to the slope that overlooks the lakes I fell out
of the ranks for a moment, and was thus able to observe,
in the plain, the terrible struggle engaged between the

4th corps and the portion of the Russian Army facing it, having the lakes at its rear. We arrived in time to give it the *coup de grâce*, and finally hurl it into the lakes. This last deadly movement was terrible. Imagine 12,000 to 15,000 men fleeing at the top of their speed over thin ice and suddenly falling in, almost to a man !

What a grievous and melancholy spectacle, but what a triumph for the victors ! Our arrival at the lakes was saluted by a score of cannon-shot, which did us no great harm. The artillery of the Guard very soon extinguished this fire and itself proceeded to fire with incomparable briskness upon the ice, in order to shatter it and render it incapable of supporting the weight of men. The battle was completely won ; a victory without example had crowned our eagles with undying laurels.

After a brief rest we retraced our steps, following almost the same path, and traversing the whole length of the battlefield. The night overtook us on this march ; the weather, which had been fine all day, now turned wet, and the darkness became so profound that we could no longer see. Having marched for a long time at hazard, trying to find the Emperor's headquarters, Marshal Bessières, having no guides and being without hope of coming upon the place, made us bivouac on the spot where he came to this conclusion. It was time, for it was late and we were all greatly exhausted.

Having piled arms by sections and laid down our knapsacks, we had to set about procuring food, firewood and straw. But where to seek them ? It was so dark and such bitter weather ! There was nothing to tell us where we should find a village. Finally some soldiers of the 5th corps, who were prowling round us, directed us to one in a deep valley. I went thither with several of my comrades ; it was full of Russian dead and wounded ; I think it was about here that the Russian Guard was cut up. I found some potatoes there and a small cask of new white wine, so sour it might have been used as vinegar. Those who drank of it in the camp had such colic they thought they were poisoned. The night was passed in conversing : each man told what had struck him most vividly during that immortal day. There were no personal feats to tell of, since we had done nothing but march, but we spoke of the frightful disaster of the lake, the courage of the wounded we had met with on our march, the immense quantity of military wreckage seen on the battlefield and the rows of the Russian soldiers' knapsacks laid down before the action, which they had not been able to recover afterwards, having been thrust in another direction, shot at, mown down with grapeshot, sabred, annihilated. There was also some question of the name by which the battle would be known, but no one knew the locality, nor the spot where the most decisive blows were struck. Since nothing was as yet known of the final result the problem remained unsolved.

With daylight my uncertainty as to the part of the battlefield on which we had spent the night was dissipated. I realized, having gone the rounds of the position, which was covered with dead bodies, and wounded men who were being removed, that we were about half a league to the right of the road from Brunn to Olmutz, and the same distance from that running from Brunn to Austerlitz, these two roads bifurcating near the post of Posaritz, where the Emperor was to have lodged.

About ten o'clock we left for Austerlitz ; but before taking the path across country that led thither we were ordered once more to bivouac for some hours. Finally we reached Austerlitz at night. The Emperor was passing the night in the castle of the little town, replacing the Emperors Alexander and Francis II, who had left in the morning.

During the day the Emperor's proclamation was read, beginning with these words : " Soldiers, I am pleased with you," and ending with the phrase : " It will be enough to say : ' I was at the battle of Austerlitz,' and men will reply : ' There is a fine fellow ! ' "

4th December.—In the morning two battalions of Grenadiers and two of Chasseurs were united and despatched on the road to Hungary. I was of them. After four hours' marching we were sent to take up a position on a hill to the right of the road, together with the cavalry and artillery of the Guard ; farther on, on the same front, were the troops of the line ; in front, and a little below us, we saw the Emperor warming himself at a bivouac fire, surrounded by his staff.

On the hill facing us were the enemy's troops in order of battle. We thought at first that an action was about to take place, but after a wait of a few minutes two handsome carriages arrived, surrounded by officers and cavalrymen, from one of which I saw a man in white uniform alighting, and the Emperor Napoleon going to meet him.

We then readily understood that this was an interview for negotiating the peace, and that the person who had alighted from the carriage was the Emperor of Austria. After their conversation, which lasted less than an hour, we took the road to Austerlitz again, where we arrived utterly worn out with fatigue and dying of hunger ; we had made eight leagues through the mud, in the bitterest cold. It was long after dark when we entered our quarters.

On the 7th December began the return to France. At Brunn we skirted part of the battlefield in which some of the dead were still lying. On the 10th, having recrossed the Danube and marched through Vienna, we came to Freysing, opposite the village and the Imperial Palace of

Schönbrunn, and there we remained until the 27th December.

During this long and welcome rest I went to Vienna several times, for the purpose of inspecting the city, and to make a few purchases and convert into French money the paper florins with which the arrears of pay due to us since crossing the Rhine had been paid. It was money well earned, but the rascals of money-changers profited by the occasion to make us lose heavily on the trans-action, the disastrous war fought by Austria having greatly depreciated this paper-money, apart from the fact that I knew nothing as to its real value.

During our stay we received our uniform great-coats, which arrived from France. They were very welcome, for the cloth smocks in which we had made the campaign were neither warm nor handsome.

During the seventeen days of our cantonment we had some days of very bad weather ; above all, a great deal of snow and some hard frosts. The Emperor often had us under arms, making us manœuvre or march past.

On the 26th the guns announced the conclusion of the peace ; it was signed on the 25th at Presburg.

On the 28th, in the morning, our battalion was sent to Vienna, to take over and escort the treasury of the army to Strasbourg ; it consisted of eight waggons and of twelve to fifteen millions in gold or silver. Most of it came from France, and had not been spent in this brief campaign, which, instead of impoverishing, enriched it.

On the 20th February, 1806, we reached the barracks at Rueil.

We had been 174 days absent from Paris ; 110 were days of marching ; 60 days of rest. From Vienna to Paris we marched, in 46 days, 306 leagues, which makes an average of $6\frac{2}{3}$ leagues a day.

Seven Months at Rueil.

At Rueil our duties were confined to mounting guard at Malmaison and the palace of Saint-Cloud. These two duties were not exhausting, since they were not too frequent. At Saint-Cloud we were fed at the Emperor's expense ; the meals were almost the same as in barracks. Another duty, rather more onerous, was to march in parade order to the Tuileries once a fortnight.

Mounting guard at Saint-Cloud was extremely interesting, owing to the remarkable spectacle of the immense assemblage of important personages who came to pay court to the powerful monarch who had overcome anarchy and the enemies of France. I often saw there kings, princes, nearly all the marshals, the ministers, the great dignitaries of the Empire, the high officers of the crown, the senators, the generals of the army, and all the great functionaries who came to salute the master of the destinies of Europe. It was truly a fine sight on the days of the great receptions. Not one of these illustrious figures passed but I discovered his name ; I very soon knew nearly all of them.

It was while I was stationed at Rueil that I was informed of the grievous loss that my mother and all the family had just suffered in the person of my father, who had died at the age of sixty-six. This unexpected death caused me much grief, for in him I lost a friend rather than a father, so kind and affectionate was he to me. His letters, so loving and so eager for information, had often delighted and consoled me.

Rumours of war that had for some time been flying about began daily to assume a more definite shape ; an infantry camp of four regiments established before Meudon seemed to foretell coming hostilities, for everything there was being organized for war. Curiosity and the wish to see a friend of mine, recently appointed officer, at the time

6

of the promotions made in Vienna, led me to go thither twice, to enjoy this military spectacle at the gates of the capital and to tell my friend how glad I was to see him with epaulettes and sword in place of the knapsack and musket which we, his less favoured comrades, were carrying. As a matter of fact there were not many promotions, since they affected only sixteen of the Grenadiers and Chasseurs ; but they pleased even those who were not of those chosen, for they proved that it was the Emperor's intention to appoint us all in turn; though sixteen out of sixteen hundred was a very small proportion.

On the 11th September, 1806, the whole Guard, considerably augmented since the close of the campaign, was mustered in the plain of Les Sablons that the Emperor might review it in detail. Everything was there, men, material and administration : no one and nothing was left in barracks but those men and horses that could not stand upright.

The companies having been deployed in single file, each man's knapsack on the ground and laid open before him, and the cavalrymen, dismounted, holding their horses by the bridle, the Emperor passed on foot along the front of the deployed ranks, questioned the men, and inspected their weapons, knapsacks, and uniform with excruciating deliberation. In the same way he inspected the horses, the guns, the caissons, the baggage-waggons, and the ambulances with the same care and attention as he had given to the infantry. This long and minute inspection completed, the regiments reformed in their usual order so that he might see the troops assembled and put them through manœuvres.

A few movements had already been executed when a furious storm rose and broke upon us, terrible in its violence ; and all that splendour, all the glittering gold, all the brilliant uniforms were smirched and soiled and made unfit for further use ; above all those of the mounted

Chasseurs and the artillery, which were especially smart and sumptuous. Less than a quarter of an hour sufficed to make the ground impracticable and prevent even the march past. We withdrew miserably, as downcast as if we had lost a great battle.

A few days later we received orders to hold ourselves in readiness to march on the 20th. This news was received with rejoicing. We had long been weary of this quiet, easy life, of that comfort which one does not appreciate except one compares it with past and soon-forgotten sufferings.

We had been just seven months in this peaceful garrison.

WAR AGAINST PRUSSIA.

We left on the 20th September. The first march, already a long one if one sets out from Paris, was three leagues longer when we started from Rueil. When we reached Saint-Marc, where the company was detached, I fell on the threshold of my billet like a man struck by a bullet. It was a long time before I regained consciousness. Thanks to the touching care of the worthy dame in whose house I was billeted, and a blood-letting, performed by the village surgeon, I was restored to life.

A night's rest and a strong constitution gave me courage and legs for the following day.

On the 22nd, at dawn, we mounted the carts which had brought the watch of the 1st regiment. These vehicles took us as far as Soissons, where we took those that the watch had just left, so that the same carts made two marches, and the 2nd regiment slept where the 1st halted on the march and halted where the 1st regiment passed the night.

We spent the night of the 23rd at Rethel; of the 24th at Stenay. On the 25th, 26th, and 27th, and all the night of the 28th, we were *en route*, with no rest beyond the time needed to change carts and hastily eat a mouthful of food when permitted. These seventy-two hours in the carts nearly broke our bones. Packed into the execrable country carts, without seats, almost without straw, unable either to sit down in comfort or to get a few minutes' quiet sleep, we ardently longed for the end of this long journey, during which we were in every respect so uncomfortable.

How could we possibly settle ourselves comfortably with such impediments as ten or twelve muskets and the sabres, cartridge-boxes and knapsacks of ten or twelve men, who were all bored, discontented and often impatient, the least contradiction or vexation resulting in a quarrel ? Apart from these moments of ill-temper, often very excusable, we were cheerful in the daytime because we were marching to the hills and because we used to talk with the people of the countryside, who came in crowds to see us go by. For them it was a new and fascinating spectacle. In many of the villages baskets of fruit were thrown into the carts ; we were offered cider in the Ardennes and beer in the German departments. However, we left the carts without regret, preparing to march and carry our whole military equipment.

On the 5th October we came in the evening to Closler-Brach, a small town with a superb abbey. The 1st regiment remained there ; the 2nd was detached in a populous village a long way to the left of the road leading to Bamberg. To reach this village we had to pass through a forest, where the ground was very uneven and hilly. The night surprised us there. In a little while the men, unable to see longer where they were on the almost imperceptible path they were following, began to collide with trees and banks of earth, and to fall into holes, or ravines, or over precipices. There were shouts, oaths and terrible groans. The Chasseurs, to avoid the accidents which had befallen those that preceded them, diverged from the path, scattering through the forest and finally losing themselves. In vain did General Curial, the second in command, who was at the head of the regiment, order it to halt and to beat a rally on the drums ; the men did not rally, because it was impossible to do so. One could not take four steps without striking against an obstacle ; fortunately I was in the vanguard, where there were guides and torches burning, which enabled us to reach our billets late, but without casualties. More than three-fourths of the regiment passed the night in the forest ; many were wounded or bruised. All those who had fallen behind rejoined the regiment before entering Bamberg ; we halted for a long time in order to rally them all.

On the 7th, at Bamberg, a proclamation of the Emperor to the Grand Army, read to the companies formed up in a circle, told us that war was declared upon Prussia.

On the 10th, having traversed the forests of Thuringia and the small towns of Lobenstein, Ebersdorf and Saalburg on the Saal, we saw the 5th corps at grips with the Prussian army, pushing it vigorously toward Saalfeld, where it was completely defeated. Prince Ludgwig of Prussia, the nephew of the king, who was with the rearguard, was killed, by a sabre-cut, by a sergeant-major of the 10th Hussars. The spot where we stood, from which our infantry division of the 5th corps had gone into action, was covered with numerous articles of equipment which the soldiers had thrown away to lighten their knapsacks, which were too heavy for fighting. As a matter of fact we were all too heavily burdened, which made marching, for the infantry, a heavy and awkward business. We came to Schleitz.

All was topsy-turvy in this little Saxon town, so terrified and bewildered were the townsmen by the evils of warfare. At supper our *bauer* (peasant) gave us silver to eat with. After the meal I told him that if he wanted to keep his silver I strongly advised him to hide it and replace it by steel ware. I think he took my advice.

On the 11th October, along the road, and in the fields near Auma, we saw numbers of Prussian corpses, the results of a cavalry engagement. We were forbidden to enter this rather pretty little village ; but, as we had no rations, hunger, which drives the wolves into the open, as the proverb says, compelled us to disobey the order.

I was in a courtyard with a number of other Chasseurs, in the act of cutting up a pig which we had just killed, when Marshal Lefèvre, commander of the Foot Guard, entered, with General Rousset, chief of staff of the Imperial Guard. We were frozen with terror, and in our alarm let our knives fall ; we could not run away, for they had closed the gates on us. At first they were very angry and threatened to have us shot ; but having heard us they said, half in anger, half-laughing : " Get off to the camp, sharp, you confounded brigands ; take your spoil, but so that no one sees it, and above all don't get caught by the patrols." This was good advice, and we followed it exactly. We had a good laugh in bivouac, over the fright we had had and the half-laughing anger of the kindly marshal.

JENA.

13th October.—In bivouac, before Jena, on a mountain, on the left bank of the Saal. To get there we went through the town and took up our position when it was already dark. Having learned that the 21st light regiment of the 5th corps was not far distant I went to see the numerous fellow-countrymen who were serving in it. They were on outpost duty, without fire, forbidden to engage in hostilities, and I soon left them. On returning to camp I learned that Jena was on fire and that the troops had flocked thither. I followed the rest, in spite of my weariness, the distance to be covered, and the execrable road I had to go down, on which more than a thousand men were busied, making it practicable for the artillery and cavalry. And, as a matter of fact, there was neither artillery nor cavalry on the flat, narrow hilltop on which the combatants were gathered, although the two armies were not a musket-shot apart. Having traversed this awkward bit of road I entered Jena. Good God, what a frightful spectacle this unhappy city offered at that hour of night ! On the one hand, the fire ; on the other, the shattering of doors and cries of despair. I went into a bookseller's shop ; the books were thrown pell-mell on the floor. I picked up one at random ; it was a guide to travellers in Germany, printed in French. It was the second volume ; I searched in vain for the first, but could not find it. (But on the day after the battle, when order had been re-established, I returned to the bookseller's to ask him to sell me this first volume. It was a little heavy to carry in my knap-sack, but I was so pleased to possess this work that it seemed to me its weight would not trouble me.) On leaving the book-shop I went into a grocery where they were distributing sugar in the loaf. They gave me five or six pounds, which I took at once into camp. That was all I had to eat the whole of the following day.

A few hours after my return to camp we were ordered under arms, and, formed into a square, awaited in silence the signal for action.

14th October.—A cannon-shot fired by the Prussians, which passed over our heads, announced the attack. The sound of guns and musketry was immediately heard along the fronts of both armies ; the fire of the infantry was heavy and continuous, but one could make nothing out, the fog being so thick that one could not see six yards. The Emperor had, by his skilful manœuvres, forced the Prussians to give battle in an unfavourable position and

on unfavourable ground, since they presented their left
flank to their base of operations, and this flank was
turned.

The Emperor broke his fast before the troops, while
waiting for the fog to rise.   At last the sun shone radiantly,
the Emperor mounted his horse and we moved forward.
Until four o'clock in the afternoon we were manœuvring
in support of the troops engaged.   Several times our
approach was enough to force the Prussians and Saxons
to abandon the positions they were defending ;   but in
spite of this the struggle was keen, the resistance desperate,
above all in the villages and the copses, but once all our
cavalry had arrived at the front and was able to manœuvre
there was nothing but disaster ;   the retreat became a
flight, and the rout was general.

The Emperor halted us on a bare, very high plateau,
where he remained about an hour, receiving the reports
that were coming in from all points, giving orders, and
conversing with his generals.   As he was right in our
midst we were able to watch him rejoicing in his tremendous
triumph, distributing praises and receiving with pride the
numerous trophies that were brought to him.   Lying on
a great open map spread out on the ground, or walking
to and fro with his hands behind his back, rolling a Prussian
drum along the ground, he listened attentively to all that
was said to him and ordered a number of different
movements.

When the masses of prisoners and the innumerable
guns had defiled before the victors, and the cannon were
no longer heard, or their detonations were at all events
few and far between, the Emperor returned to Jena,
followed by the infantry of the Guard.   We had more
than two leagues to cover, and it was after five o'clock ;
so we were not able to get in until after seven.   We were
billeted on the town, each corporal taking his squad with
him.   A rather handsome house invited us to enter :

we were the first, so took possession of it ; it was a girls'
boarding-school. The cage was left, but the birds had
flown, leaving their plumes, or at least some part of their
belongings : pianos, harps, guitars, books, tasteful drawings
or engravings, and desk equipment to satisfy every need
and task. The rooms were charmingly furnished and
very tasteful. I profited by the circumstances to write
a long letter to my elder brother, in which I told him of
our brilliant victory.

On the following day, at daybreak, I loitered round
headquarters to watch for the departure of the Imperial
courier. I had not to wait long. I begged the first courier
to start to put my letter in the post as soon as he reached
Mayence. He consented with pleasure, saying that the
good news could not be too widely distributed.

On the 15th we were ordered to cook large quantities
of meat, which had to be fetched from the country, in order
to make broth for the wounded. All day long the Guard
was occupied in this pious duty. My God, how many
the wounded were ! All the churches, all the large buildings were full of them. The duties of sick-nurse are very
painful when one identifies oneself with the sufferings
of the unfortunates whom one is trying to solace !

On the 18th to Merseburg, on the left bank of the Saal,
in a charming position. I was on the bodyguard of the
Emperor, who arrived after we did, coming from Weimar.

During the day we passed close to the battlefield of
Rosbach. Jena fully avenged this defeat !

The Emperor enters Berlin.

27th October.—For some days we had been marching
through the sand on the banks of the Elbe and the March
of Brandenburg, which made our feet very tender and
painful. Once on the horrible Potsdam highway, made
of little sharp pebbles, our sufferings were truly atrocious.

We did not march so much as skip and hobble like men whose feet are being scorched. If it had not been so painful it would have been truly comical.

In the morning we set out from Charlottenburg in full uniform, our plumed bonnets on our heads, the whole Guard being united and formed up to make a solemn entry. Having reached the fine Charlottenburg gate, or rather the magnificent triumphal arch, on which is a quadriga, a very fine piece of sculpture, the Emperor reviewed his splendid Guard on horseback and put himself at our head, surrounded by a staff as resplendent as it was numerous. The Grenadiers followed us; the special gendarmerie brought up the rear.

To reach the King's palace, where the Emperor was to be lodged, we followed the wide, magnificent Avenue of the Linden-trees,[1] the finest in existence, which excels in beauty, if not in length, the boulevards of Paris. The crowd gathered to see us pass was so great that one might have thought the whole population of Berlin was assembled at this point to watch the conquerors of their country go by; which shows that all the loafers are not in Paris.

I was on guard at the palace. In the evening I was sentry on one of the walks crossing the great lawn in front of the palace, when a very well-dressed man offered me a drink from a bottle which he had hidden under his coat. I repulsed him rather roughly; he must have thought I behaved so only because I feared the liquor might be poisoned. He said: "Don't be afraid, it's wholesome drink!" and at the same time he took a good pull at it. I thanked him again, at the same time telling him to take himself off. 'Pon my word, I said to myself, here's a Berliner who is hardly a Prussian! it looks as if it should have been easy to give his king and countrymen, and all those who wear the Prussian uniform, such a sound thrashing!

---

[1] Allée des Tilleuls, *Unter den Linden.*—Tr

On the 28th we were billeted in a wide street, the Roos-Strasse, in a fine, spacious house. It was midnight; my five comrades and I were sleeping profoundly when we were awakened by cries of "Fire! Fire!" I was the first to reach the window and then saw that all the upper part of the house was in flames. We began to run round the room as though demented, trying unsuccessfully to dress ourselves, colliding with and tumbling over one another; it did not strike us particularly to go to the door and assure ourselves whether escape was possible. Very fortunately the staircase was intact, and we were able to get out unhurt. There we were in the street, almost naked, without shoes, up to our knees in the snow, our possessions in bed-sheets slung over our shoulders; hampered with muskets, sabres, cartridge-boxes, bearskins, plumes, hats—it was the very devil, in short; not knowing whither to betake ourselves, bewildered by the shouts of the crowd which came pouring out of every side-street, the galloping of the horses that were bringing the pumps and barrels of water fastened on sledges, the tocsin sounded on all the bells of the city, the general, which was being beaten in all the sections, the arrival of the first pickets of cavalry, and orderly officers, generals, and the governor of the city, General Huttin, colonel of the dismounted Grenadiers of the Guard, and all the soldiery, who thought this was a signal for an insurrection against the life of the Emperor and the garrison. The din and confusion were such that one did not know what one was doing.

While all steps were being taken to check the progress of the fire we finished dressing ourselves amidst all this confusion; but the salvage of our equipment was not complete, so that we had to go up to our room again to search for our effects, an adventure not without danger, and in recovering them we had the pleasure of helping some persons to escape who might have fallen victims to the disaster. I should mention, to the credit of the

authorities and the citizens, that the work of rescue was
prompt and well directed.

An exasperated remark of the governor's made us
fear that he held us guilty of this unhappy accident. In
the morning we went to him to be interrogated ; a few
words sufficed to exculpate us. We were billeted on a
banker in the same street.

Every day there was a grand parade in the outer
courtyard of the citadel, which lay between the palace and
the lawn of which I have spoken. The service battalion
and the pickets of the cavalry of the Guard were present
and remained while the others marched past. All the
troops that arrived from France, all those that had remained
in the rear to pursue the remnants of the Prussian Army,
or to blockade the fortified places, which the enemy was
surrendering daily, were reviewed by the Emperor, who
kept them a long time under arms. At the same time he
made all the promotions necessary to fill up the regimental
cadres, distributed decorations to the soldiers who were
recommended as having merited this glorious recompense,
delivered speeches to the corps, made them manœuvre in
order to assure himself of their practical training, and,
in short, neglected nothing that might touch their well-
being or fire them with the longing to rush forward to
other battles.

These parades and reviews were very interesting to
watch ; we loved to follow with our eyes the man who
was shattering thrones and nations. Twice we executed
great manœuvres in the country round about Berlin,
under the Emperor's eyes.

I was one of those who bore the colours taken from the
enemy at the battle of Jena, when the Emperor presented
them to the deputation from the Senate, which came to
Berlin to receive them. This was a present which the
Emperor made to his Conservative Senate.

During the twenty-seven days we remained in Berlin

I visited all the public buildings and important collections and all the best districts of that fine city. Several times I went to the play to see the great French operas performed, translated and arranged for the German stage.

On the day following his entry into Berlin the Emperor inserted in the orders to the army a new proclamation announcing that the Russians were marching to meet us and that they would be defeated as at Austerlitz. It wound up with this sentence : " Soldiers, I cannot better express what I feel for you than by saying that I bear in my heart the love that you show me day by day."

Going to meet the Russians.

Entering Poland on the 29th November, Barrès reached Posen on the 3rd December, where he remained until the 15th.

On our arrival the Emperor's new proclamation was read in the orders to the army, on the 2nd December, to announce the anniversary of the battle of Austerlitz, the capture of Warsaw, which the Russians had been unable to defend, and the arrival of the Grand Army on the banks of the Vistula.

This fine proclamation was followed by a decree which destined the site of the Madeleine in Paris for a temple of glory, on the façade of which was to be placed this inscription in letters of gold : *The Emperor Napoleon to the soldiers of the Grand Army.* This decree proved to the army how the Emperor was wont to watch over its glory and encourage it to new triumphs. . . .

On the 24th December we came to Warsaw. Since crossing the Wertha on the 29th November we had been in Prussian Poland. Our rapid march did not give us a very good opinion of its prosperity. What poor, melan-

choly villages we found, what wretchedness we had before
our eyes, without counting our own ! Always up to the
knees in mud or melting snow, marching all day, with
neither shelter nor fire ! When we reached our halts the
food was in keeping with what we saw, with all that
surrounded us.

On the 25th the crossing of the Vistula before Warsaw
was made over a bridge of boats which was restored after
the Russians had passed. The river contained considerable quantities of drifting ice, the frosts having returned
two days earlier, and was flowing fast enough to make us
fear for the safety of the bridge. Having crossed the
bridge, we traversed, obliquely, part of the Praga suburb,
celebrated for its importance, but even more so for its
misfortunes, almost the entire population having been
massacred by Suvarov in 1794. At the farther edge of
the suburbs is the Austrian frontier, which we had to
respect, so that we were compelled to deviate to the left
lest we should violate the neutrality of that Power.

The crossing of the Bug was a matter of considerable
difficulty and danger. The bridge, hastily repaired for
the passage of that part of the army which was operating
on the right bank, was often carried away by the force
of the current, or shattered by the great bergs of ice
drifting on the wide stream. We were able to pass only
by small detachments and when the engineer officers
(*pontonniers*) considered that we could cross in safety.

On the 26th we were in bivouac, near a village called
Loparzin, the headquarters of the Emperor.

At nightfall, as we were traversing a very dense pine-
forest, I was called by name, by three or four fellow-Lor-
rainers, from Blesle, who had fallen to the rear of their
corps ; they were what one calls marauders or stragglers.
Having halted near a canteen, they offered me some bread
and pickled pork, which I accepted with pleasure, having
eaten nothing during the day. Having spent some time

with them, I tried to regain my company, but I went astray, with a number of my comrades, in this infernal forest, which seemed to be limitless. At length, at daybreak, we came to a hamlet where a number of soldiers had taken refuge. I learned with pleasure that my regiment was not far distant. I stopped for a short rest, for I was dropping with sleep and fatigue. When I saw that the regiment was getting ready to depart I made for it across country. The surface only of the ground was frozen, on account of the thaw which had set in the previous day, so that at every step I plunged deep into the soft earth, so that I could hardly drag my feet out again. My shoes would have remained there had I not decided to carry them in my hands and to walk barefoot. In this way I went more than five miles on a crust of ice that broke at every step. I was not able to put my shoes on again, taking advantage of a moment's halt, until long after I had rejoined the company.

During the day the roads, or rather the ground we were crossing, had become impracticable. Two men could not march close together without the risk of sinking through the crust. We marched as though in skirmishing order. All were falling behind, both victors and vanquished. The guns, the caissons, the baggage-waggons, and the Emperor's carriages, no less than the humble canteen-cart, all were mired and could not be moved. The roads and fields were covered with the Russian equipment and baggage. If the pursuit could have been continued for three or four days the enemy army would have been compelled to abandon all its equipment, without even the power of defending it. But the French themselves were in no condition to attack. We had to halt, or cease to be an army. The order was accordingly given the same day that the army was to go into cantonments and the Guard to return to Warsaw, where the Emperor was to establish his headquarters.

31st December.—My billet paper sent me to Monseigneur the Bishop of Warsaw. I was greatly rejoiced by this happy chance, which sent me to a great dignitary of the Church, doubtless to see him put into practice that Christian charity which seeks to solace those who suffer : but nothing of the sort ! Monseigneur did not deign to interest himself in our dilapidated stomachs nor to make us forget our miseries on the right bank of the Bug. On the contrary, he contrived that we should be lodged elsewhere, so that he should not be compelled to provide the air we should have breathed in his house.

Good luck sent us to one of Monseigneur's canons, who spoke French very well ; but that was all. . . .

During our stay in Warsaw the cold was very severe. In twenty-four hours the Vistula was frozen solid and could be crossed everywhere on foot. This did not prevent the Emperor from attending reviews and parades, at which we marched past him. He did much as he did in Berlin, with the difference that our evolutions were not so lengthy, as it was often impossible to remain on the ground.

Numbers of graceful sledges ploughed through all the streets, passing like a flash. This manner of locomotion, which was unfamiliar to me, interested me keenly.

Warsaw is a fine city in some of its quarters. We remained there until the 27th January, 1807. However, I was not very eager to visit the public buildings and museums ; the weather was not accommodating. Huddled in a corner of my poor, cold room, where I used to read for part of the day, I did not go out unless duty and service obliged me to do so.

There were a few promotions of Skirmishers to the rank of officer ; this was the second batch. It affected only a few protégés of the generals in greatest favour, or men in the Emperor's suite.

On the 2nd February, 1807, after a battle, in which we were in reserve, we were ordered to bivouac in front of Passenheim. As usual, I went to look for wood, straw or provisions, in short, whatever I could find. On returning to the camp, loaded with wood, I fell into a deep ravine and remained buried under ten or twelve feet of snow. It was more than an hour before I succeeded in leaving my tomb. I contrived to do so at last, but half-dead of cold and exhaustion. The weather was frightful, the cold bitter ; the snow was whirling about us so that we could not see two paces in front of us. I passed a very bad night, for I had the greatest difficulty in getting warm again.

On the 3rd, near the village of Geltkendorf, where the Emperor lay, after the terrible battles of Geltkendorf and the bridge of Bergfried, we remained in position till two o'clock in the morning, in three feet of snow, in a biting north wind that took our breath away. It was a terrible night.

Since our entry into Poland we had been allowed to wear our hats with one corner in front, and to add on either side a bit of fur which was tied with strings under the chin, to protect the face, and above all the ears, from the frost. The Emperor, the Prince of Neufchâtel, and most of the generals had bonnets of costly fur, shaped like a helmet, from which hung two flaps of fur to be fastened under the chin when the cold became too bitter. These two princes wore a polonaise of grey velvet lined with ermine or some equally rich fur, and boots also fur-lined. They were able to bear the severities of the winter, but for us poor devils, with our old great-coats, it was a very different matter. But, after all, we were young, we were marching all day long, and we were used to it.

On the 5th, which was a day when no action took place, our camp was pitched near Arensdorf, on a lake, a fact

no one suspected. During the night our bivouac fire
melted the ice and the thin coating of snow which here
covered it, and sank into fairly deep water. We escaped
with the loss of what we were cooking to eat before our
departure.

On the 6th we were in bivouac round about the little
hamlet of Haff. After the terrible battle of this date,
when the Russian rearguard was cut to pieces and almost
destroyed, we remained in position on a hill until eleven
o'clock at night. Retracing our steps after this long
watch we passed the night without fire, able only to warm
ourselves in secret at the bivouacs of the other troops
who had arrived before us. The few houses of the village
were full of French wounded. Their numbers were
great, very great, and these were not all, the rest having
been left on the battlefield, exposed to all the rigour of
that icy day. What a hideous night I spent! Many
times I regretted that I was not one of the thousands
of corpses that surrounded us.

Eylau.

7th February, 1807.—In bivouac on a hill half a league
beyond Eylau.

On leaving we once more passed the battlefield of the
day before, and the position we had occupied until eleven
o'clock at night ; and, a little farther on, the place where
two Russian regiments had been destroyed in a charge of
Cuirassiers. At this spot the dead lay two or three
deep ; it was frightful. Finally we traversed the little
town of Landsberg on the Stein. Having left this town
behind us, we came to a great forest, traversed by the
road which we were following, which was so choked with
abandoned vehicles and by the troops ahead of us that
we were forced to halt, for this reason or others of
which I was ignorant. For the rest, the guns were

muttering loudly ahead of us, which made us think a serious battle must be proceeding. I took advantage of this halt to sleep, lying on the snow with as much pleasure as in a comfortable bed. My eyes were inflamed by the smoke of yesterday's bivouac, by lack of sleep, and the glare of the snow, which greatly increased my sufferings. I had reached a state when I could no longer see where I was going. This rest, of perhaps an hour, did me good and enabled me to continue with the regiment in the forward movement then being carried out.

On emerging from the forest we came to a plain and then a hill, which we climbed. It was to carry this position that the heavy firing we had heard some hours earlier had taken place. The 4th corps carried it and drove the enemy beyond Eylau, but there were heavy losses to deplore. The ground was covered with our dead; it was there that we camped for the night. Fighting was still going on, although it had long been dark.

Once we were free to do so we went in search of wood and straw for the night; it was snowing so that we could not see our way and the wind was very penetrating. We found a deserted bivouac fire, still burning fiercely, and a quantity of gathered wood. We profited by this lucky find to warm ourselves and provide ourselves with what we were seeking. While we were philosophizing over the war and its delights we heard the bleating of a sheep. To run after it, catch it, cut its throat and flay it was the work of a few minutes. To set the liver on hot embers or roast it on the end of a stick took even less time : thanks to this providential find we were able, if not to satisfy our devouring hunger, at least to assuage it a little. After our disgusting meal, we were told, on our return to camp, that there were potatoes and dried peas and beans to be found in Eylau. We went thither, while waiting for the sheep we had brought to be cooked. We did in fact find quite a quantity of what we were seeking ; proud of our

discovery and pleased to contribute our share to the
rations of our comrades, we returned to camp, but they
were sleeping in the open, almost buried in the snow.
We, who were sweating despite the cold, thought that to
sleep thus, after exertion, and so much running, would be
harmful, so we resolved to return to Eylau with all our
equipment, deciding to return to the ranks as the regiment
marched through, as it was going, according to us, to lie
at Königsberg that day.

We had hardly slept two hours when day broke and
with it a frightful cannonade, directed upon the troops
covering the town. Our only thought was to get under
arms and out of the town, but the block at the gate was
so great, owing to the mass of men of all ranks and all corps
who were in bivouac before or around Eylau, that to pass
through was practically impossible. All this while spent
bullets were increasing the confusion. We reached our
post before the regiment had received the order to move
forward. I had run and struggled so that I was quite
out of breath.

8th February.—The regiment descended the hill in
column formation and turned to the right of the church,
when it deployed. Already a number of bullets had struck
the regiment and carried off a good many men. Once in
action, in a somewhat exposed position, the number was
much greater. We were under the fire of a huge battery
which was directing against us a withering fire, working
terrible havoc in our ranks. Once the file touching me on
the right was struck full in the chest ; once the file to
the left had their right thighs torn off. The shock was so
violent that those next to the men struck were thrown down
together with the poor wretches who were hit. The order
was given to carry the last three to the ambulance post,
established in the barns of the suburbs on our left. One
of my comrades asked me to help him ; he was an old

Breton soldier, who was greatly attached to me. I eagerly acceded to his wish and carried him, with three of my comrades, to the house where Dr. Larrey was working. We learned next day from the captain that he had given us his gold watch in the event of his succumbing to the amputation of his thigh.

During our absence the regiment moved to the right, and found itself behind a slight elevation which to some extent protected it from the gunfire. The Emperor, who felt the necessity of saving his reserves, to employ them later, should events, which were becoming critical, compel him to do so, had given this order. To return to the ranks we had to pass through a hail of shot, which struck so close together that one could not go half a dozen steps without being checked by the explosion of a shell or the ricochet of a cannon-ball. In the end I arrived safe and sound, but two of my comrades had fallen dead on the hill.

For some time a fall of snow of a density unknown in our climate gave us a little respite ; the remainder of the day passed slowly ; from time to time we received unequiv-ocal signs of the presence of the Russians in front of our lines. At length, toward the end of the day, they yielded their ground to us and retired, in pretty good order, far out of range of our guns. Once their retreat was plainly evident we returned to our position of the morning, most cruelly decimated and painfully affected by the death of so many good men.

Thus ended the bloodiest day, the most horrible butchery of men that had taken place since the beginning of the Revolutionary wars. The losses were enormous in both armies, and although victorious we were as badly damaged as the vanquished.

9th February.—Same position. During the day I was sent on fatigue to Eylau, but as this duty did not require of me an immediate return to the camp, I profited by it to visit the battlefield. What a frightful spectacle was offered by this expanse of ground, formerly full of life, where 160,000 men had breathed the air and displayed such courage! The countryside was covered with a dense layer of snow, pierced here and there by the dead, the wounded, and débris of every kind; in all directions the snow was soiled by wide stains of blood, turned yellow by the trampling of men and horses. The spots where the cavalry charges had taken place, and the bayonet attacks, and the battery emplacements were covered with dead men and dead horses. The wounded of both nations were being removed with the aid of Russian prisoners, which lent a little life to this scene of carnage. Long lines of weapons, of corpses, of wounded men, showed the emplacement of each battalion. In short, no matter where one looked one saw nothing but corpses, and beheld men dragging themselves over the ground; one heard nothing but heartrending cries. I went away horror-struck.

I remained at Eylau until the 16th inclusive. I returned once more to that field of desolation, to engrave clearly on my memory the place where so many men had perished; where sixteen French generals had been killed or mortally wounded; where an army corps and whole regiments had succumbed. In the city square were twenty-four Russian guns which had been collected on the battlefield. One day, as I was inspecting them very attentively, I was clapped on the shoulder by Marshal Bessières, who asked me to make way for him. He was followed by the Emperor, who said, as he passed me : " I am pleased with my inspection." I said nothing; my surprise was too great at finding myself so close to a man so highly placed, whom I had seen three days earlier exposed to the same dangers as ourselves.

Before our departure there was a third promotion of

Skirmishers. As I was not yet expecting anything I took little note of it. Our sojourn at Eylau was becoming miserable; we were without food, and almost without a place to lay our heads, for we were packed on top of one another. The thaw was very pronounced, which made our position even more uncomfortable. At last the signal for withdrawal was announced by a proclamation which explained why we were advancing no farther and why we were to go into cantonments thirty leagues to the rear. This was only a temporary truce; hostilities would recommence with the fine weather.

19th February.—At Liebstadt, a small town on the Passarge, the river beyond which the army was withdrawing, and where it was taking up strong positions to cover its winter quarters, and to prepare to resume the offensive, so soon as Father Violet (a name by which the Emperor was called) should give the signal to do so.

One entire squadron was lodged in an isolated house, the dwelling of a quarryman. The approaches were not very pleasing, but the interior was better. In the cellar there was a barrel of smoked salmon, in a perfect state of preservation, with an exquisite flavour. This was a precious discovery for us, who for a long time had been eating only potatoes, and not many of them. After we had regaled ourselves on the fish and shared what was left with others, the burgomaster of the town came with an aide de camp of the Grand Duke of Berg to demand the barrel. We replied that all was eaten. The aide de camp begged us, if any was left, to be so good as to give him enough for the prince's supper, as he had nothing at all. We turned a deaf ear to him, since we thought it would be easier for the commander-in-chief of the whole cavalry to procure food than for us poor infantrymen, who could not turn aside from the highway. He retired in great displeasure.

21st February.—To Osterode, a small town in Prussia on the road from Königsberg to Thorn. The Emperor established his headquarters in this town, and sent into cantonments, in the surrounding villages, all that portion of the Guard not required for duty about his person or his staff.

The announcement of our going into cantonments was received with lively satisfaction. We had suffered so many privations and undergone such exertions that we might well be permitted to rejoice and to hope for a little rest. Moreover, our equipment was in a state of deplorable dilapidation, while our feet were pulp, and our bodies eaten by vermin, of which we could not rid ourselves, as we had no time and no body-linen. This campaign, which I might call a snow campaign, as the other was a mud campaign, was made still more difficult by the lack of food, which we felt most cruelly on account of the intense cold. . . .

23rd February.—Schildeck, a village two leagues from Osterode. We established ourselves in the castle of the landlord of the village, which was seigneurial only in name, being no more than a simple one-storey building, handsome and fairly large. We were all quartered there, officers, non-coms. and men, and we all fed together, at the same table, like brothers-in-arms. We found corn in the granaries and cows in the byre ; in the cellar, beer and potatoes ; in the barn, straw ; so that we were able to settle down to pass the days of rest that were granted us in quiet and comfort.

This unhoped-for comfort had often to be shared with passers-by, even with generals, who came to sit by our cosy fireside. Later, when the sort of abundance we were living in became known at Osterode, we were asked to provide some corn. But to fulfil the orders given us we had to thresh it in the barn. This was a task unfamiliar to most of us, and moreover a very fatiguing one ; we supplemented our efforts by those of peasants whom we requisitioned. At first they obstinately refused, but when they found they were kindly treated and paid in kind we had more arms than we needed.

With rest and food came restored health, cleanliness and neatness. Our cadres, so weak on our arrival, were completed by the return of men who had been left in hospital, by old soldiers, and by new Skirmishers from the corps or from France. We were as happy as could be expected in our situation, with the exception of myself and two or three comrades of the company, who had our feet frozen.

In this painful condition I could undertake no duty or fatigues, nor could I follow the company in the event of its departure. The surgeon decided that I should be sent to the rear, to the small depot of the Guard on the other side of the Vistula. I was greatly put about by this, but the state of my health demanded it ; I had to obey.

On the 9th I left the cantonment in which I was so comfortable to go to Osterode, where we were given carts, for there were several of us, sick or wounded, escorted by a corporal. On the 15th March I reached Inovraslov or Inovladislov.

15th March to the 14th April, at Inovraslov :—Instead of going into the hospital established for the troops of the Imperial Guard, I received a billet. Chance served me well, for I had warm, quiet quarters, which hastened my recovery, to which I carefully devoted myself. The town, as I have already stated, was exclusively given over to the troops of the Guard. The number of sick and wounded was considerable at first, but the influence of the spring was beginning to make itself felt, so that the number soon diminished, and the convalescent depot must have become almost useless soon after my departure.

All our men wounded at Eylau were evacuated on to this town. The hospital was full of them when I arrived, but it soon began to empty, rather because the men died than because they were healed. The poor Chasseur, my good comrade, whom I had helped to carry to the ambulance, had died on the road; only one of the three wounded by that ball was doing well and was apparently saved.

On the 15th I went to rejoin my company. During my absence the Emperor had transferred his headquarters to Finckenstein, the superb castle of the Count of Dohna, ex-premier to the King of Prussia, near the small town of Rosenberg. In this town were quartered the greater number of the officers of the Imperial Household.

On the 27th April there was a great review of the entire Guard in the Finckenstein plain; a Persian ambassador was present at this review.

THE EMPEROR TASTES MY BREAD.

18th May.—On a hill near Finckenstein, living in hutments which we had to build. We set to work directly we got here, and in a few days this was a rest-camp of the most interesting sort. There were plenty of workers, plenty of wood felled, plenty of houses demolished so that we could build our own. There were acts of vandalism, painful to see, but war was the excuse.

On the 25th May the Emperor came to inspect our camp. He ought to have felt satisfied, for we had taken pains to make it worthy of the august visitor. I was in one of the kitchens that day. He inspected mine with the rest and asked me a number of questions as to our food and above all as to our munition bread. I told him without hesitation, very plainly, that it was not good,

especially for putting in the soup. He asked to taste it
and I gave him a loaf. He took off his glove, broke a
piece with his fingers, and having tasted it, gave it back
to me, saying : " Of course this bread is not good enough
for these gentlemen." This reply crushed me. He then
put other questions, but fearing lest I should reply as
before General Soulès spoke for me.

For some days in the camp I was known only as " the
gentleman." However, next day we had white bread to
put in our soup, rice, and a ration of grain spirit known
as schnaps. The word " gentlemen " had not been uttered
in derision of my audacious demand.

On the 31st May to Finckenstein, to be on duty near the
Emperor. During the six days that the regiment spent
there, there were parades every day and reviews of the
troops arriving from France. They were lengthy but
interesting to watch. I witnessed a good deal of impatience
and anger, not always suppressed, when the manœuvres
went awry. More than one officer withdrew with hanging
head, and others had the painful experience of being sent
to the rear. The Emperor also commanded firing practice,
with blank and with ball cartridge, by squadrons, in the
case of troops arriving, in the garden of the castle, which
was full of shrubberies, fountains and statues. He gave
them as their target a fine fountain of sculptured stone
at the end of the garden facing the palace.

HEILSBERG.

5th June.—Resumption of hostilities : In bivouac before
Saafeld, a small town in the Prussian Grand Duchy.
During the day all our outposts on the Passarge and the
Alle were attacked, unexpectedly and with vigour, by the
Russians, and driven in at all points. The news reached
the Imperial headquarters in the evening. An hour later
the Emperor, his suite, and the entire Guard marched off

to Saafeld, which we reached during the night. The Emperor passed through our ranks in his carriage, driving very swiftly ; the Grand Duke of Berg had taken the place of the driver of the Emperor's calèche. The speed of our march and the activity of all the officers attached to the Imperial staff told us that matters were urgent, and that heavy blows would be struck on our front.

When we reached the heights above the plain before the town of Heilsberg, not far from the left bank of the Alle, there had been sharp fighting since the morning. Placed in reserve, we could make out the two armies engaged, and the incessant attacks delivered by the French, to seize some elevated redoubts, which, down on the plain, covered the front of the Russian Army. The troops in the front line having failed to capture them, the Emperor sent thither the two regiments of Young Guards—Fusiliers, Chasseurs and Grenadiers—which had been organized a few months previously, and had joined the army some days before. The redoubts were taken after a heavy sacrifice of men and heroic efforts. General of Division Rousset,[1] Chief of Staff, who was commanding them, had his head carried away, and many of the officers and non-coms. who had organized the Guard, several of whom I knew, lost their lives there.

While this fine feat of arms was being accomplished three or four fusiliers of these regiments passed through our ranks asking where their corps were. The Emperor, who was just in front of us, following with his glasses the progress of the attack, turned sharply, and said : " Ah ! Ah ! men who are not at their post ! General Soulès, you will see that they hear all about this to-night ! " A moment later he said : " Ask them why they stayed in the rear." They replied that having drank too much cold water it had made their legs helpless, etc. " Ah !

---

[1] General Rousset was born at Charmes and married at Strasbourg, where I knew his wife and two daughters. (*Note by J.-B. Barrès.*)

Ah ! That's another matter ; I forgive them. Put them into your ranks; it's better here than over there." At moments a few rare shots fired from the right bank of the Alle came our way, killing men and disturbing the Emperor at his observations. To divert the direction of these shots he sent two batteries of the Guard to smother the fire of the Russian guns. This was a matter of two or three volleys ; then it was over.

The day closed without result, each side retaining its positions, and we bivouacked on the ground we occupied, amidst the dead of the morning's battle. We had been twelve hours under arms, without changing our position.

On the following evening the enemy evacuated the town of Heilsberg, its magazines, and the entrenchments whose defence had cost so much bloodshed.

FRIEDLAND.

12*th June*.—At ten in the morning we left the heights we had occupied since the 10th ; we crossed the ground on which the battle had been fought, then traversed the town of Heilsberg, and arrived, after a long night march, on the battlefield of Eylau, at six o'clock on the morning of the 13th, to bivouac on almost the same spot where we were shot to pieces four months previously. This night march was remarkable in that we were assailed, while traversing a great forest, by a storm so violent, so fierce, that we had to halt until it had passed lest we should lose our way. We arrived dejected, wet through, horribly fatigued, and in no state to fire a shot if that had been necessary, but the enemy was on the right bank of the Alle and we were on the left, at some little distance.

13*th June*.—In bivouac on the battlefield of Eylau. It was with some satisfaction that I saw once more a spot so celebrated, so soaked in blood, now covered with rich vegetation, and mounds under which rested thousands of men. In place of the vast carpet of men were meadows, streams, lakes, and clumps of wood, of which we saw nothing on the day of the battle.

14th June.—We started early in the morning, turning to the right, toward Friedland and the banks of the Alle. The guns were heard very early, and the sound seemed to grow louder as we advanced. The order was given to put on our plumed bearskins ; this told us that an important action was about to take place.

Our hats were for the most part in such bad condition, and it was so awkward to carry two sorts of headgear and have one always on one's knapsack, giving more trouble than it was worth, that all the Chasseurs decided, as by a spontaneous impulse, to throw their hats away. This was done throughout both regiments. It would have been useless to forbid us to do so, useless to shout at us ; the sacrifice was accomplished amidst cries of joy from the whole of the infantry Guard.

Once ready we resumed our march ; shortly afterwards we began to meet the first wounded. Their number was becoming greater every moment, which told us that the engagement was a hot one and that we were approaching the place where the army was in action. Eventually we emerged from the wood in which we had been marching almost ever since our departure, on to a fairly extensive plain, and saw before us the Russian army in action, having crossed the Alle by several bridges, in order to dispute with us the ground we were occupying, and move on Königsberg, to relieve the blockade. Placed at once in line of battle, within artillery range of the enemy, to the left of the road from Domnau to Friedland, we remained for some hours in that position ; but when once the action was hotly engaged, about five or six in the

afternoon, we moved forward to take possession of a plateau, which to some extent dominated the town, and to support the attacks of the army corps which were in action.

By ten o'clock at night the battle was won, the Russians driven in at all points and hurled into the Alle, the whole left bank being swept clean of them. Their losses were immense, in men and material both. This bloody and brilliant victory completely crushed them.

On the 17th and 18th the Emperor lodged in the village of Sgaisgirren, in the baron's château. I was on guard about his person. On the day after his departure I inspected his apartments; they did not call for such attention, being more than simple; but I found there a big bundle of newspapers from Paris, Altona, Frankfort, and St. Petersburg, of which I joyfully took possession, having had no chance of reading a paper since leaving Warsaw. This was a piece of luck, for we knew nothing of what had been happening to the army except from the Parisian journals.

The guard bivouacked round the village. The Emperor left before us; there was a rumour of a suspension of hostilities. The picket of the Guard did not leave the post until the carts, waggons, saddle-horses and mules of the Emperor and his suite were ready to leave, escorted by the special gendarmerie.

Tilsit.

On the 19th June, at Tilsit, we were billeted in the suburb that runs along the left bank of the Niemen, above the city, but, as the place was very cramped and uncleanly, we preferred to bivouac in the gardens and fields round about. The inhabitants, before our arrival, had hidden their possessions, and considerable quantities of food, in

their gardens, buried in the soil. When they saw that we respected person and property they came to us to beg for leave to dig up these hidden objects. We readily consented, but with the reservation that if there were eatables they would give us part of them. As a matter of fact, so many pieces of bacon and so many hams were revealed that our messes were provided for some days with a food of the greatest value for giving a savour to our scanty diet. There was no lack of meat, but the bread, which contained more bran and straw than flour, was detestable; one had to be as hungry as a dog before one would eat it.

The Russians were encamped on the other bank of the river, where we could easily see and hear them, above all when they assembled of an evening to chant their prayers. The fine wooden bridge across the river had been burned; no communication between the two banks was possible, for all the boats and barges had been taken away or sunk; however, when it was agreed that an interview between the two emperors should take place on a raft, vessels were found to bring the materials required for its construction.

These preparations engrossed us to a singular degree; we were tired of the war; we found ourselves, in a sense, at the end of the civilized world, five hundred leagues from Paris and worn out with our exertions. This was reason enough why we should long to see, proceeding from this raft, a peace worthy of the great efforts of an army which had done its utmost to vanquish the enemies of France.

25th June.—I was on the bank when the Emperor embarked to meet the Emperor Alexander, and there I remained until his return. This spectacle was so extraordinary, so wonderful, that it well deserved all the interest that we took in it.

26th June.—According to the conventions drawn up yesterday on the raft, the Emperor Alexander was to come and live in Tilsit with his suite and 800 men of his Guard. The town was declared neutral, and divided into a French portion and a Russian portion. We were forbidden, even without arms, to enter that part of the town inhabited by the Emperor of all the Russias. Later on, however, we were permitted to pass through it in order to reach our quarter, which lay in that direction, but only in parade uniform.

On the 26th June we were ordered under arms at midday and formed up in the wide, handsome street in which Napoleon was living ; the infantry was on the right, the cavalry on the left. At a preconcerted signal Napoleon proceeded to the bank of the Niemen to receive Alexander and conduct him to his lodging. Shortly afterward the two great sovereigns arrived, preceded and followed by an immense and resplendent staff, having exchanged orders and holding one another by the hands, like the best of friends. Having passed in front of the troops, the two emperors took up their position at the foot of the Emperor Napoleon's steps, and we marched past before them.

Once the march past was over, we returned to our bivouacs, and the Emperor Alexander was re-escorted to his own quarters with the same ceremonial.

27th June.—Grand manœuvres and firing exercise of the whole Imperial Guard, on the heights of Tilsit, before their Imperial Majesties. Napoleon was extremely anxious that his Guard should justify the great renown it had acquired, for during the musketry fire he passed behind the ranks to incite the soldiers to fire quickly, and while they were marching, to incite them to march in close formation and in perfect alignment. With voice, glance and gesture he urged us on and encouraged us. On his part, the Emperor Alexander was greatly pleased to see,

at close quarters, these men, who, whether they charged upon his cavalry or marched against his infantry, sufficed by their mere presence to check or contain them. At one moment he placed himself in front of our fire. Napoleon went to him, and, taking him by the hand, led him back, saying : " An accident might cause a great misfortune." Alexander replied : " With men such as these there is nothing to fear."

After the march past, which was very well executed, the order of the day contained expressions of the satisfaction which the Emperor Alexander had displayed several times during the manœuvres.

28th June.—Arrival of His Majesty the King of Prussia. I was on sentry-go at the foot of the stairs leading to the street, when the Emperor Napoleon came to receive him as he alighted from his carriage. He took him by the hand and made him go first up the staircase. This was not the reception of the 26th; it was a vanquished king who came to beg for a portion of his shattered crown.

The infantry Guard gave a dinner, on the open ground behind our quarter of the town, to the 800 Russian Guards who came on duty about their sovereign. During the dinner the Prussian Guards arrived ; they were welcomed and treated with the greatest consideration ; as a general thing they were preferred to the Russians, probably because they were German. There was a great deal of drunkenness, especially among the Russians, but there was no quarrelling and no disorder. For the rest, the officers of the three Powers were there, to check any manifestation contrary to the general harmony.

During my stay at Tilsit I received a letter from old General Lacoste, of Le Puy, for his son, general of the division of engineers, aide de camp to the Emperor. I was very well received, and he promised to interest himself in me.

One night, when I was sentry on the banks of the Niemen, I had occasion to note how short the nights are in the north at this time of year. It was the 23rd June. Placed on sentry-go at eleven o'clock at night, it was still light enough to read a letter, and when I was relieved, at one o'clock in the morning, the night had passed and the day had reappeared.

The interviews and other events at Tilsit made me acquainted with an enormous number of the notable personalities of Europe, whom I was fond of observing, and was very well situated for the purpose. Few occasions can have occurred where so many men of mark were to be seen assembled in so small an area.

3rd July.—The negotiations for the conclusion of peace being almost completed, the 2nd regiments of each arm of the Guard received orders to set out on the following day for Königsberg and then for France. This news was received with a great demonstration of joy. The glorious peace which was signed at Tilsit well rewarded us for all the ills that we had suffered during these four great and hard and vigorous campaigns, but we would none the less have liked to rest a little longer, to leave our heavy muskets in the racks and our clumsy knapsacks on the floor, unless, indeed, it were to carry them again, because the independence of our country had need of our arms and our lives. For the moment we had had enough of them.

BACK TO FRANCE.

From the 7th to the 13th July we were at Königsberg. During this time the Emperor, his staff, and all that was left of the Guard, arrived from Tilsit. All arrangements were made to leave the north and return to our country, which was the object of all our desires. The distribution of rations, which had almost ceased since leaving Warsaw,

once more became regular. They were even abundant
and varied. The enemy, on evacuating the town on the
news of the loss of the battle of Friedland, had left there
immense store-houses of food richly provisioned. Independently of the ordinary rations they contained stockfish,
herrings, wine, rum, etc. There were a number of ships
in the port, loaded with the cargoes needed for the
nourishment and upkeep of the army. All these factors
taken together produced a return of abundance and
comfort.

During the six days that we remained in this town I
had an adventure which might have been serious, had
I not been recognized as innocent of the charge brought
against me. We were six of us lodged in a small
cabaret, confined to a closet in which we could hardly
turn round. We asked for a larger room without obtaining
one. Our complaints were constantly renewed, for we
were stifled with the heat; we lacked air to breathe and
space to dress and accoutre ourselves. The ill-natured
wife of the landlord, quite young and pretty as she was,
went to denounce us to the governor of the city, who
was none other than General Savary, colonel of the special
gendarmerie, said to be the harshest officer in the whole
army. She turned up with a corporal and four men to
have us arrested. But to have six men taken off at once
seemed to me a trifle audacious; she pointed out the
youngest as being the most guilty. The corporal invited
me to follow him, and explained the order which he had
to execute. I told him to proceed, with his men; that
I would follow to the governor's quarters. I went there,
explained our position, the malicious character of the
woman, and the absurdity of her denunciation. All that
I said sounded so true, so natural, so reasonable, that the
governor had the shrew turned away, dismissed me
without a single word of reproach, and had us sent to
other quarters.

The day before we left there was a great promotion of Skirmishers to the grade of lieutenant, announced only at the moment of marching. I had great hopes of making one of them, but my impatience was disappointed. I was considerably put out by this, and left without regret a town in which I had experienced so many disappointments and vexations.

On the 14th of July, as we were about to enter Brandenburg, some of the Emperor's carriages, escorted by the special gendarmerie, passed through our ranks. A Chasseur of the battalion shouted : " Room for the Immortals ! " A lively quarrel would have ensued had not the officers intervened. This sarcastic epigram was repeated whenever the gendarmes went by, till we came to Jena. It was because this special troop, being entrusted with the military police duties of the Imperial headquarters, and the protection of the Emperor's carriages, never went under fire, that it was baptized by the name of " the Immortals." This insult was unjust, but what can one do against a widespread opinion ? However, after the battle of Eylau the Emperor ordered, on the day of a battle, that the gendarmes should have a squadron at the front. The men died at their post, but this did not kill the jest.

On the 12th August, the day before our departure for Berlin, several of my comrades told me that they were sure I was appointed sub-lieutenant, but nothing happened to confirm this good news ; I had already been told as much on the march. I did not dare to make inquiries.

On the 25th August we came to Hanover, there to remain until the 12th October, that is, for forty-nine days. This long unexpected rest, very contrary to our eagerness to return to Paris, was necessitated, so it was said, by the appearance of an English fleet in the Baltic and the bombardment and capture of Copenhagen by the English, and perhaps also by the need to watch over the execution of the treaties of Tilsit, the consolidation of the newly created kingdom of Westphalia and so forth. We would rather have continued our journey ; we were too thoroughly broken to marching to wish to halt.

I profited by this long delay to inspect this pretty town with attention ; I went often to the Electoral theatre, to see the German operas performed in a very richly-gilt opera-house. Colonel Boudinhox, of the 4th Hussars, born at Le Puy, and a friend of my brother's, invited me to breakfast, and kept me with him part of the day. An émigré priest, born in Auvergne, an acquaintance of my father's, a professor in the university of the city, asked me to visit him often, to talk of our country. He placed his fine and copious library at my disposal. I valued his acquaintance greatly, for his conversation was full of interest. Several Spanish regiments, under the command of the Marquis de la Romana, their general-in-chief, kept garrison with us. Their lack of discipline and their ferocious behaviour caused frequent quarrels, in which their daggers always played a part. A sergeant-major and two or three soldiers of the Guard were treacherously killed by them. These Spaniards were part of the army corps which their Government had placed at the Emperor's disposal.

There was in Hanover a fifth promotion of Skirmishers. I was not included in it, despite all my captain's efforts. My notes were among the most favourable, but there were many who were more effectually " protected " than myself.

At last, on the 25th October, we came to Mayence, on the soil of the French Empire, and on the 17th November to Meaux.

The city of Paris had voted golden wreaths for our eagles, and a great fête on the entry into the capital of the Imperial Guard. In order that all the corps forming the Guard might be united, it was necessary to slow down the march of those at the head of the column, and to make them wheel round Paris to give place to those that followed. Thus it was that we passed through Dammartin, Louvres, Luzarches, Gonesse and Rueil, while waiting for the later troops to reach the gates of Paris.

TRIUMPHAL ENTRY OF THE GUARD INTO PARIS.

25th November.—The city of Paris had erected near the north or Saint-Martin barrier a triumphal arch of the largest size. This arch had only a single arcade, but twenty men could pass through it marching abreast. At the spring of the vault, on the exterior, one saw great figures of Renown offering wreaths of laurel. A gilt quadriga surmounted the monument, and inscriptions were engraved on each of its sides.

From the morning onwards the arch was surrounded by an immense crowd. Arriving from Rueil about nine o'clock, we were drawn up in close column formation in the fields bordering the highway, as close as possible to the arch, leaving the road free for traffic.

At noon, all the corps having arrived, the eagles were united at the head of the column and decorated by the prefect of the Seine. Golden wreaths had been voted by the Municipal Council, which, with the mayors of Paris, surrounded the prefect, M. Frochot, and our entire General Staff, with our commander-in-chief, Marshal Bessières, at its head. After the customary speeches and the return of the eagles to their habitual positions, 10,000 men in parade uniform moved forward to march past under the triumphal arch, to the sound of the drums and the bands of the corps, numerous salvoes of artillery, and the acclamations of the immense mass of people who had assembled on the spot. From the barrier to the palace of the Tuileries the same acclamations accompanied us. We marched past between the ranks of the population of Paris. All the roofs and windows of the houses of the Faubourg Saint-Martin and the boulevards were packed with sight-seers. Poems in which we were compared to the ten thousand Immortals and warlike songs were sung and distributed as we went by. Prolonged cheering greeted our eagles. In short, the enthusiasm was absolute, and the festival worthy of the great days of Rome and Greece.

On reaching the Tuileries we marched past under the splendid Arc de Triomphe, which had been built during our absence. At the grills of the Carrousel, after we had deposited our eagles at the palace, where they habitually remained in times of peace, we passed through the gardens of the Tuileries, where we piled our arms and left them there.

All then repaired to the Champs Elysées, where a table set for ten thousand awaited us. It was placed in the two side avenues. By the *rond-point* was that of the officers, presided over by the Marshal. The dinner consisted of eight cold courses, which were repeated indefinitely; everything was good and we were comfortably seated, but unhappily the rain refused to consider the givers and the heroes of this magnificent feast.

After the dinner we went to pile our arms in the École Militaire, where we were in barracks, and returned to Paris to enjoy the general gaiety, the illuminations and fireworks, the public dances and games of every kind. The poor of Paris also had their part in this gigantic feast.

We had been absent from Paris or Rueil one year, two months and five days.

The rejoicings continued for several days. On the 26th all the theatres of the capital were open to the Guard. The parterre, orchestra, and first tier of boxes were reserved for us, and the first rows in the other boxes. I was of those who were allotted to the opera. They gave the *Triomphe de Trajan*, a typical piece, full of allusions to the campaign just completed. The beauty of the subject, the brilliant decorations, the pomp of the costumes, and the grace of the dances and the ballet intoxicated me with delight. When Trajan appeared on the scene in his triumphal car, drawn by four white horses, thousands of laurel-wreaths were thrown from the centre of the theatre, with which all the spectators crowned themselves like so many Cæsars ; it was a grand night and a fine spectacle.

On the 28th the Conservative Senate gave us or wished to give us a superb and brilliant fête. Everything was done to ensure that it should be worthy of the great body that offered it, but unfortunately the wretched weather made it a most melancholy and even disagreeable affair. A Temple of Glory was erected, where all the victories of the Grand Army were recorded on shields, surrounded with laurel-wreaths and mingled with trophies combining the weapons of the vanquished nations ; there were inscriptions evoking the great battles which the fête was intended to celebrate ; the beautiful garden was full of games of every kind, orchestras, and an endless number of well-covered buffets. The snow, which was falling abundantly, the damp soil, and the cold autumnal night froze our hearts, our stomachs, and our legs. Many of the soldiers wanted to withdraw, but the grills were shut ; someone had to appeal to the Senate ; all this involved an irritating delay. Finally, as it was reported that we threatened to scale the walls, the pass-word was cancelled, the gates opened, and the veterans of the Guard escaped like prisoners restored to liberty. I believe there remained only the Fusiliers, and those who, having no money to dine in the city, thought it better to eat a cold dinner rather than none at all. They ought to have managed to do so, for there was plenty to eat, and it was good. The officers were entertained in the palace. I dined at Véry's, with several comrades, and went on to the Théâtre Français.

A little later the Empress gave us dinner in barracks by squadrons; this was the mess dinner, but largely augmented, and washed down with a bottle of Beaune per man.

Finally, on the 19th December, the Guard gave a great feast to the city of Paris. It took place in the evening, in the Champ de Mars and the palace of the École Militaire; the preparations were protracted, as they were magnificent and wholly military in character. In the vast enclosure of the Champ de Mars there were set, on classic pedestals, vases filled with inflammable materials, or eagles with winged thunderbolts full of fireworks. The vases and the eagles alternated, and were connected by means of a flying dragon, which was to light all at the same time. Beneath the eagles were the numbers of the regiments forming each brigade, with the name of the general commanding it, and under the coloured fires the name of a battle and of the general of division who commanded the two brigades in the action. In the centre was a huge map of Northern Europe, showing in enormous letters the principal towns and the site of our great battles; and the route followed by the Grand Army in the campaigns of 1805, 1806 and 1807 was traced by white stars, under which, as under the names of the towns, there was a great coloured fire which was to burn while the set-piece surrounding the map was itself ablaze. Above the map were winged Victories, also set off by fireworks, and so forth.

The foot Guard marched into this enclosure under arms, to carry out firing exercise with firework projectiles. When it was quite dark the Empress set fire to a flying dragon which, at the same moment, set fire to all the fireworks.

At the same moment also the 4,000 to 5,000 infantrymen of the Guard began a brisk and sustained fire in two ranks, with firework cartridges. The vault of the heavens, lit by the thousands of blazing stars, the frightful detonations which resounded from every part of the Champ de Mars, the shouts of the multitude covering the slopes, all contributed to make this military fête one of the greatest magnitude, and to give one the noblest opinion of the power of mankind when it employs all its faculties in creating the beautiful and the sublime.

The Grand Army played its part in this fête of the Imperial Guard, since all the army corps, divisions, brigades and regiments figured in it by their numbers.

The fireworks and salvoes of artillery having ceased, we returned to our quarters. The ball then began and was continued far into the night. More than fifteen hundred persons of the Court and the city were present; it was admitted to have been magnificent. . . .

Shortly after our return all parts of our equipment were entirely renewed. The cut of the coats was improved, and was modelled on that of the Russians. Our bearskin bonnets, which had become hideous, were likewise replaced. I had the satisfaction of lighting on a bearskin as fine as those of the officers. As for our hats, it was absolutely necessary to give us others, since we had had none since the battle of Friedland.

I AM APPOINTED SUB-LIEUTENANT.

A few days after our arrival I went to call on General La Coste, who received me well and expressed his surprise at seeing that I was not yet an officer. In answer to a few questions which he put to me, I thought it well to remark that he might possibly believe that his recommendations had been without effect because my conduct might not have been good. I assured him that this was not the case, and withdrew in a rather dejected mood.

On the 31st December General Soulès, our colonel-in-chief, sent me word to report to him. . . . Having asked my name, he took from a drawer of his desk several nominations to the grade of sub-lieutenant, among which I at once distinguished that which was intended for me. He then asked me : " Have you been through the whole campaign ? Were you at Jena, Warsaw, Eylau, Königs-berg, Berlin, and in the march home ? " I replied " yes " to all these questions, for that was the truth. . . . " But then how is it that when I have asked after you on various occasions I have been told that you were unknown to the regiment ? "—" That is due to two causes, my general ; the first is that those are not my Christian names. The decree is made out in the name of Pierre-Louis, but my name is Jean-Baptiste-Auguste ; the second is more serious. I had the misfortune to be disliked by the sergeant-major."—" Ah ! ah ! and why is that ? "—" This is the reason, my general : at the battle of Eylau a bullet cut the sergeant-major's musket in two ; he was then resting under arms, with his left arm bearing on the socket of the bayonet, so that he twirled round on his heels in such a peculiar way that I could not help bursting into a laugh, which escaped me quite involuntarily, with-out any thought of ill-nature and not thinking he could be wounded ; which, as a matter of fact, he was. In going to the rear to get his wound dressed he told me : ' I shall remember that laugh of yours.' I understood at once how injurious his threat might be to me, for I knew he was an ill-tempered and revengeful man ; so I was on my guard to avoid being punished by him. At Königsberg, Berlin, and elsewhere, when they called my name at roll-call, to give me my appointment, he replied : ' There is a Barrès, certainly, in the company, but it isn't that one.' He was careful not to speak to me of this lest I should take steps to prove that there were not two of my name in the two regiments. That, my general, is why they said I was unknown. . . ."

After a few moments' reflection, he said : " Sit at my desk and write." It was a letter to the Minister for War, asking him for a duplicate of my appointment and the correction of the names. Having signed it he gave it to me, saying : " Take it yourself to the office of the infantry and tell them to hurry things up. As for you, you are now an officer ; I release you from all service until the moment of your departure." My appointment was for the 13th July, dated Königsberg, to the 16th regiment of light infantry.

I returned, delighted, to my quarters, where I received the congratulations of my comrades, and with all my heart I fell to kicking my knapsack, which had weighed so heavy on my shoulders. . . . I went into a barber's to have my pigtail cut off : a ridiculous ornament which the infantry no longer wore, excepting one or two regiments of the Guard. When I was rid of this inconvenient appendage, I went to call on a friend of my father's, to tell him of my change of rank and wish him a prosperous year. I dined at his house and did not return to quarters until ten o'clock at night. Thus from the very first day I took advantage of my new rank.

I remained in Paris until the night of the 6th February, 1808. I profited with delight by the few days of liberty which I allowed myself, the better to acquaint myself with this vast city, to pass the evenings at the play, and to see more frequently the few friends I had there. What a pleasant change I experienced ! One must make three of four campaigns with knapsack on back, one must have marched half over Europe on foot, in order fully to appreciate my felicity. I had actually served in the Guard three years, six months and seventeen days.

My route paper was given me, at my request, on the

2nd February, for Neuf-Brisach, the depot of the 16th light infantry, and my place was booked for the 5th, to leave at seven o'clock in the morning, by the Vélociféres of the Rue du Bouloi.

NINETEEN MONTHS IN FRANCE.

From Neuf-Brisach, where he is well content, Barrès is suddenly sent to Rennes, in May 1808.

14th June.—To reach Rennes took me thirty-five days of marching or of halts. The march was enjoyable, peaceful, and without incident ; the men behaved well, but I grew very weary on account of my isolation, above all at our halting-stages, where I had to live and stroll about alone.

Directly I got to Rennes I paid the usual calls, to make the acquaintance of the men I was to live among. At my age pleasant social relations are soon established, above all if one is more or less of the same rank and seniority. By the evening of the second day I was one of the family, so to speak, and delighted to think of the quiet time I was going to have. But my star, or the course of events, decided that all my plans were but illusory. On the following day, the 16th, orders were received that all the valid troops of the legion were to be despatched within twenty-four hours to Napoléonville (Pontivy).

I was appointed paymaster of the battalion, to perform the duties, provisionally, of adjutant-major, and take the command of a company. This was a great deal too much for a young subaltern of four months' service, but I was so pressingly urged to accept by the battalion commander, the commander of the depot, and the commissary of war charged with the administration of the legion, that I allowed myself to be overwhelmed with honours and with

duties. The battalion commander, M. Dove, came from
the Guard, where I had known him as a captain. It was
to this, and to something about me that pleased him,
that I owed this preference and the confidence he accorded
me. All the rest of this day and part of the night were
employed in clothing and arming our young conscripts,
making out the roll, taking stock, striking bargains,
drawing a fortnight's pay, etc. For me it was a night of
work.

On the 3rd July I received orders to leave on the 4th,
with the whole battalion, for Belle-Ile-en-Mer.

On the 6th July, having come to Quiberon, which is
a dirty, dismal village amid fields, I saw the sea for the
first time, in all its vastness, its beauty, and its many
aspects. I spent part of the evening on the shore, to
contemplate it in all its immensity, and study some of
its miracles and its products.

On the following day, the 7th, the detachment was
embarked in luggers stationed at the port of Portaliguen,
which is not far from the village of Quiberon. When we
were assured that the passage was clear, and that the
crossing could be made without danger, the sea and the
tide being favourable, we hoisted sail and steered for
Le Palais, the capital and port of the island. I was
afraid I should be sea-sick, but I was only afraid. It
was not the same with the men ; they were almost all
in a state of such utter prostration that if we had been
accosted by an enemy sloop they would not have been
able to use their weapons, which I had taken the precaution to have loaded before we embarked.

Our arrival being notified I found all the officers of
the 3rd battalion on the quay to receive me. Their
welcome was most cordial.

Seventeen days later, the entire 3rd battalion left for
Spain. They took a hundred of my men to complete it.
I was left alone with my two companies, still 220 strong,

to instruct and discipline them and administer the battalion's affairs. The trouble this caused me, and my desire to make a campaign as officer, made me regret keenly that I could not follow my comrades. I parted from them, and especially from certain among them whose character was congenial to me, with real sorrow. (Of these twenty officers I saw only two again, the commandant, who had become colonel, and a sub-lieutenant, who became a captain. All the rest died in 1814.)

A few days sufficed to place me on a friendly footing with the officers of these corps and also with almost all the townsfolk, with whom, indeed, I was on such good terms that I felt, in their houses, that I was in my own home. It was a very pleasant life and I appreciated its charm to the full. There was not a friendly or family dinner-party, not a picnic or fishing expedition, at which I was not of the company.

The generals were no less amiable to me. I used often to dine at their houses, above all with the general of division, Quentin, original, fantastic, capricious, but at heart an excellent fellow. He conceived a friendship for me, petted me, made much of me, sometimes turned sulky, and when I once let a day go by without going to his house he sent for me, saying, when I reached his headquarters, as he called his house : " Monsieur, I have a better character than you ; I soon forget the offences of others ; how then is it that you do not forget mine, if I am guilty of any ? " I was for three months his aide de camp *per interim*. This was often worse than tiresome. The first time he invited me to dine was a few days after my arrival. I was on duty at the guard-house. At the port, the aide de camp, M. de Bourayne, came to inform me that the general invited me to dinner at two o'clock precisely, and to be there punctually, since he sat down to table without waiting five minutes for his guests. I replied that I was on duty, that I was not my own master. He replied : " Come all the same ; I'll warn General Roulland." At two o'clock I was in the dining-room. He addressed me, drily enough : " What have you come here for ? "—" To dine, general."—" How to dine ? Are you not on duty ? Do you think I am capable of dissuading an officer from performing his duty ? "—" But I came only because you told me to do so through your aide de camp."—" My aide de camp has too much tact to have undertaken such a mission."

I did not know what further to say. I had begun to make for the door, greatly displeased by this reception, when I cried out, half-laughing, half-vexed : " Since I'm invited, I shall stay."—" That is pretty audacious for a subaltern," he said, " but since he is one of the heroes of Austerlitz, and was at Jena, Eylau, and Friedland, I suppose one must pardon him."

He placed me beside him and paid me all sorts of friendly attentions. He made very merry over my embarrassment and the sorry figure I had cut for a moment. For the rest, this almost brutal reception was calculated to intimidate a young officer who was not yet familiar with the ways of his superior. Under other circumstances he tried to repeat this sort of practical joke, but it no longer came off.

During the month of September several officers coming from the reserve came to take command of the companies and of the detachment. One of the captains, who had the advantage of seniority, was the strangest creature as to his moral and physical qualities, the greatest drunkard and the sorriest soldier I had ever seen in those days. Fortunately my duties as paymaster set me in some sort above him. He was a *Septembriseur*. In one of his drunken moments he spoke of those terrible incidents as an active participant. He was a tall, thin fellow, withered, old, with a face half-covered with a repulsive-looking port-wine stain. His wife, for he was married,

9

was neither younger, nor more sober, nor less hideous
than he. A horrible pair, a vile household, a shameful
officer !

About this time I was sent into cantonments, with a
section, in the village of Bangor at the centre of the island.
I profited by my isolation to invite a merry party of my
acquaintances in the capital to dine with me in my dismal
solitude. I announced to them the arrival of a case of
Bordeaux, which had been sent me by the father of a
conscript in my company whom I had made corporal.
They were punctual at the rendezvous, and the dinner
was good for the time of year and the place, but what
was still better was that they drank not only the contents
of my case of wine, but an equal quantity of *vin ordinaire*,
which was also of Bordeaux, to say nothing of Frontignan,
and of punch, and so forth. I had then to hire chaises
and dump my guests into them, and away they went.
They got home in a deplorable state, smothered in such
a coating of mud that they were unrecognizable. It was
several days before I ventured to speak to their wives,
who were furious with me. The anger of the women and
the dismal faces of the men caused much amusement.
This Pantagruelic banquet won me great renown, since
no one would have believed that a young sub-lieutenant
could have been responsible for fuddling such venerable
heads or men of such respectable years and position.

January 1809.—I was still in this village when a great
storm of wind burst on the shores of the island and
probably on many other parts of the continent. The
upheaval of the sea was terrifying to watch ; the waves
were monstrous. The shock of the waves against the
rocky crags fronting the wild sea at the south of the
island was like the incessant fire of artillery ; the shattered
waves were cast into the air so that one tasted the brine
more than half a league inland. The oldest seamen had

never seen anything like it. It was the 6th January, the Day of the Kings. I was invited to dine in the town at the house of a captain of gunners in the sedentary coastguard. Just as I was about to leave, the thatched roof of my house was carried away; I had my things taken to a neighbouring house and set out with a non-commissioned officer. By dint of clinging to one another we reached our destination safe and sound, but on entering the house where I was expected I found the whole family and a number of strangers in tears. One of the chimneys of the house had been blown down, and had fallen almost intact into the dining-room and had crushed the table on which dinner was laid, so that if I had turned up fifteen or twenty minutes earlier we should all have been under the fall, since they were only awaiting my arrival to have dinner served. No one was hurt, but the house was scarcely habitable. The house front was badly shaken, two ceilings were smashed in, the furniture broken, and so forth.

This storm, which so shook the island, was felt even in the depths of the sea; on the next and following days our outposts recovered from the sea more than a hundred single and double barrels of port. These fine, strong barrels, hooped with iron, were covered with a very thick layer of madrepores, oysters, barnacles, and other shellfish of these waters. Having cleared them of this marine envelope, we read on all of them the word " Marlborough." It was then recollected that in 1794 an English warship of this name had sunk in Quiberon Bay. It is probable that the hulk had remained intact until the storm of the 6th January, that it was then shattered, and that the barrels, no longer imprisoned, were cast up not only on the shores of Belle-Ile, but all along the Breton coast, for some were salvaged thirty or forty miles from the bay. The wine was in perfect condition and sold at a good price. The detachment received, for its share in saving the wine, over 300 francs, which was paid by the Customs administration. I too received a share as officer of the detachment.

After returning to the town and living for some time in the citadel I was detached to the battery of La Belle-Fontaine, not far from Le Palais, where I went for my meals and to spend part of the day. The room I inhabited would not hold more than a bed, a chair, and a little table, but it was in a charming position, fronting on a delightful little garden, at the foot of which was the sea, so that I could go down from my little room to bathe at low tide. When the tide was high and the sea rough it dashed as high as the casement.

On the 1st September we received orders to leave on the 6th for Locminé, and I foresaw that I was bound for Spain. Despite all the pleasure I took in this friendly and excellent countryside, where I had come to know so many worthy folks, I was not sorry to leave it. I was tired of this soft, quiet, drowsy life. My mind felt the need of returning to a sphere of activity more in keeping with my age, and of sharing a little of the glory and the perils of my comrades.

These last few days were employed in settling accounts, in packing the stores in the magazines, in replacing the beds and other articles of furniture in the barracks, and other details, as troublesome as they were necessary, and in saying good-bye ; and this was a matter that moved me deeply and sincerely, as it did all those with whom I had lived for so long in such a pleasant intimacy. General Quentin, always extraordinary in everything, much regretted my departure ; I too regretted leaving him, despite his originality, which was not always agreeable ; after all, I was so accustomed to his fantastic queerness that I no longer troubled about it, and lived with him almost as with one of my equals. He was greatly vexed

that he was not a count or a baron ; that he was not
at the head of a division on active service, in Spain or
elsewhere. In vain did the Minister for War gild the pill
by telling him that the Emperor had placed him at the
outpost of the Empire ; that was not enough for him.
How many letters he dictated to me, complaining of the
oblivion in which he was left ! How many times he made
me taste my share of the insult inflicted on him in failing
to recognize his military capacities ! One day he received
a packet addressed to " M. le général de division Quentin,
in the Army of Spain." He believed that he was
appointed, had his pigtail cut off, which was two feet
in length, sold his kitchen utensils, took rooms in a hotel,
and made ready to depart. " Directly my nomination
arrives," he told me, " I shall write to have you appointed
my aide de camp." I thanked him sincerely for the
honour, for which I was not in the least anxious. . . . I
left him greatly discouraged, impressed with ideas of death
or disgrace. At heart he was an excellent man, but, with
great mental ability, he was lacking in judgment and
behaviour.

There was another man whom I did not see so often,
but who was also greatly attached to me ; this was the
father of General Bigarré, my captain in the Guard. To
speak of this good old man, who was commissary of war,
and of his son and son-in-law, quartermaster in the
16th light infantry, is to make him live again in memory,
to recall all his kindness and affection. For him, too, I
had a close friendship.

I have said a good deal about Belle-Ile, but if I meant
to consign to this diary all the particulars of my private
and military life during the fourteen months of my stay
there I should need to write a volume. The recollections
of this happy countryside will never fade from my memory.
Its fêtes, its rocky crags, its worthy inhabitants will always
hold a favoured place there.

SPAIN AND PORTUGAL.

December 1809.—I had just been appointed lieutenant when the order arrived to despatch our battalion to Spain, on the 10th December. On the 31st December I was at Bordeaux. On the morning of the 4th January, before the battalion left for Saint-André-de-Cubsac, I had to take a hundred refractory conscripts from the citadel of Blaye, to be incorporated in the corps after our entry into Spain. Lest they should again desert they had to march together under an escort and to be shut up every night behind bolt and bar.

8th January, 1810.—A batallion of the 46th regiment of the line, commanded by a major [1] who was more than original, marched with us to Bordeaux. The officers of the two corps ate together at our halts. At Tartas, as we finished dinner, the innkeeper came to announce that twelve to fourteen pieces of silver were missing. This insolent statement excited murmurs of indignation from all the diners. The doors were at once locked and the innkeeper was ordered to search all the officers. He refused to do so, so the commandant did so in his presence. The search was almost completed when someone came to say that the silver had been found. Thereupon the commandant fell upon the innkeeper and gave him a terrific beating, despite the cries and entreaties of his wife. We had to intervene, or he might have beaten the man to death. He left immediately afterwards for Mont-de-Marsan, to lay a complaint before the Imperial attorney. I don't know what came of it, but the officer's vengeance was somewhat exaggerated, his rage was misplaced, and above all his behaviour was undignified.

On the 15th January we were at Ernani, a small town of the province of Guipuscoa (Biscay). I proceeded to

[1] *Chef de bataillon.*—TR.

distribute through the companies the hundred refractory conscripts who were entrusted to me at Blaye. There were none of them missing ; on the contrary, there was one too many! I cannot explain this mistake, which was not noticed on the road, since we did not have the roll called, but contented ourselves with counting them like sheep, unless it was that the man slipped in among the rest at the moment of departure, to recover his liberty and try to win a little glory. However this may be, I had to report the matter, and write to a number of authorities to explain this mystery, and to protect the parents of the soldier from the severe treatment meted out to them when their son was declared a deserter.

On the 16th, at Tolosa, on rising in the morning, I saw that my shirt was covered with vermin. This was a sad beginning, which gave me a very poor idea of Spanish cleanliness.

On the 20th January orders arrived that we were to go into garrison at Durango. I was appointed to command the fortress. The officers and men were quartered in a convent. For myself, I thought it better to take handsome apartments in town, with a sentry at my door. During the night I was aroused by a dirty peasant covered with rags, whom I took at first for an ill-intentioned guerilla, but who was no other than the agent of General Avril, commanding at Bilbao, who sent me orders to proceed to Vittoria. I left my aristocratic lodging without regret, and my honourable functions, to become a mere lieutenant again.

26th January.—I arrived in Burgos and remained there until the 27th February. These thirty-two days passed very quietly and even pleasantly. We had need of rest. The forty-eight days of marching which we had just spent had severely fatigued us. General of division Solignac, governor of Old Castile, gave a number of great evening receptions, very remarkable for their brilliance, the multitude of guests, and the rage for gambling displayed. The Duc and Duchesse d'Abrantès, having arrived a few days later than we did, were present at some of these evening dances. There were also a great many other generals and prominent notables of the two nations. These assemblies were gay, lively and opulent. The Spanish ladies, who were present in great numbers, were not as a rule remarkable save for their awkward manners and the bad taste of their French clothes. Those who had the good sense to retain the national costume looked much better.

In this backward country nothing is known of fireplaces or cooking-ranges. The rooms are warmed with brasiers fed with charcoal ; the warmth they give is not sufficient, and they give one a headache when they do not asphyxiate one. To escape the cold and the tedium of our dismal quarters we used to go to the café, which was kept by a Frenchman, and was always full, despite the enormous size of the many rooms. Piles of gold were gambled away there nightly. The greed of gain and the need of repairing heavy losses led a few officers into committing shameful actions, which led to frequent duels and severe disciplinary measures. A few were dismissed their regiment.

20th March.—At Gradefès, a town near the frontier of the kingdom of the Asturias, on the Elza. The 4th battalion was lodged farther up the course of the river. A few Grenadiers and a woman canteen-keeper, having dropped behind, stopped in a village to pass the night. Next day they were given a guide who led them into a prepared ambush ; there their throats were all cut, with refinements of cruelty. The commandant of the battalion, informed of this horrible ambush, marched on the village, caused it to be burned to the ground, seized all the able-bodied men, and announced that he would have them all put to death if they did not point out the murderers. Four had already fallen under the bullets of the Grenadiers without confessing, but the fifth revealed the assassins. They were present ; they were shot. This severe reprisal gives some idea of what the Spanish war was like.

We remained in this village, with a squadron of Dragoons, until the 5th April.

8th April.—To Leon. In the morning I received orders to rejoin my battalion. On the way, being a hundred paces from the detachment, and in a position where I could not be seen by it, owing to the formation of the ground, I was accosted by a man on horseback, armed to the teeth, in Spanish costume, in the style of Figaro, with a wide cloak over all. I had barely caught sight of him when he was upon me. He swiftly threw open his cloak, felt in his pockets as though for his pistols, and presented to me a document proving that he was in the service of France, I forget in what quality. I must have looked rather embarrassed, as I thought I was surely dealing with a guerilla ; with the more reason as I had only my sword wherewith to defend myself—a poor weapon against pistols, a blunderbuss and a lance. This unexpected surprise made me reflect that it was not prudent to go so far from my men in a country where every tree, thicket or rock may hide an enemy.

The 4th battalion left in the course of the morning for the blockade of Astorga. We remained in Leon until the 13th April, with the 5th battalion of our division.

14th April.—At the bridge of Orbigo, a small town two leagues from Astorga. . . . We remained in this town to safeguard communications with Leon and with the rear of the troops employed at the siege of Astorga, to escort

the convoys of provisions and munitions of war, to look
after the sick and wounded of the besieging troops, and
to furnish armed detachments for the trenches.

The Duc d'Abrantès having arrived, the blockade of
Astorga was converted into a siege.   The artillery necessary
to batter a breach had preceded him.   The saps were
commenced immediately.   On the 20th April (Good
Friday) the battery was unmasked and fired continually
for thirty-six hours on the enclosure wall ; but it was not
heavy enough, or perhaps was too distant ; the effect
was mediocre ; in spite of this the assault was declared
practicable.

It took place on the 21st, at five o'clock in the afternoon.
Six picked companies, of which two were of our 4th battalion, were entrusted with this terrible mission.   It was
long, murderous and incomplete.   At five o'clock in the
morning the besiegers were entrenched in the breach, yet
we could not enter into the town by reason of the difficult
nature of the obstacles which our troops encountered on
the way.   However, when daylight had come the commandant asked leave to capitulate.

His proposals were accepted, and it was agreed that
the garrison should come out on Easter Monday, at noon,
with the honours of war, and that the troops should be
prisoners of war.

Easter morning was employed in improving the works
while negotiations were proceeding and in giving burial
to the victims of this dismal night.   At mid-day the
garrison marched out under arms, and laid them down
outside the walls ; it was still a strong one.   Among their
number were five or six French deserters, who were
recognized and shot on the spot, without even taking
their names.

The losses of the French were very considerable ; far
too great, having regard to the importance of the fortress.
But the commandant of the 8th army corps wanted to

be heard of ; he wanted to win, on the walls of this paltry little town, the bâton of a Marshal of the Empire. Our two companies had more than a hundred men killed and wounded, among them three officers of the infantry, killed in the breach, and two of the Grenadiers wounded.

During the siege I went to escort a convoy of powder to Astorga. The ten or twelve peasants' carts, drawn by oxen, were of the kind whose wooden axles turn round with the wheels. On the road one of the axles caught fire ; there was no water to throw on it ; the position was critical. I wished to hasten the carts ahead of the burning cart and to delay those that were behind it, but the drivers, afraid of an explosion, ran away, and a few of the soldiers did the same. However, a sufficient number remained to do what I prescribed. During this time a few nimble fellows had made their way down the valley and brought me some water in their shakoes ; this saved us. The convoy continued its journey without further incidents.

We remained at the bridge of Orbigo until the 29th April. We were then twenty days at Morias, a small village half a league from Astorga, on the road and at the entrance into the mountains of Galacia. It was a very poor village, where we were worse than uncomfortable.

I went to Astorga several times, because I had nothing to do, and also to dine at a French restaurant. In all the towns occupied by the French at least one French restaurant and café was set up on the morrow of occupation. They were dear, these poisoners who followed in the wake of the army, but at least they gave us something to do with our money.

On the 1st June, at Zamora, where I spent a week, I found several officers of my acquaintance ; among others General Jeannin, who had been my battalion commander in the Guard. He was pleased to see me and invited me to sup with him. General Jeannin had married one of the daughters of David, the famous painter.

From the 7th July to the 31st I remained at Salamanca. A few leagues before it reached the city the battalion, passing through a large wood, was attacked by a herd of wild cattle, which put us to flight. We had to fire our muskets in order to drive them back into the thickets. Three or four men were thrown down and hurt. When this novel sort of assault was over we had a good laugh at this headlong charge, as unforeseen as it was impetuous. The officers, once the danger was apparent, had rallied a party of their men and ordered them to fix bayonets and march against the herd, while firing a few shots, which dispersed them.

Having lodgings overlooking the public square of Salamanca, so fine with its uniform architecture, its covered porticoes, its continuous galleries, and balconies to all the stories of the buildings, I witnessed, from the window of my room, several bull-fights, which interested me keenly.

Twice I mounted guard at the house of the Prince d'Essling (Masséna), commander-in-chief of the army of Portugal. These two guards resulted in friendly relations with the eldest son of the prince and the only son of Marshal the Duke of Dantzig (Lefebvre), and several other officers of his general staff.

On the 3rd April, 1810, we left for Ciudad-Rodrigo. The country that lies between Salamanca and Ciudad-Rodrigo is desert, sterile, without cultivation, yet covered with evergreen oaks and another species which produces sweet acorns. These trees are fine, vigorous and dense, which shows that it is not through the fault of the soil, but through lack of workers, that it is practically uninhabited.

On the evening of my arrival at Rodrigo my sub-lieutenant and I could find only two rooms : one occupied by a gendarme and the other by the valet of the Prince d'Essling. We told the mistress of the house that we were taking one of the rooms, and that the other would be left for the two persons just mentioned. Utterly exhausted by the march, the heat, and illness, I went to bed immediately, without eating, so sorely did I feel the need of rest. A few moments later two great rascals of lackeys came to pick a quarrel with me because I had taken the bed of one of them. Having explained to them the arrangements which had been made in the interests of the four persons having a right to lodging, I begged them to withdraw, but I had to deal with a couple of insolent flunkeys, and sound reasoning was powerless to reach their egoistical minds. They insulted me, threatened me with the prince and the provost-marshal of the army, and with their fists, if they did not receive their just rights. They went out and I went to sleep again, but an hour or two later I was sent for by the provost-marshal, the order being brought by a sergeant-major.

Being confronted by Colonel Pavette, of the gendarmerie, I explained what had happened. "How is it, colonel," I said to him, at the end of my tale, "an officer of the army, who daily risks his life in the defence of his country, who wears down his health on the highways in pursuit of the enemy, who often passes days without food and nights without sleep, is summoned, at the request of a lackey, as though he were a criminal? Is this how one respects the epaulette, the honour of the army, the soldiers whose blood is required every day?" After a rather lengthy conversation, in which the colonel was as polite as he was prudent, I left, and resumed my place in the miserable bed that had been the subject of dispute.

On the following day, speaking of this affair to one of the aides of the prince, I learned that on the provost-marshal's report the audacious valet and his worthy acolyte, the groom, had been sent to prison. A little while before this a similar scene had been enacted, with the same motives, in respect of a captain of a regiment of our division, but being a more violent man, and wearing his sabre at the time, he inflicted a serious wound on a servant of the Duc d'Abrantès. The latter, having punished the officer by close arrest, wished to have him dismissed the army. The officers of the corps, hearing of this improper severity, had him informed that if this were done they would all submit their resignation and their reasons for it. The Duc took alarm and there the matter ended.

During the siege of Almeida I was twice sent with detachments in the direction of that city, as far as Rodrigo, to escort convoys. I was there on the night our guns began firing, and caused the frightful explosion of the powder-magazine. No real idea can be formed of the intensity of this detonation, of the general commotion of the air, of the monstrous column of fire, smoke and stones which rose into the air. Stones and corpses were hurled almost into our lines. This occurred on the 26th August ; the town was occupied on the 27th.

On the 15th September Barrès crossed the frontier of Portugal, where the French Army, 50,000 strong, was commanded by Masséna.

16th *September.*—During the morning, having left Almeida on our right, we crossed the torrent of the Coa, the approach to which is terrific, the banks almost perpendicular and the depth tremendous.

During all the time that followed it was more often than not impossible for me to discover the names of the towns or villages we passed through, for we did not meet in them a single inhabitant. The whole population had fled, destroying whatever might have been of use to us.

The English had organized this general emigration along our path in order to create greater obstacles to our march and make us more hateful to the Portuguese.

25th September.—This day we were pretty hotly attacked by a party of the enemy, but, sharply repulsed, he retired, after killing and wounding several of our men.

On the following day we had an alarm which caused us as much trouble as uneasiness. The material which we were escorting had been parked on a heath scorched by the great heat we had experienced since entering this deserted kingdom. The heath caught fire, and the fire made such progress, despite all the means taken to check it, that we had hastily to fetch the horses and harness them hurriedly in order to park the convoy on another site. The danger was great ; the loss to the army would have been immense, for all its resources for the continuation of the war were in this park of stores.

27th September.—In bivouac, not far from the spot where the battle of Bussaco and Alcoba was fought on the same day, where we were, if not beaten, at least pushed back from all the points we were endeavouring to occupy. This disastrous day, which cost the army more than 4,000 killed or wounded, discouraged it greatly. However, Marshal Masséna did not abandon his project of marching on Lisbon. Having recognized a little too late, when the mischief was done, that the position of Alcoba was impregnable to frontal attack, he resolved to turn it by the right, by occupying the passes of Serdao, which Wellington had neglected to occupy. This mistake forced the English general to draw off, re-cross the Mondego, evacuate Coimbra and abandon to us the whole country from the mountains to the sea. Thus, despite our serious check, we continued to pursue a victorious army, abundantly provided with everything, having the sympathy of the population, while we were living on the country, which meant distant foraging parties, and added to the dangers and fatigue incurred by the men.

2nd October.—In the early part of the day we finally emerged from the long pass of Serdao, where we had been for five days, and also from the mountains, which we had been crossing since leaving Rodrigo. Far off we beheld the sea, and at our feet a beautiful countryside. Here we were in a rich, fertile plain, covered with numerous villages, deserted, in truth, like all those we had come to, but more abundantly provided with victuals.

On the 4th October, in the forenoon, we rested some hours at Coimbra, a large and fine city, on the Mondego, which cuts it in two. The cathedral and the fountains are magnificent, and the outskirts covered with vines, orange-trees and olive-trees. The English, in abandoning it, had forced the inhabitants to leave the city. The army secured here valuable stores of rice, stockfish, coffee, sugar, tea and chocolate, with which the warehouses were abundantly furnished. The sick and wounded were all left in a convent situated on a height on the left bank of the Mendego, with an armed guard to ensure them against molestation, but twenty-four hours later the guard was taken prisoner and the sick in danger of being massacred.

On the 8th October, before Leiria, in a torrential rain, the company could find no other shelter available than the church, of which it gladly took possession. There was corn and wood in plenty, so we had soon established a bivouac so comfortable that we had no cause to regret the houses, which were crammed with troops. We found excellent wine there, and as there was plenty of sugar and cinnamon in the bags and baggage, we made a lot

of mulled wine, which restored all our bodies, worn out
with exertion and soaked to the bones.

12th October.—For three days we were wandering
through unbroken and apparently limitless forests of
olive-trees, when we came to the little town of Alemquer,
headquarters of Marshal the Prince d'Essling.

We had at last reached the valley of the Tagus, for
which we had been sighing so long, thinking that we
should find on its banks comfort, a little rest, or at
least better roads and shelter. I saw, for the first time
in my life, round about this pretty little town, a great
number of palm-trees, which struck me as remarkable
for their beauty and their size.

Before we reached shelter, General Sainte-Croix, of
the cavalry, an officer of the greatest merit, quite young,
was cut in two, in the midst of our ranks, by a cannon-
ball fired from an English gunboat stationed on the
Tagus. The surface of this magnificent river was covered
with armed vessels intended to prevent our approach.

On the following day, the morning being delightfully
fine, I went for a walk with several officers along the
neighbouring slopes, covered with vines not yet stripped
of their grapes and fig-trees bending under the weight of
their fruit.

14th October.—At Villafranca, a small town on the
banks of the Tagus. We stayed in the country houses
of the surrounding country until the 28th October
inclusive.

The majestic and smiling banks of the Tagus, the
magnificent country houses on its enchanted shores,
the lovely gardens that cover the plain lying between
the high ground and the river, full of orange-trees in
regular ranks, lemon-trees, oleanders and other equally
interesting growths; the hillsides carpeted with vines,
fig-trees and olive-trees, a sky of ravishing beauty, and

10

a magnificent highway, made the position of Villafranca one of the most beautiful I had hitherto feasted my eyes on. This beautiful country seemed to me a home of joy, a new earthly Paradise, despite the frightful detonations of the English flotilla and the lugubrious whistling of the great balls which they sent our way.

On reaching Villafranca we had expected to leave the following day for Lisbon, but invincible obstacles, unknown to us, mobile and obedient machines, detained us.

The company was sent on outpost duty by a little stream which separated the two armies in that direction. We stayed a week in this position, where we could, despite the neighbourhood of the enemy, whom the course of the stream alone divided from us, enjoy a little rest and look to our subsistence. We occupied five or six fine country houses, richly furnished and luxurious, in which we found some provisions and a little corn hidden away. In one of these houses there was a flour-mill which was worked by one or several horses. The infantry-men served as draught-horses and kept the mill turning night and day. The meal was coarse and of poor quality, but with it we made unleavened bread, cakes and gruel. In short, we did not do so badly, and, officers and men alike, thought ourselves very lucky to have this resource, which was not to last very long.

Our general-in-chief, Comte Regnier, used to send his aide, Captain Brossard, who spoke English, once or twice a day to the outposts, to carry despatches and bring back replies and the English newspapers. He used to pick me up, with a trumpeter, and the three of us used to go as far as a barricade built upon the road. On coming to this I had the trumpet sounded, an English officer handed us the newspapers and letters, and the captain, for his part, did the same. We talked, drank rum, ate some excellent ship's biscuits which the English-men had brought, and withdrew, excellent friends. It had been agreed that no attack should be delivered without previous warning, and that the sentinels should not fire on one another ; so that there was, for the time being, security and a tacit suspension of hostilities.

One night when I was on guard a shot was fired on the line of posts under my command. I immediately ordered all my men under arms and sent patrols on reconnaissance. After some time my men returned with a prisoner. This was one of our asses, which, while peacefully grazing, had crossed the lines, violated enemy territory and shown himself to an English sentry, who drove him back in our direction. My sentry cried "Who goes there ? " on his appearance, and, receiving no reply, fired on him, missed, and caused the troops on both sides of the line to seize their weapons, evidently for quite a distance, since long after this one heard the comical alarm : " Sentries, be on your guard ! "

These useful and patient animals, the asses, I may here remark, rendered immense services to the army of Portugal, whose miseries rendered it ungrateful to its saviours. All regiments had at least a hundred and twenty to a hundred and fifty asses in its train, to transport the sick and wounded, the knapsacks of the convalescents, and the stores of victuals, when we were lucky enough to possess more than a day's rations. This mass of quadrupeds took a number of men out of the ranks, and greatly delayed the march of the columns, but it saved many an unlucky wight. A few days after our arrival before the English lines our poverty became so poignant, so general, that all these inoffensive creatures were killed and eaten with a sort of sensual hunger. Those who wished or were able to save some of them kept them well hidden, and looked after them as though they had been blood horses, for they were stolen and killed without scruple.

I have already said that the English had covered the

river with their flotilla and had gone much higher than the limits agreed on by the two armies. One could not show oneself on the embankment of the Tagus, or pass along the high-road, without at once being a target for their guns. This murderous hostility greatly embarrassed our movements. One night, when I was on guard at the outposts, I had withdrawn to the courtyard of a house with two or three men to warm myself, for the night was cold and we were forbidden to light fires in the open. The outer gate of the courtyard was open; the opening faced the river and the fire was opposite this open carriage-gate. The fire was a fierce one, blazing brightly; and while I was sitting on a chair talking with these men, who were standing beside me, a shot came and cut one man in two, hurling him into the blazing fire. The poor fellow never spoke a word; his death was instantaneous. I had the fire put out and spent the rest of the night with my men, who, while regretting the death of their comrade, also regretted this faint assuagement of their hard lot.

In our bivouac at the foot of the hill overlooking Villafranca there were houses isolated in the vineyards in which we lived during the day, to take shelter from the sun and eat our meals, when there was anything to be eaten. In our house we found a hiding-place full of French books, nearly all by our best authors, well produced and finely bound; there were the two Encyclopædias, Voltaire, Rousseau, Montesquieu, etc. I saw nothing of this kind in Spain.

29th October.—At Ponte de Mugen, on the road to Santarem. In the forenoon our battalion received orders to take arms and hold itself in readiness to set out to fulfil a special mission. This hurried departure for an unknown destination vainly excited the sagacity of those officers who saw through everything. The men rejoiced in the change of position. Worn down by dearth, exhausted with service, devoured by almost invisible vermin, they could not have been more wretched elsewhere.

A few hours after we left our quarters we passed through Santarem, on a height bathed by the Tagus. We spent the night in an immense country house, remarkable for its huge store-houses, filled with colonial products, chests of oranges, and grain; and its cellars were equally remarkable for their wines. This was abundance after dearth. We bivouacked round about, and sentries were set at the doors to prevent waste.

31st October.—At Tancos, a pretty little town on the Tagus. From the other bank a number of musket-shots were fired at us, to which we paid no attention. During the day we passed through another little town, called Barquigny, where there were, as at Tancos, warehouses full of rice, coffee, sugar, chocolate, stockfish, rum, etc. We loaded with these the donkeys that were still left, and some others that we had already recruited since our departure, by beating the country to the left of our route. I myself, since we entered Portugal, had possessed a very powerful mule, which cost me rather a high price, but was of the very greatest use to me. I loaded it as heavily as I could, thinking we were going to take part in the siege of Abrantès, to which we were marching. The country we had hitherto come through was magnificent, rich and fertile; the vines had not been stripped nor the figs plucked, but this was no longer a resource; the fruit was for the most part rotten. What magnificent harvests lost, above all of the olives, which were devoured by millions of plovers! I had never seen so many birds; when they crossed the sun it was as though a cloud were passing. The towns and villages were empty of men and animals.

1st November.—At Punhète. For crossing the Zezer, which was swift and fairly deep, there were neither boats nor bridges. We planted stakes across its bed and stretched ropes between them so that the men could steady themselves lest they should be swept away by the current. Some good swimmers were posted below the crossing, to seize in passing those that might be swept away by the stream. It was a lengthy operation, difficult and even dangerous for the majority of the men, who, since the water rose above their waists, were lifted and carried away if they did not hold firmly to the cord. Many of them were fished out by the swimmers. A few muskets were lost, but none of the men were drowned. I crossed on my mule, after it had carried its load to the other bank.

In the evening General Foy, our commander, whom we had scarcely seen till then, as he was always with the cavalry, came to inspect our bivouacs. After I had had a long talk with him about various service matters he noticed, as he approached more closely to one of our bivouacs, a man on his knees near the fire with his hands clasped together, clad in a shirt. " Good Lord ! " he said to me ; " what's the matter with that man ? What has he been doing ? "—" Don't worry about him, general ; that man is a wooden god, praying ; it is a Christ, which an infantryman took from the church to dry his shirt on." He laughed heartily, while deprecating this somewhat irreverent jest, which the disorders of warfare rendered excusable. General Foy's sweetness of character, his affability and his kindly welcome charmed me. This was the first time I had spoken to him.

After Tancos we followed the Tagus, along the banks, on account of the mountains, among which its bed was very narrow and its current very swift. Its banks were now more picturesque, but the beautiful plains which bordered it had disappeared.

2nd November.—While we were in bivouac the reveille
was beaten even earlier than usual. The battalion
stood to arms, and when it was formed General Foy
gathered the officers about him and announced that we
were to go to Spain as his escort and that he had a
mission to the Emperor. The enterprise was perilous;
it involved no less than crossing a kingdom in a state of
revolution; but with audacity, courage and perfect
obedience to his orders he undertook to lead us to Spain
without fighting but not without exertion. He warned
us that we should always march before daybreak and
that we should not halt before night, in order to conceal
our traces from the numerous parties that were scouring
the kingdom. He recommended us to march with closed
ranks and not to stray from the column under penalty
of being killed by the peasants.

This was the marching order which we were as a rule
to observe: A company of Dragoons in the vanguard;
a section of Grenadiers ahead of the battalion; the
horses, mules and asses, and the sick and wounded to
follow the battalion; the infantry, as the rearguard,
were to pick up stragglers and keep the men and the
baggage in close contact; lastly, on the flanks fifty
Hanoverian Lancers were to scout, scouring and beating
the country beyond us in order to announce the approach
of the enemy.

The detachment contained 350 infantry and 200 horse.
The general recommended me to study the country we
were passing through, to take notes, and to give them to
him every night after we had halted. This arrangement
involved my seeing him twice or thrice a day and placed
me on an almost intimate footing with him.

To undertake an expedition so hazardous with so few
men was very bold; but the general was active and
enterprising and kept beside him a Portuguese who knew
the country and an aide who spoke the language, so that

he could question any inhabitants we might encounter or the prisoners we might make. To facilitate this almost cross-country journey and rid the country of the armed bands that might lurk there troops were sent to the fortress of Abrantès, to give the impression of an approaching siege. This apprehension should cause the mobile columns to move in that direction, to defend Abrantès ; other demonstrations made on our left would have the same result, so that we should find the country we had to traverse almost free.

For the rest, I do not doubt that if we had been harder pressed the general would have abandoned the infantry, which would have extricated itself as best it could, and that he would have set out with the cavalry to fulfil his mission, which seemed to him more important than the preservation of a few hundred men. A few words which he spoke to me in a private conversation made me think so.

On the 3rd November we passed through a village where there was a bakehouse and stores of food and wine for the partisan corps. On our approach the magistrates of the place set fire to the magazine and staved in the barrels. However, we were able to seize some bread which was not yet destroyed by the flames, and the soldiers lay on their bellies and quenched their thirst with the wine that was running in the road as they would have drunk the water after a storm.

On the 4th, a few minutes before reaching the place where we were to spend the night, and when it was already growing dark, a shot was fired at the company by a man ambushed behind a hedge beyond a stream to our right. The ball cut the waist of my coat, which was open, and struck the left arm of the recruiting-sergeant on my right. The cavalry scouts having come in without seeing anything, we proceeded on our way.

On the 5th, as we were setting out, we learned that

in a few hours' time we should cross a plain where we might encounter the cavalry of Silveira, a Portuguese general; that it would thenceforth be prudent to march in close formation so that we could subsequently form a square and resist his charge. And indeed, on emerging from a village, we beheld a wide plain, preceded by a brook which we had to cross by a single plank, one man at a time. The commandant, who was not much of a soldier, continued to march without reforming his battalion; so that the men advanced into the plain singly and in some degree scattered. When the general saw this he returned at a gallop and most violently upbraided the battalion-leader and the officers. He was so angry that he could not get his words out. At this moment I was crossing the brook. I stopped the first few men beyond it, and as they arrived I ordered them to fix bayonets and form up three deep. When they had crossed I moved forward thus, with the ranks in close order. When the general saw me coming he cried out: " There at last is a company that knows its duties and understands where it is. Very good, men; very good, Lieutenant Barrès."

On the 7th, in the forenoon, we entered a Spanish village, to our very great satisfaction, for we were terribly fatigued by these six days of forced marches, and now we felt as though we were at home, although the countryside was equally inhospitable. By the evening we were only three leagues from Almeida and five from Rodrigo. Unhappily for me that same night I became dismally certain that I was in the grips of a violent fever.

On the 8th November, in the morning, the general assembled us to bid us farewell. After a few polite phrases, rather coldly spoken, he took me aside to ask me for the latest notes I had been able to take, and added, in a low voice: " I shall recommend you to the Minister." He then left with the cavalry. On reaching Rodrigo we found he was no longer there; he was in haste to get to Paris, to explain to the Emperor the state in which he had left the army in Portugal and the necessity of sending it reinforcements.

Thus ended an expedition full of danger, though we did not once encounter the enemy, or even receive a musket-shot, excepting that of which I have spoken, which might have been fatal to me. We had very few sick, despite our exertions and the very bad food. Our march was so irregular that it would have been very difficult for an enemy to pursue us, for, like a hunted hare, we changed our direction several times in the course of the day, in order to put those who might learn that we were *en route* off our track. It was said, though I did not see it, that the guides we took were afterwards killed by the Hanoverians when they arrived on the left of the column.

9th November.—On this day and the following I did not leave my lodging, being too overcome by the fever to fulfil my duties. The malady was plainly declared and recovery might be slow, so I determined to go into the hospital at Rodrigo, much as I disliked the idea. I there sold my mule.

Entering hospital on the 11th, I remained there for forty days without experiencing any improvement of health. Thinking that perhaps the medicines were not good or the air unwholesome I left it, still as sick as ever, on the 21st December, to get myself treated in the town at my own expense.

The battalion had long before left for Almeida. I therefore found myself alone in Rodrigo save for one infantryman who was also leaving hospital. A few days after I had left, being kept in bed by illness, I said to him : " You threatened one day to kill me on the first opportunity that offered ; you threatened me in Portugal because I required you to carry the musket of a sick

comrade ; well, you can do it to-day without fear, for
I know I haven't the strength to defend myself."—" Ah ! "
he replied, flushing, " that's the sort of thing one says
when one's angry, but that one doesn't do, unless one's a
scoundrel."

I had heard that quinquina of the best quality, infused
in good wine, was an excellent febrifuge ; I procured
both the day I left hospital and at once took some. A
few days later I no longer had any fever, but very great
weakness, which I could not repair by abundant and sub-
stantial food for fear of a relapse. Nothing but time and
a great deal of care could give me back my strength.

1st January.—The first day of the year 1811, as I
returned after spending the evening with a friend of mine,
a captain, who was wounded, my soldier informed me :
" There's an officer lying in your bed." I scolded him
for having allowed this. He excused himself, saying
this captain was too exhausted to go and get his billeting
paper changed ; that he was leaving at daybreak next
day ; that he was a young officer, neat and clean as to
his person ; finally, that he had begged him so politely
to allow him to sleep beside me that he had neither the
courage nor the wish to prevent him. Thinking the
matter over, knowing that there was only the one bed
and the one room in the house, I thought of myself in
the like position. I got into bed beside the stranger.
At daybreak he got up very quietly in order not to wake
me, but having opened my eyes I recognized an officer
of the 16th light infantry with whom I had served, a
good comrade who had shown evidence of considerable
regret when we said farewell at Belfort in 1808. Each of
us was greatly delighted to meet again, thanks to a chance
which was like an encounter in a comedy.

On the 3rd January I thought myself sufficiently
recovered to go and rejoin my company ; but the rain

and the cold during the day made me fear, that evening at Galiegos, that I had again done an imprudent thing.

On the 4th, when I went to see the captain on my arrival at Almeida, he told me : " You were wrong to come ; you are not recovered yet." I assured him that I was, but my physical state and my weakness gave me the lie.

Next day I was delirious ; I was carried to a granary which served as hospital. I lay there thirty-six days between life and death, recognizing nothing, but retaining the sense of hearing in a remarkable degree. Thus, for several mornings in succession, I heard the doctor say : " He has no pulse left ; he won't last long." Or : " He won't last out the day." I recovered, however, as though by a miracle, with everybody dying all round me, thanks principally to my strong constitution, for the care and the remedies I was given were too insignificant to help me, if they were not harmful. During my convalescence General Foy returned from Paris. Having learned that I was in hospital he came to see me. This kindly attention touched me to tears.

I had been in Almeida or in hospital seventy-eight days when on the 23rd March the cadre of the 4th battalion, which was returning to France, passed through the town. Being of the battalion I had to leave with it. I was not sorry to do so ; my health was still so bad that I did not regret that I did not belong to a cadre on active service.

On the 27th, passing through Ciudad-Rodrigo, Samonios and Malitra, we reached Salamanca, where we learned of the birth of the King of Rome. We remained there until the 8th April. On the 11th April we were approaching Valladolid when I again committed an imprudence that might have been disastrous to me. During the halt at Valdesillas I met several officers of the Imperial Guard, whom I had known when I was serving in it.

They invited me to breakfast, and I accepted with pleasure, while telling them that I could only stay three-quarters of an hour unless I wanted to find myself alone on the highway. We talked a great deal, and when I rose from the table the column had left. I had two leagues to go through a desert countryside, scoured every day by numerous guerillas, whose mission was to intercept communication between Valladolid and Madrid and Salamanca. The danger was serious ; it meant almost certain death ; but the idea of being forced to wait, perhaps for a long time, for another convoy, before I could return to France, made me risk everything. I set out anything but confident as to my situation. On the way I was overtaken by a mounted gendarme who was going at a great pace. I seized the tail of his horse and ran with him, but I was soon tired and had to abandon the attempt. However, I was gaining ground ; but finally, when I had nearly overtaken the column, five or six Spaniards on horseback appeared on my left. Whether because they did not see me, or for some other reason, they were not advancing. I was redoubling my efforts to escape from their clutches, when I saw, beyond a little clump of trees, five or six French cavalrymen coming to meet me. The worthy gendarme had told them of the danger I was incurring, and the officer of the rearguard at once sent a few cavalrymen back, to save me, if it was not too late. Without them I should have been killed ; these bloodthirsty bands did not make prisoners. I thanked my rescuers, and after resting awhile I continued with them as far as the banks of the Douro, where I overtook the column.

On the 12th April Marshal the Duc d'Istria reviewed us and entrusted us with the escort to France of 3,500 prisoners, taken at Badajoz. This was a disagreeable task with which we could very well have dispensed. While inspecting us he recognized a captain of the regiment who had been a fifer under his orders in Egypt. "Ah, there you are, you rascal ! "—"Thank you, my lord. I am glad to see you remember me." The marshal laughed heartily, and then said to him : " I shall expect you to dinner."

There was also at this inspection an officer, one of our friends, lieutenant in the 70th, by name Poiret, whom we used to call "the Saviour of France." At Saint-Cloud, on the 18th Brumaire, he had taken Bonaparte in his arms to protect him from the blows showered upon him and to get him out of the hall of the Council of Six Hundred. This won him the rank of officer, a pension, the title of chevalier, with a coat of arms, and many valuable presents. He was an excellent fellow, uneducated, but a good comrade. The marshal invited him also to dine with him, together with a few officers of higher rank.

Since that day I have often seen, in Paris, this sturdy Grenadier of the Guard of the Directorate, who saw his private pension stopped by the Restoration, but was indemnified by the Comte de Las-Cases. Las-Cases gave him a larger pension, with reversion to his wife in case of survival, out of the legacy which the Emperor Napoleon left him by the famous testament of St. Helena.

Finally, on the morning of the 27th April, we crossed the Bidassoa. It would be difficult to express the joy experienced by all those who formed part of this immense column. A general "hurrah" sounded all along the line. Once the bridge was crossed, we had no longer any need to fear assassination or want or the fear of seeing our prisoners taken from us. I was so poor that I had to borrow money of my captain to pay for the first meal I took in France. We halted for breakfast at Saint-Jean-de-Luz.

I had been in the Peninsula a year, three months and thirteen days.

Detached to the Ile de Groix, Barrès was promoted captain on the 19th April, 1812. He rejoined the Grand Army at the beginning of 1813; and in the capacity of captain of the 3rd battalion of the 47th regiment of infantry he took for the third time, in April, the road to Germany.

CAMPAIGNS OF 1813 AND 1814.

On the 5th March, 1813, in the evening, I left for Paris on the diligence, being sent thither by the commander of the battalion for sabres, belts and straps, drums and trumpets, and various articles of uniform for the officers. For four days I was busily occupied on the errand with which I had been entrusted, which I was fortunate enough to complete in every particular.

On the morning of the 10th I sent to Saint-Denis, where the battalion was stationed, all the articles required, which gave general satisfaction.

The officers had asked me to arrange a good dinner for the 9th. I ordered it at Grignon's, a restaurant in the Rue Neuve-des-Petits-Champs, at a fairly high price, so that most of them could say it was the best they had ever had. It was as merry as if we had been about to travel for pleasure instead of being about to embark on a terrible campaign, which was plainly going to be a very murderous one, considering the weight of combatants who would be at the front. (On our return from Paris sixteen months later at least half the guests at this delightful and epicurean banquet never again beheld their native land.)

Despite my many errands I found time to have my portrait taken by the physionotrace.[1]

The battalion arrived in Mayence on the 5th April. It was the third time I had passed through the town.

[1] Presumably a silhouette or profile portrait, but whether made by outlining a shadow, or an image cast by a lens, or by a species of pantograph I cannot discover.—TR.

On the afternoon of the 29th April, being in bivouac, we heard the guns for the first time during this campaign. A young soldier of the 6th, at the sound of this cannonade, which was apparently at some distance, went to take his musket from the piles as though to clean it, saying to his comrades, as he moved away : " The devil ! there's the beastly sound already. I shan't hear it long ; " then, hiding behind a hedge, he blew his brains out. This was regarded as an act of madness, for it was incomprehensible. If the man feared death, at all events he killed himself. If he did not fear it, he should have waited for it to come to him, naturally or accidentally.

On the 1st May, on our arrival at the bivouac, we saw a waggon going by at a gallop to Weissenfels. It contained the body of Marshal the Duc d'Istria (Bessières), who had been shot through by a bullet on the heights ahead of us. In him the Emperor lost a faithful friend, an old and valiant comrade in arms. The death of this worthy marshal grieved me greatly, for I had for a long time been under his orders ; he was a charming and courteous man.

2nd May, 1813.—Lutzen. We marched off early in the morning, following the Leipsic highway. Reaching the high ground at the entrance to the plain of Lutzen the division drew up in column on the left of the road. On the horizon in front of us we saw the smoke of the enemy guns. Insensibly the sound grew louder and nearer, proving that they were moving toward us. During this time the 2nd and 3rd divisions of our army corps came up and formed in column behind us ; the artillery fixed its lashings and prepared to open fire. The whole Imperial Guard, which was behind, was moving by forced marches on Lutzen, following the high-road.

At last we moved forward ; our division was on the extreme right. In close column formation we went along

the road and moved straight on the village, to the right
of Strasiedel. On our left we passed the monument
erected to the memory of the great Gustavus Adolphus,
who was killed here in 1632.

In front of Strasiedel we were saluted by the whole
artillery of the enemy army and horribly cut up.
Threatened by the cavalry we formed a square, and in
this position received incessant charges which we always
successfully repulsed. At the beginning of the action
Colonel Henrion had his left epaulette carried away by
a bullet and was forced to withdraw. Commandant
Fabre took over the command of the regiment and was
replaced by a captain. In less than half an hour I, the
fifth captain of the battalion, found my turn had come to
command it.

At last, after three and a half to four hours of stubborn
fighting, having lost half our officers and men and had
our guns dismounted and ammunition-caissons blown up,
we retired in good order, at the march, as on parade, and
went to take up our position behind the village of Strasiedel, without closing up our ranks too much. Major
Fabre was admirable in this movement of withdrawal :
what coolness, what presence of mind this uneducated
man displayed ! A little respite having been granted us,
I saw that I was forty-three men short, and an officer,
wounded in the head. I too was wounded in two places,
but so slightly that I did not think of leaving the battlefield. One of these wounds was inflicted by the head of
a sub-lieutenent, which had been hurled into my face.
I was for a long time covered with my own blood and the
brains of this nice young fellow, who, having left the
École Militaire two months before, said to us the
previous day : " At thirty I shall be a colonel, or
killed."

Forced to beat a retreat, I thought the battle lost, but
an unattached major, having arrived the day before from

11

Spain with at least a hundred others, reassured me, saying that on the contrary the battle was nearly won; that the 4th corps (Comte Bertrand) was debouching on our right behind the left wing of the enemy, and that the 5th corps (Comte Lauriston) was debouching on the extreme left, behind the enemy's right wing. After half an hour's repose the division again moved forward, passing again over the ground we had occupied so long and strown with our dead. We found one of our adjutants, whose leg was broken by a grapeshot, taking cover in a furrow. For more than half an hour the cannonballs and bullets of the two armies had been going by over his head. When we had stood several cavalry charges and sustained several volleys of grape, one of which killed or wounded all our drummers and trumpeters, cut the major's sabre in two and wounded his horse, the enemy withdrew without being pursued, as we had not the cavalry to follow on his heels.

We bivouacked on the battlefield, formed in a square, so as to be prepared to repulse the enemy should he turn up during the night. This did indeed happen, but not to us.

Our young conscripts behaved very well; not one left the ranks; on the contrary, some that we had left behind, sick, came to take their places. One of our buglers, a boy of sixteen, was of the number. He had a thigh carried away by a ball and died at the rear of the company. These poor children, when they were wounded but still able to walk, used to come to me to ask to leave the company to get their wounds dressed; it was a renunciation of life, a submission to their superiors, which touched one more than it astonished.

My company was disorganized; it had lost half its sergeants and corporals; many of the muskets were broken by grapeshot; while the kettles, cooking-pots, shoulder-straps, tufts, etc., were lost.

3rd May.—In bivouac, before Pegau. . . .

The army moved off in the forenoon, all ready to attack the enemy if he had waited for us on the Elster, but we did not encounter him. I was with the vanguard of the army corps. Having passed Pegau, I received orders to halt, to take up a position on the heights, and to retire when relieved.

While I was in this position a squadron of the Baden dragoons came forward to reconnoitre and the outpost which was to relieve me arrived. I warned the sergeant of the 86th that some foreign cavalrymen would possibly appear on their return to camp ; to make sure of their identity, but to beware of taking them for enemies. I was on the way to rejoin my battalion when I heard musket-shots behind me. It was the Baden dragoons, who had been taken for Russians. The outpost gave ground when it thought it was being charged, and took to its legs. The alarm spread through the bivouacs of the division and the troops sprang to arms. I sent word at once that it was a misapprehension, but the troops were already in formation. A quarter of an hour later all was quiet again ; one cavalryman was wounded. The sergeant was degraded and punished.

4th May.—In bivouac around Borna, a small town in Saxony, four leagues from Altenburg.

I was ordered to make the rearguard of the division. The general recommended me to keep at least a league to the rear of all the troops, to advance with prudence and in good order, because I had a wide plain to cross where I might be charged by Cossacks hidden in the forest which I should skirt on my right. I saw, indeed, several Cossacks, but not being in sufficient force they did not attack us.

At night, in bivouac, the commandant made me write some memoranda of applications for promotion and for the decoration of the Legion of Honour, also an order of the day for appointments to the rank of sergeant and corporal. My sergeant-major was made adjutant. I mention this promotion because later on he became an important figure in the world of finance. Still adjutant in 1814, he demanded and obtained his discharge. Having become clerk to a receiver-general he was in 1824 treasurer-general of the Navy and had his marriage-contract signed by Charles X and the royal family. If he had been promoted officer he would have remained in the Army. But even if he had been fortunate his position would probably never have been equal to that which he attained. His name is Marbeau ; he is still in the service of the Government.

I RECEIVE THE LEGION OF HONOUR.

18*th May*.—A letter from the major-general of the Grand Army, the Prince of Neufchâtel and Wagram, told me that by a decree dated the 17th May I was appointed Chevalier of the Legion of Honour, under the number 35,505. Never did any reward give me so much pleasure. The major was appointed officer of the legion, while the captain of the Grenadiers and two or three others, sergeants, corporals and soldiers, were appointed legionaries. Those of the captains who were not distinguished complained greatly of the major, but this was unjust, for he asked for the distinction for all of them.

THE TWO BATTLES OF BAUTZEN.

20*th May*.—All preparations for a general engagement having been completed by the evening of the 19th, we were warned that it would take place on the morning of the 20th. We made ready for the great day. About ten o'clock we moved forward, to force the passage of the Spree, having the town of Bautzen opposite us on the farther bank. The crossing could not be made, for lack of bridges. Bridges were thrown across on trestles, and when the gangways were practicable we crossed rapidly. All the positions were carried, and we left the town behind us. At seven o'clock at night the battle was gained, and the corps took up their positions so as to pass the night in square formation, for it was feared the cavalry might surprise us.

Before crossing the Spree, General Compans, commanding our division, required of me fourteen men with a sergeant and a corporal. He led them himself to the foot of the walls of the town, showed them a breach through which they could pass, told them to climb over it, throw down any obstacles, and then to make for a gate, which he pointed out to them, in order to open it. The sergeant climbed the breach first; he was killed. The corporal replaced him and gave a hand to the men, to help them to climb. They fired a volley, lost two or three men, reached the gate, opened it and admitted the troops of the 11th corps, who were waiting at the foot of the wall, unable to scale it for want of ladders. The town taken, the men returned to me. A moment later General Compans came up to the company. He said to me : " Captain, you will make this brave corporal a sergeant, and whichever of the men has the best education a corporal, for they all deserve to be rewarded, one as much as another. If the sergeant had not been killed I should have made him an officer. Finally, you will forward this corporal's name for a decoration, and also that of one of the men, as you may decide." All this he said to me privately. I was some distance from the battalion, having been detached as guard to a battery. I made the two promotions, which was not entirely regular ; but the orders were imperative and the motive too honourable for me to do other than execute them at once.

During the evening my orderly [1] brought me some bread and sausage, a bottle of liqueur and a truss of straw which he had bought at Bautzen. I shared them with my two officers. I then spread out my truss of straw behind the piled arms of the company, of which one rank stood while the other two lay down, by turns of an hour each. These things were thankfully received, for we were faint with hunger and fatigue.

21st May.—Before daylight we stood to arms, and later on moved to the foot of the hills the other side of the stream, by which we had halted the previous evening. Being ignorant of what was happening, we waited for the order to move forward in pursuit of the enemy ; but the detonations of hundreds of guns and the brisk fusillade to be heard all along the front of the army told us that what we had done the day before was only the prologue of a bloody drama which was about to be played out before us by 350,000 men brought hither to enact it.

The Emperor having arrived, we climbed the hill before us, meeting with no resistance, and moved down into the plain facing us, where we could see the Russian army covered by the redoubts and entrenchments with which its whole front was bristling. This entrenched front stretched from the slopes of the Bohemian mountains to the left of the enemy to a line of hillocks on the right, perpendicular to the line of battle. Our army corps was in the centre ; it was to threaten the entrenched enemy front sufficiently to make it believe that we were seeking to force it, and by drawing the enemy's whole attention to this point to enable the army corps at the extremities to turn it and cause the front to cave in without a direct attack. To this end more than a hundred guns were formed in battery and fired constantly from nine o'clock in the morning to four in the afternoon. We were in

[1] *Soldat de confiance.*—Tr.

square formation in the plain behind the batteries, receiving all the shots intended for them. Our ranks were opened, battered, horribly mutilated by this incessant mass of projectiles which reached us from these diabolical trenches. A few showers of rain that for the moment obscured the air gave us some periods of respite by which we profited to lie down, but they were brief.

At last, about four or five o'clock, the order came to carry these formidable redoubts, whose fire was not yet entirely extinguished, with the bayonet. We began to form the attacking columns, when the cannonade suddenly ceased; the enemy was leaving the field to us, and retiring in order. We pressed him close for an hour or two, halting at last, distressed and dying of hunger, but proud of our triumph.

I suppose there are no finer moments in life than the evening of a day when one has just won a great victory. If the joy is tempered a little by the regret caused by the loss of so many good and valiant comrades, it is none the less keen and intoxicating. We gathered round General Joubert to congratulate ourselves mutually on the result of this terrible day. A bottle of rum was passed round to drink the Emperor's health. We had gathered in a circle and were gaily conversing when a spent cannon-ball arrived, slowly ricocheting, but still having enough force to cut a man in two if it had encountered one. Warned in time, we avoided it nimbly, and no one was hit.

I had twenty-one men killed or wounded during these two days. The wounds were horrible.

22nd May.—We went into position to take part in the battle of Reichenbach, which took place in the afternoon, but were not engaged. It was in this rearguard action that the Grand Marshal of the Palace, Duroc, Duc de Friuli, and General Kirgener of the engineers of the Guard were killed by the same ball. At night, by the light of our bivouac, Major Fabre and I wrote memoranda proposing men for vacant commissions and for decorations. I did not forget to include the sergeant who behaved so well in the attack on Bautzen and the man whom I selected as the most deserving among the twelve survivors.

26th May.—The enemy sought to prevent us from crossing the Katsbach, near Wüdschüs, by firing on us. I was sent with sharpshooters to drive them from the left bank and follow them in their movement of retreat. After a pretty sharp fusillade in which I lost three men they withdrew. I followed them closely and meant to cross the river after them, but I found before me a considerable stream, which I was unable to cross. As night was falling the marshal did not think it opportune to go into action at so late an hour ; he told me to bivouac a little below the point at which I was, where I should find a road. I went there and saw that the obstacle which had stopped me was an artificial body of water made to turn a mill.

28th May.—In the morning I took the head of the column and received the marshal's orders direct. After two hours' advance the marshal decided to abandon the valley we were following and diverge to the left in order to cross the plain of Jauer. There were a few cavalry charges, which were repulsed, and we presently found ourselves under the walls of the town of Jauer.

In going through the town I struck against a fairly large object which I picked up and carried along with me, having a presentiment that it might be something good. It was in fact an enormous turkey, the biggest I had ever seen. Plucked, cleaned, trussed and enclosed in a napkin and a cavalry nose-bag, I showed it to my comrades, who were of the opinion that we should all of us eat it on the following day, that is, if, as it was reported, we were remaining in this position.

On the 29th those officers who knew a little of cooking set to work to prepare the dinner planned the night before ; there was no lack of victuals nor of culinary art. This day we did what we had not done since crossing the Rhine—made a very good meal, washed down with an excellent Moravian wine. The preparations, which were difficult of achievement, the pleasure of being gathered together, and of eating, quietly seated, the products of our culinary friends, enabled us to spend a few agreeable hours, such as are rare in warfare.

30th May.—We remained at Eisendorf, a village near Neumarckt, waiting until the armistice of Plessvitz should be signed, and on the 6th June began our retrograde movement, to take up the positions which the Grand Army was to occupy during the fifty days of repose which were granted to it by the armistice.

At night, in bivouac before Neudorf, the infantryman I had proposed for decoration was guilty of theft from one of his comrades. Suspected of the crime, he was searched, and was found in possession of the stolen article. The indignant soldiers seized him, gave him a drubbing, and sent a deputation to me asking that he should be thrown out of the company. I had retired to a house at some little distance, which is the reason why justice was thus administered unknown to me. I should have opposed the sentence, as although the theft was proved, the article stolen was of small value. But the harm was done, and I had to appear, tacitly, in order to maintain this honourable susceptibility in the company. I reported the matter to the major, and it was agreed between us that if the unhappy young man was appointed legionary his diploma should be returned and the reason of so doing explained.

7th June.—Before leaving Neudorf, General Joubert gave me the order to scour, with my company, all the villages situated a league or more from the right flank of the column, and to take away any cattle I might find in them, and drive them to Gnadenberg, where I was to report at eight o'clock at night.

On the 8th I rejoined the division at night, long after it had established its bivouacs, with four hundred cows or bullocks, three thousand sheep, and a few goats, horses, etc. General Joubert was delighted with this excursion ; General Compans came to congratulate me on it and told me to take my captives to the army park. This was all I got out of the affair, though if I had wanted to make money I could have done so without difficulty ; the landowning barons offering me gold if I would leave them the half of what I took from them. But I had to execute a confidential mission and I did so conscientiously. However, when the soldiers brought me cows belonging to poor people who came to beg for them, I gave them back. In an outbuilding of a very fine château an Italian general, slightly wounded, who was present, wanted to oppose my requisition. " I am quite willing, General, but give me orders in writing." He dared not do so.

On the 10th June my company had as its quarters a very large, isolated farm, where it was very comfortably housed. We began to feel a great need of repose. The army was very greatly weakened by daily fighting, by marching and sickness, by numerous mutilations, by the facility with which the enemy was able to make prisoners, the soldiers seeking ways of getting themselves captured. It was also in urgent need of body-linen and shoes ; everything needed repairing and very largely renewing. On the very next day I organized tailors' and cobblers' shops for repairs. One had also to busy oneself with curing skin complaints, ridding the poor young soldiers of the vermin that were devouring them, nursing slight illnesses and sending to the hospital at Buntzlau such men as were more seriously affected. There was also the matter of armament to think of; shoulder-straps and belts too, and the thousand details involved in the administration of a company.

My sub-lieutenant, wounded at Lutzen, having rejoined me, I had three officers with me. We slept, all four, in a little room, on straw, but this was better than the best bivouac, for we were under cover. I had slept in the open air for forty-four nights.

On the 15th June the major received eight nominations to the rank of Chevalier of the Legion of Honour, two of which were for my company. The nomination of the Chasseur who was expelled from the company was among them. It was sent back the same day to the general of the brigades accompanied by a detailed report. On the 17th a special decree, dated from Dresden, annulled this nomination. The proposal, nomination and annulment were not known to the unhappy man interested nor to any of the battalion officers.

A few days after our establishment in this village of Ober-Thomaswald a young relative of mine, who came out with me from home, after displaying great courage and energy in this war, which called for them in a more than ordinary degree, fell sick. I kept him by me for some time; then, as his condition grew more serious, I sent him to the hospital at Buntzlau, where he died. This death was grievous to me and made me keenly regret that I had taken him with me.

During the armistice the marshal had all the mutilated men paraded; their number was very great. It was really afflicting. There were more than twenty in the battalion, and perhaps more than 15,000 in the whole army. They were sent to the rear to work on the fortifications, to drive waggons, etc. When M. Larrey, surgeon-in-chief to the army, assured the Emperor that

this was untrue he was knowingly deceiving him. There
was not an officer in the army ignorant of the fact, for
it went on, so to speak, under their eyes. This deplorable
monomania had existed for a long time, but it was more
generally practised in this terrible campaign. It was
precursory to our future disasters.

18*th July.*—The armistice, which was to have ended
on the 20th July, was prolonged until the 15th August.
The Emperor's fête, celebrated as a rule on the
15th August, was anticipated by five days and fixed for
the 10th. To give it all the proper brilliance, to impose
on this great solemnity a character in keeping with the
extraordinary circumstances in which France and the
army then stood, great preparations were made in all
the headquarters and cantonments.

On the 10th August the army corps was united in a
wide plain and reviewed by its commander, Marshal the
Duc de Ragusa, who, in full uniform, cloak, and hat in
the style of Henri IV, with his marshal's truncheon in
his hand, passed before the front line of each corps.
After the review there were some large manœuvres and
a general march past. The army corps, composed of
three divisions (Compans, Bonnet, Friederich), was remarkably fine and full of enthusiasm. Its strength was
27,000, with 82 guns.

After the review all the officers of the division assembled
at Gnadenberg to take part in a great dinner which the
general of the division gave in the fine Protestant temple.
Three roast roebuck were served, whole, standing on
their four legs, on a huge iron trestle. Lovers of very
high venison were able to regale themselves, for they
stank out the banqueting hall.

During the evening we repaired to headquarters, where
games of all sorts were played. It was a good day, to
be followed by many bad.

DRESDEN.

18*th August.*—Resumption of hostilities. In bivouac, near Gnadenberg, facing Bohemia, to cover our right flank, threatened by the Austrians, who had just joined the coalition. This war of a father-in-law against his son-in-law surprised the army as greatly as it offended them. This new enemy on our hands, without counting a number of others of whom we were told, made one foresee events of which many of us were not to see the conclusion. But we were confident in the genius of the Emperor and in our previous successes. And this presumption, which nothing could overturn, reassured us as to the issue of this war.

26*th August.*—In bivouac, two leagues before coming to Dresden. The rain fell in torrents all day. The road was covered with troops, likewise on their way to Dresden. The guns which were loudly audible in that direction, the continual passing of aides and orderlies, the excitement to be remarked on all faces, foretold important events. The bivouac was dismal, inconvenient, altogether wretched.

27*th August.*—We left our position before day, but the road was so encumbered with foot-soldiers, cavalry and guns that at noon we were in the streets of Dresden without being able to debouch on to the plain. The rain was as violent as the day before. The detonations of an immense artillery deafened us. At last we arrived on the battlefield and were put in line of battle, but already victory had descended on our eagles. What remained to be done was reduced to profiting by this brilliant success. We pursued the enemy a little ;| the soil was too sodden for us to advance rapidly and do him much damage ;

night came as our division was beginning to get into action.

In bivouac in the mud, on the field of battle.

28th August.—In pursuit of the enemy from daybreak. We reached him several times but without serious engagement; he made no stand. On the last heights surrounding Dresden the general sent me to search a village which we were leaving on our right, in the valley of Plauen, in which a number of Austrians had been reported to him. I went thither with my company, supported by that of the grenadiers, who were to remain in reserve. On the height, after an insignificant exchange of musketry, I made more than five hundred and fifty men prisoners, who surrendered rather than defend themselves. According to what they said I could have made three or four thousand by continuing along the bottom of the valley, and should have found there a great deal of artillery and baggage, but I received the order to return, as the army corps had to move more to the left, where the Russian rearguard persisted in defending a difficult pass. Its resistance ceased only with the daylight.

We bivouacked on the farther side of the great forest and near the small town of Dippoldwalde in the valley of Plauen. In general the Austrians made no resistance, but the Russians were more obstinate than ever. The battle of Dresden had destroyed the Austrian army but had done very little to damage the other allies.

I had only two men wounded during the day, on the morning of which we learned of the death of General Moreau, who was killed in the ranks of the Russian army. It was a punishment from heaven.

30th August.—Battle of Zinnwald. I am not very certain of this name, having taken it from a map with which I was provided, but having no one to tell me whether I was making a mistake as to the locality. This battle was very creditable to my company, which, on the admission of General Joubert, did more by itself than all the other infantry of the division. The description of the battle would be interesting to write, but would take too long. After carrying the position we threw the enemy in disorder into the forest of Löplitz, and there we bivouacked. I had had eight men killed or wounded and I myself received a lance-thrust from a Cossack, which fortunately only grazed my right shoulder. A week later the company received two decorations for its good conduct in the day's fighting.

We had been two days in the midst of the impenetrable forests of Bohemia, sometimes in gorges whose wild profundity was truly awe-inspiring.

31st August.—Almost with the break of day the Russians attacked us with a violence that surprised us and contrasted with their conduct on the preceding days. Victorious at first, we pushed them beyond their position of that morning, to within sight of Löplitz. Pressed back in our turn to our first position, we remained there in spite of all the efforts they made to drive us back. The whole division was fighting on foot excepting a few reserves intended to relieve companies that were too exhausted. At four in the afternoon I withdrew from the battle a moment to clean my weapons ; they were so encrusted that the bullets would not enter the barrel. I returned to the front until the night.

We bivouacked on the same ground as the night before ; we had been cruelly dealt with. The battalion had had several officers killed or wounded and almost a third of its men ; I had lost one officer and twenty-five men from my own ranks. In the middle of the night we received orders to light great fires (there was no lack of wood) and then to withdraw in silence, without drums or trumpets, by the same track that we had followed during the preceding days.

The march was slow and dangerous, by these frightful tracks where one could see nothing. At dawn we came to the battlefield of the 30th. We halted there awhile to organize our ranks and to rest, for we sorely needed rest.

It was then that we learned that General Vandamme, commander of the 1st army corps, had been completely defeated on the 30th, at Kulm, not far from us, on our left, but completely separated from us by gorges so frightful and forests so dense that we could not have brought him assistance. This explained the violence of the battle of the previous day and our movement of withdrawal.

2nd September.—For six days we had been without food. I ate nothing but the strawberries and bilberries which abounded in the woods. At last the canteen-woman of the company, in whose cart I had some provisions, rejoined us. This wretched woman had abandoned us when she saw us entering such a wild country.

4th September.—A decree of this date ordered that of every ten men found away from their corps one should be shot. This measure sufficiently shows how demoralization had spread through the army.

10th September.—In camp, in hutments before Dresden, we had three days' rest. This completely restored me. I had been very ill, without giving in. It also did a great deal of good to the army, which had been on the roads from dawn to nightfall for twenty-four days.

On the 13th, at Grossen-Hayn, an event occurred which wrung my heart. A poor soldier had been condemned to death for a rather insignificant crime or offence. Led out to be shot, and having listened to the reading of his sentence, he cried for mercy and fled as fast as he could run. He was followed by musket-shots and finally hit. Once fallen, he was finished off.

27th September.—In the night we were told that the enemy cavalry was approaching and preparing to attack ours, which, composed of young soldiers, was in no condition to hold its own. Our battalion moved off first to take up a position at the entrance of a defile in order to protect the retreat of the cavalry. I was placed in the cemetery of a village through which the road passed. I hid my men and gave them orders not to fire on the Cossacks until our cavalry had entered the village. Shortly afterwards I saw our wretched cavalry arrive in frightful disorder, followed by an immense cloud of Cossacks. When it had almost all passed I gave the order to fire, when it was the turn of the Cossacks to fly. What a raking they got, and how swiftly they disappeared!

Once they had taken themselves off I rejoined my battalion, which was the other side of the ravine. The cavalry was rallied, and once in order we resumed our march, but half an hour later the cavalry was again in flight and allowed two of its guns to be taken. The whole battalion set off at the double and re-took them. In this position the good Colonel Boudinhox, commanding a provisional regiment of dragoons, came to see me and to offer his services. He was greatly distressed at commanding such poor cavalry.

I was then sent by the Duc de Ragusa, on to a height, to guard the outlet of two roads, with orders not to leave this position as long as there were any of our men in the plain, and then to form the extreme rearguard. I marched at a venture a great part of the night to rejoin the army corps, which I found close to the Elbe, opposite Meissen, where we bivouacked. I was very lucky not

12

to have been taken by the Cossacks in my deserted state, for unless I had dashed into the woods and marched at hazard through country which I did not know I could not long have held out against numerous and repeated cavalry charges.

28th September.—We descended the left bank of the Elbe. A league below Meissen, at a spot where the river is squeezed between two ranges of fairly high hills, we were horribly bombarded by fifteen to twenty guns, placed on a height of the right bank, firing point-blank with solid shot and grape, with all the more success as we were not firing back. The best thing to do was to quicken our pace, in order to get out of range as soon as possible ; this the cavalry was able to do rapidly, but for us it was not so easy. We left on the road more than thirty dead, independently of a score of wounded, of whom two were officers, whom we took along with us. For some time we tried shooting at the guns to make them draw back, but without success. We remained for the best part of a quarter of an hour under this incessant bombardment.

At night we lay at Riesa, on the banks of the Elbe ; these were the first lodgings we had had since the 17th August.

8th October.—We were in bivouac under the walls of Torgau, on the Elbe. On the morning of the 9th the Comte de Narbonne, aide de camp to the Emperor, and governor of Torgau, came to review us, and begged us to clear him a little of the enemy. There was there an engagement which might be regarded as a battle in miniature, between the glacis of the fortress and the blockhouse constructed by the blockading troops. Too weak to hold the open country, the enemy sought to draw us toward his entrenchments, to overwhelm us with his heavy artillery, but we, in turn, were not strong enough to attempt to attack these numerous positions, which were also well armed ; so that the day passed in demonstrations on one side or the other, without any very sharp engagement. All arms—infantry, cavalry, artillery—were in action, without suffering much loss. My company played the part of scouts. But the undertaking was beyond our strength.

On the 12th October we crossed to the right bank of the Elbe at Wittemburg, and I began the affair at the orders of General Chastel, commanding a brigade of cavalry in the army corps of General Regnier. This battle (battle of Coswick) was brilliant and successful. Many prisoners were taken and much baggage, and our advance was very rapid, for the enemy was routed at the very outset of the action. We bivouacked some two leagues beyond the battlefield. We were greatly fatigued, as we had tried to keep pace with the cavalry.

On the 13th we pursued the enemy till we were opposite Ackern. There were during the day a number of very successful cavalry charges against the enemy rearguard. We went at a forced march. During the day we halted in the pretty little town of Roslau. In order to obtain a good breakfast my comrades told the owner of the house which we had entered in military capacity that I was a general and they were my staff. I owed this honour to a wide gold stripe on my trousers and a high-collared cloak which hid my shoulder-straps. In the evening a terrible bombardment carried off several men. When night fell we returned by a forced march to Coswick. It was four o'clock in the morning.

On the 14th, in the forenoon, we recrossed the Elbe at Wittemburg and camped near Daben, a small town. We marched very quickly, the Cossacks surrounding us and opening to let us pass. They picked off a number of stragglers.

On the 15th we encamped near Leipzic. Our march was as hurried as the day before ; as before we were surrounded by Cossacks. The passage was closed after us and all communication with the rear cut off.

THE DISASTER OF LEIPZIC.

16th October.—Battle of Wackau. During the early hours of the forenoon we passed through a suburb of Leipzic, leaving the city on our right, making for the village of Holzhausen, where we had orders to report. Hardly had we arrived when the thousand guns in battery burst forth simultaneously. All the armies of northern Europe had met together on the ground about Leipzic.

A general of the 11th army corps ordered us to move forward, toward a wood of some extent, and to dislodge the enemy therefrom. We were on the extreme left of the army. The wood was attacked by the six companies in six different places ;· owing to my place in the line of battle I found myself the most remote. Entering at once with my men as skirmishers, I soon dislodged the Austrian Croats whom I met there, but as I advanced I met with more resistance, and when my fire was hot there were very distinct shouts of : " Don't fire, we are French." Then, when I ceased fire, they fired on us. The wood was very dense ; it was thick undergrowth in which you could see nothing ten paces off. No longer knowing with whom I had to deal, unable to make anything of this warning not to fire, with the air riddled with bullets, I advanced alone, with some precaution, toward the place from which these French voices came. I saw behind a ridge a battalion of Croats, who fired on me ; but I had time to throw myself flat on my face, so that I was not hit. I shouted to my skirmishers to advance, and once surrounded by them I had the charge sounded. Then we advanced with more confidence, paying no further attention to the shouts of

" Don't fire ! " for it was evident that it was some of our
soldiers, prisoners, who were being compelled to speak
thus. However, once someone called me by my name,
shouting : " To me, Barrès ! Rescue ! " We hastened
our pace and I recaptured a captain of the battalion, with
some Croats.

At last I emerged from the wood, driving before me a
hundred of the enemy, who were running away as fast as
their legs could carry them across a plain to which we had
come after this dense undergrowth. No enemies to our
left, none in the plain, and, far away on my right, hell
unchained ; all the efforts and all the effects of a great
battle. Having rallied all my skirmishers I marched on
the village of Klein-Possna, occupied by some Austrians
and Cossacks, who withdrew after a fusillade of less than
fifteen minutes. Emboldened by this success, I passed
the village on the heels of those I had driven out and saw
on the other side, on the verge of a wood, a considerable
force of the enemy. I was obliged to halt and hold myself
on the defensive. I then had the village searched by some
of my men, to obtain victuals, and waited for nightfall,
which was approaching, to withdraw.

My men having re-entered the village, I marched by my
right toward the point where the fighting was proceeding
and installed myself at the entrance to the village, in a
meadow surrounded by hedges, at the branching of two
roads. I had chosen this position because it safeguarded
me against a night surprise, and I thought the battalion
might perhaps come in that direction. Since the morning
I had no means of knowing where it was. I had fought
alone with my men all day and on my own initiative,
without having seen a single superior officer. Before the
night had quite fallen the divisional general, Gérard, of
the 15th corps, came to my bivouac. I reported to him
what I had done and my reasons for taking up this position.
He approved and told me to remain there. I asked him

the result of the battle. He replied: "You see we are victorious here; I do not know what is happening elsewhere."

This day had cost me eight men wounded, one of whom was an officer. We were melting away day by day.

When night had fallen the cavalry of this part of the army came to occupy the village I had taken. A few hours later, when the most absolute quiet seemed to prevail in the two armies, a brisk cannonade was heard and startled the men, quietly resting after the heavy exertions of the day. Suddenly awakened by the noise and by a shell which shattered three of my muskets, the men, numb with cold, and alarmed by so unexpected an impression, ran to their weapons. The cavalry did the same, so that the night we had so longed for was passed in dangers and alarms. The incident had no consequence, but the men and the horses lost the restorative sleep so necessary in such circumstances. It was no doubt a deserter or a faint-hearted prisoner who had pointed out the village to which our cavalry had retired. By shelling it the enemy hoped to set it on fire and cause our horses to perish in the flames.

At the break of day I sent some sergeants and corporals to the rear to look for the battalion, but they did not find it. Later I saw General Reiset going by at the head of his cavalry brigade. I asked him for news of the battalion. He could give me none. I explained my embarrassment and my anxiety as to my comrades. He replied: "Come with me."—"Thank you, general, but if the battle were to reopen while I was in the plain I should be pounded to bits among so many horses. I can get along better with my forty men by themselves." He laughed at my remark and agreed.

At length, during the day, I heard that the battalion had been at Holzhausen since the previous evening. I went thither; they were surprised to see me, for it was

believed that we were all prisoners. The day was spent
in concentrating troops and preparing for the next day's
battle, which ought to decide what had not been decided
the day before.

18th October.—The forenoon of this day, fatal to our
arms, was quiet. Nearly 300,000 men, on the point of
flying at one another's throats, were waiting under arms
until the signal should be given. Before the action
opened Major Fabre, our battalion commander, promoted
to this rank a month ago (though he remained at our head
until a battalion commander should come to replace him),
assembled the officers to ask whether it were not more
suitable to go and fight in the ranks of the 6th corps, to
which we belonged and in which we were known to the
generals, than to remain in the 11th, to which we found
ourselves attached without knowing why, and where no
one paid any attention to us. All the officers were of
this opinion, and we immediately left this part of the
battlefield, moving over to the other side of the Parthe,
on the Duben road, by which we had come on the morning
of the 16th, and where the 6th corps was situated. On
this march we came across the Imperial Guard, which was
in reserve, ready to go wherever its presence might become
necessary.

When we had reached this point the battle commenced.
The circumference of the battle had lessened ; we were in
a circle of fire, for everywhere, at every point, in all directions, there was fighting. At the crossing of the Parthe
the Saxon army went over to the enemy before our
eyes. Those of the Saxons who were on the hither side
of the river could not carry out their movement of
desertion. They were halted and sent to the rear. A
sergeant-major of artillery, passing through our ranks
at the rear of his battery, shouted at the top of his voice :
" Paris ! Paris ! " A sergeant of the battalion, indignant,

as was the whole army, at this cowardly desertion, and his insolence, replied, " Dresden, Dresden ! " and laid him dead at his feet with a musket-ball.

A few minutes later we came to the ground where lay the relics of the 6th corps, which had been annihilated on the 16th. It was in the pretty village of Schönfeld, fighting at close quarters with the Swedes, in the midst of flames and rubbish. The 1st division, of which we formed part, was on the right, outside the village, supporting the artillery, which was withering the masses of the enemy as they drew near, to turn the village and throw us into the Parthe. Marshal Marmont and General Compans were glad to see us arrive, for our battalion, weak as it was, was still stronger than what was left of this fine division, more than 8,000 strong at the resumption of hostilities. As soon as we arrived our thin column was ploughed by the enemy's balls. Officers and soldiers fell like ears of corn before the reaper's sickle. The cannon-balls ploughed through our ranks from the first to the last, each time sweeping away at least thirty men when they took the column full on. The officers who remained were doing nothing but go from the right to the left of their squadrons to make them close ranks toward the right, drag the dead and wounded out of the ranks, and prevent the men from massing together or wheeling round on themselves. Marshal Marmont and General Compans having been wounded, we passed under the orders of Marshal Ney, who came to encourage us to hold our ground. At last, after several hours of this formidable cannonade, we were constrained to withdraw, when Schönfeld had been carried, and our left taken in reverse by the troops that came to seize it from the suburb of Halle.

Our retreat was made in good order, under the protection of the heavy artillery in reserve, which stopped short the army of Bernadotte, once the French Marshal, the Crown Prince of Sweden. We halted on the right bank of the Parthe, where we spent the night. It was dismal, painful, cruel ! The grief of having lost a great and bloody battle, the frightful prospect of a morrow that might perhaps be still more wretched, the guns raging at every point of our unhappy lines, the defection of our cowardly allies, and lastly the privations of every kind that had for days been crushing us : all these ills, all these causes taken together, made me reflect bitterly indeed upon war and its vicissitudes ! We lost, in this disastrous day, the bloodiest that had been hitherto, the majority of the officers and more than half our men. I had not twenty men left of the two hundred and more who had answered the roll since the beginning of this disastrous campaign. The army corps no longer existed save in name. More than two-thirds of the generals had been killed or wounded.

19th October.—At daybreak we received orders to begin our movement of retreat, which was to be made by army corps and at fixed hours. On coming to the boulevards, which were choked with guns, baggage waggons, travelling carriages, carts, canteens, horses, etc., we could go no farther, so complete was the disorder and pell-mell confusion. Our general of brigade made us go into a paddock to wait for a favourable moment to cross the only bridge, by which we had to retreat. This bridge was the Caudine Forks of the army.

During this time the enemy army was pressing us still harder in Leipzic ; an impetuous attack through the suburb of Halle, with the object of seizing the bridge, was making progress ; we were sent thither. They were fighting in the streets, in the gardens, in the houses ; the bullets were flying over the boulevards. I do not know how it came about that on going from one point to another, to hearten my men, I found myself alone, surrounded by enemies and on the point of capture. I slipped through the gate of a garden, and after walking for some time I found myself, alone of the battalion, on the boulevard, in the midst of the army, which was in a state of the completest rout. I followed the stream without knowing where I was going, crossed the bridge, whose entrance was blocked by one of the leaves of the iron grille, and littered with corpses, which were being trampled underfoot. At last I found myself on the other side, carried along by the mass of flying men. The confusion made one's heart bleed.

Once on the other bank I met the captain of Grenadiers who, like myself, had no men and, like myself, did not know what had become of the battalion. We stopped on the bank to the right of the road, to wait for it. We were crying with rage and grief ; we shed tears of blood over this immense disaster. Less than five minutes after we had laid ourselves down on the grass, for we were too exhausted, too physically and morally sick to be able to stand upright, the bridge blew up and we were covered with its débris. This was the climax of the lugubrious tragedy which had begun on the 17th August.

We then made our way toward Langenau, where we came to the end of this narrow causeway, artificially raised above the low-lying fields flooded by the Elster and its affluents. The disorder there was as great as on the boulevards of Leipzic. Emerging at last from this narrow road, we found the Emperor in the plain, on horseback (it was the last time I saw him), bidding the officers who passed near him : " Rally your men ! "

Signposts on which were written in large letters the numbers of the army corps told us what roads were to be taken. Coming to Markrundstadt, we found the battalion, which had crossed the bridge before us. This unexpected encounter filled us with joy. I found, too, my servant, who had saved my horse and my portmanteau. Lastly, an infantryman who had found an abandoned horse on the boulevards of the city, and caught him, offered him to me for a small reward. This fine horse belonged to a military commissary, to judge by the contents of his portmanteau, which was very well provided with clothing. I distributed this among some of the officers of the battalion, who had lost everything in this frightful rout. The papers were kept in case of inquiry. I put them in the holsters.

We spent part of the night on the spot where I found the battalion ; but before daylight the order was given to march off without noise and to make for Weissenfels.

20th October.—Past Lutzen and part of the famous battlefield which, nearly seven months earlier, we had made glorious by a brilliant victory. The times were indeed altered.

We crossed the Saale at Weissenfels, and camped on the left bank, near the town.

In the morning, being on my horse of the day before, I was accosted by his owner, who claimed him. I observed that, having abandoned him, he had lost all right to possess him. After a good deal of discussion he asked for his portmanteau ; I told him what I had done with it and returned him his papers. That evening, in camp, a corporal of my company, badly wounded in the foot, begged me with tears in his eyes to give him the horse to carry him to Mayence. To save this unfortunate man, who did his duty well during the campaign, I gave him the horse on the condition of his returning it at Mayence. I condemned myself to make the journey on foot in order to be of use to him.

Having crossed the Unstrutt at Freibourg not far from Roosbach, on a bridge pounded by the enemy artillery, Barrès was sent to Erfurt to fetch supplies of clothing. Meanwhile the retreat continued, aggravated by cold and hunger.

On the 27th October, at Vach, the ground was covered with snow. Having neither wood wherewith to warm ourselves, nor straw to rest on, I took refuge for the night in a church. In the morning my faithful servant told me to come at once and drink some soup which he had prepared for me. This was a piece of good luck, as for several days I had not even had any potatoes. When I approached the fire where he had passed the night I saw that he was weeping with rage and despair. In the few minutes he had spent in coming to warn me someone had stolen his cooking-pot and the only provisions he had been able to obtain by running about part of the time in order to find them. His distress touched me, since it was for my sake that he was so disappointed.

On the morning of the 30th I witnessed an incident that made a very painful impression on me. Halting a moment in a village between Auttenan and Hanau, owing to congestion, which often occurred, a poor soldier, wounded in the side, came out for a moment, on some necessary errand, from the house in which he had taken refuge while his wound was healing. In returning to the house he was caught by a basket attached to a passing horse. He was struck on the site of his wound, which reopened ; gave a cry of pain ; went up to the second floor, where he was lodging, and threw himself out of the window on to the road, where he fell a few feet from me, and was killed outright. A few soldiers of my company, having caught sight of a peasant who came to the window when the unhappy soldier threw himself out, cried out that it was the peasant who had thrown him out. This was absurd, but misery listens to no reasoning. They seized the unhappy peasant and shot him a hundred paces farther on, outside the village. In vain did I try to defend him and explain how the matter must have happened ; I was not heeded. The staff-officer who took the affair in hand insisted that he alone was in the right. He committed a crime instead of an act of justice.

Having left this village, where a suicide and a cruel execution had just been committed, we heard in front of us the firing of heavy guns, which, by its intensity and duration, told us that the enemy had got ahead of us and was seeking to bar our passage, as he had attempted to do twice or thrice, but without success, since the beginning of our retreat. Farther on some staff-officers, sent to the rear to hasten the march of the troops, told us it was the Bavarian Army which had arrived post-haste, and was disputing the pass on the heights of Hanau. We no longer marched ; we ran. Before we reached the battle-field we were fired on by guns on the left bank of the Kinzig. I was sent with my men to force them away from the bank. My men having taken cover behind the trees along the bank in order to fire on the gunners, the latter, after a few shots, decamped quicker than they had come. The remnants of the 6th corps formed up in columns of attack, and going forward at the charge with fixed bayonets, along the right bank of the Kinzig, they assisted the other troops already engaged to throw the treacherous Bavarians into this river and to re-establish communications, which had been cut for forty-eight hours.

The Bavarians will long remember the lesson they received this day of hot fighting. Their losses were considerable, but as they were occupying the fortress of Hanau, which they did not evacuate until night, and the left banks of the Main and the Kinzig, it was not thought prudent to pursue them. For the rest, the night had fallen before the victory was complete.

31st October.—We remained until mid-day on the field of battle, which we left to continue our movement on Frankfort. There was fighting all the forenoon, with

artillery, between one bank of the Kinzig and the other.
In a moment of relaxation, when the troops were not under
arms, I was warming myself near a camp fire, where I
was cooking a few potatoes, and while waiting I was
reading a diary which I had found on the battlefield; a
cannon-ball interrupted my reflections arising from the
reading of this record and swept away the frugal breakfast
for which I was longing with a sort of sensuality. This
accursed cannon-ball, after carrying away the head of a
commandant of a battalion of naval artillery, who was
leaning against a tree, holding his horse by the bridle,
ricochetted into the middle of my fire, depriving me of
my potatoes and covering me with burning embers and
cinders. An infantryman standing opposite me had the
same misfortune and the same good luck. This was a
lucky shot for us, for if we had been placed differently
we should have been cut in two.

The effect of this cannon-ball gave rise to a strange
discussion and an incident as strange. The commandant
being killed, the terrified horse ran away into the woods,
where we found it, and as it was frightened anew by
several cannon-balls whistling past our ears, we had infinite
trouble to catch it. The soldier who caught it claimed
that it was his property, that anything captured on a
battlefield was a lawful prize. The officer of the corps
at once assembled under the presidency of the general of
brigade, to decide this weighty question, which was
decided, after differences of opinion, in favour of the
commandant's heirs.

While we were deliberating under the fire of our ex-
allies' guns my first bugler, who had been three days
missing, returned to the company, bringing me a cooked
fowl and a loaf to propitiate me for his absence. I was
going to refuse to accept it, but my officers, who had not
so many reasons for severity, urged me to close my eyes to
a few acts of indiscipline of this kind, in view of the weak-

ness of their stomachs. This consideration made me go over to their opinion. But as I knew that our excellent commander, Major Fabre, had no more in his stomach than I had, I invited him to come and eat his share. He informed me that General Joubert was dying of hunger. I went to him and pressed him to eat a wing of my fowl, which he heartily accepted. But on thinking of the pleasure he was about to experience, he suddenly remembered that the general of division, Lagrange, commanding the remnant of the three divisions of the army corps, had likewise had nothing for breakfast ; he advised me to be *bon prince* in respect of him and invite him to eat his share. Thus there were six of us, all famished, round a poor fowl which would not have sufficed to appease the devouring hunger of a single one of us.

Some troops still in the rear having come to relieve us we set out at mid-day for Frankfort. (A little later we should have been present at a second battle, which began shortly after our departure. This new attack, which was very hot, but less murderous than that of the day before, had no more success. The Bavarians were thrust back into the town or hurled into the Kinzig.) Our march on Frankfort was difficult. The road, encumbered with stragglers, sick, and wounded, and vehicles of all descriptions, horribly bad on account of the thaw, the rain and the melting snows, was anything but favourable to rapid movement. It was night when we took possession of the ground on which we were to bivouac. We were in the vineyards around and above Frankfort, in mud up to our knees, without fire or straw or shelter, with the rain drumming on our bodies. What a frightful night ! What hunger !

1st November.—In bivouac round Höchst, a small town of the Duke of Nassau's, which I passed for the fourth time. There was great disorder on crossing the bridge

over the Nidda, a river flowing near the town, but this
night was less disagreeable than the previous one. We
had at least shelter, food, and above all some excellent
Rhine wine to warm us and restore us.

That night I was accosted by our paymaster, whom we
had not seen for a long time. He told me, with tears in
his eyes, that the day before the battle of Hanau he, the
baggage-master, the men of the escort, the treasury, the
counting-house and the ambulance chests had been captured by the Bavarians, but during the night he contrived
to escape from their hands. He begged me to warn the
major of this misfortune and to spare me the first moments
of his wrath. Once established in the position where we
were to pass the night, I went to impart the vexatious news
I had just learned. The major flew into a violent rage,
but when I had explained the means to employ to repair
this misfortune and to avoid shouldering the responsi-
bility, and when I told him that I would see to all the
writing and the steps to be taken to this end, he was
somewhat appeased. I then sent for the young officer,
whom he pardoned. But after this explanation I told
him to go at once to see General Joubert, to report the
matter to him and give him a certificate stating that it
was in consequence of the military events of the retreat
that the chest was lost.

2nd November.—At last, after seventeen days of fatigue,
battles and privations of every nature, excitement, and
peril of every kind, we came to the banks of the Rhine,
so greatly longed for, of that majestic river which would,
at least for some days, set a term to our many woes.
Here we encamped near the glacis of Cassel.

To recapitulate the disasters of this terrible, I do not
say retreat, but rout, would be to paint the most
horrible picture of our reverse. After the miseries of
Leipzic no serious measures were or could be taken to

rally the men and restore order and discipline in the army. We marched at will, confused, driven on, pitilessly crushed, abandoned without succour, with no friendly hand to support one or close one's eyes. Our moral sufferings rendered us indifferent to physical suffering; destitution made egoists even of kindly and generous men; the personal ego was everything; Christian charity and humanity towards one's fellows were no more than words.

We arrived on the banks of the Rhine as we left the banks of the Elster, in a state of complete dissolution. We had covered our track with the relics of our army. At every step we took we left behind us corpses of men and carcases of horses, guns, baggage, tatters of our one-time glory. It was a horrible spectacle, that wrung the heart with agony. To all these woes combined were added yet others that further aggravated our grievous situation. Typhus broke out in our disorganized ranks in a terrifying fashion. Thus one may say that on leaving Leipzic we were accompanied by all the plagues that can devour an army.

I had the pleasure of being joined in camp by several infantrymen whose wounds were healed, and among others by the corporal whom I had given my horse to ride. He was better, without being quite recovered. In a few moments I found myself possessed of seven horses which these wounded soldiers gave me. But as I had not the means of feeding them, I gave them in my turn to officers of the battalion who had need of them.

3rd November.—Crossing the Rhine at Mayence, we were sent into cantonments at Dexheim, a village near Oppenheim, ascending the left bank of the Rhine.

Our being sent into the villages to rest was welcomed with joy. It was necessary; we were worn out with marching and privations of every sort. Always in bivouac, in the snow or mud, for nearly a month, having for nourishment only the disgusting leavings of those who preceded us on the road of suffering, it was not surprising that we were greedy for rest. During the five days which the battalion remained in the village I could not succeed in appeasing my hunger, despite the five or six meals I made each day; not heavy enough, it is true, to make me ill, but copious enough to satisfy two or three men under ordinary circumstances. I had been seven months on the farther side of the Rhine.

9th November, 1813.—Before we were sent to Mayence to hold the garrison there, the Prince de Neufchâtel assembled our army corps in a plain on the banks of the Rhine, below Oppenheim, there to be reorganized and provided with the officers it lacked.

We bade farewell to the battalion of the 86th, with which we had made the whole campaign, and which, even more unfortunate than ourselves, was almost entirely destroyed on the 16th October at Leipzic. On arriving at Mayence we found on the parade ground the 4th battalion, which had just seen some hot fighting on the heights of Hochheim, as a beginning, and had lost some men. We celebrated our reunion by a good dinner which made them forget the emotions of the day.

At this time I was sent to Oppenheim and billeted on a wealthy landowner, a great lover of the wines of his country, which he set far above the best vintages of Bordeaux. He made me too drink his excellent wines at every meal, for I had my meals in his house, to please him, as he insistently asked me to do so. In order that his old wines should lose nothing of their quality the glasses had to be rinsed with ordinary claret. This excellent man, the father of a large and pleasant family, was descended from a French family expatriated for religious motives at the time of the revocation of the

Edict of Nantes. He was a Frenchman at heart and proposed to leave the country if it again became German.

On the 28th December the two battalions received orders to go up as far as Mannheim, to survey both banks of the Rhine, while I was sent on service to Mayence. On the 31st I was on the road on my good " prize " horse, on the way to rejoin my regiment, when I met General Merlin, who was returning to Strasbourg. He asked me to sell him the horse, so I consented to let him have it for 300 francs, which he paid me then and there. Shortly afterwards—it was on leaving Worms—I met my battalion commander, Commandant D——, who was complaining of acute rheumatism. " What annoys me," he told me, " is that I want to start for Paris, and I haven't a copper for the journey."—" If that is all that is troubling you," I said, " I can remove that trouble. Here are 300 francs in gold ; you will repay them when you can." He accepted and continued on his way. (Shrewder and more ambitious than any of the other battalion officers, he saw that we should before long be blockaded in Mayence, where no advancement was to be looked for, and perhaps he was already in the confidence of those who were conspiring for the return of the Bourbons.)

I came to Ogersheim on the last night of December, as a detachment of a hundred men, commanded by a captain, a friend of mine, having three officers under his orders, was leaving to garrison a redoubt erected in front of Mannheim to prevent the crossing of the Rhine at this spot. He was given instructions not to enter into negotiations for any sort of capitulation. He had to conquer or die. An absurd alternative for so few defenders.

Toward the end of this night (31st December–1st January 1914) a heavy cannonade told us that his redoubt was being attacked and that the Prussian Army, under Blücher, was crossing the Rhine. We at once seized our arms and marched toward the guns ; but already the redoubt was enveloped and was being hotly attacked, the plain being covered with enemy scouts. We drove back the latter without difficulty, but presently found ourselves confronted by forces so superior that in order to avoid being cut off from Mayence, whither we were ordered to return, we retired in good order, still resisting the enemy, on Franckhal and Worms, where we arrived in the course of the night.

The redoubt held out for three hours and was finally taken by assault. Happily those of the defenders who were left were spared. More, the King of Prussia, who was at Mannheim, had the officers' swords returned to them, and the inhabitants hastened to reclothe the soldiers, who arrived in the town half naked. This was in homage to their fine conduct, to which even their enemies did justice. The Prussians admitted to having left seven hundred dead and wounded in the woods ; the detachment was reduced to half its strength.

However, we continued our retreat on Mayence, and at nightfall we were installed in bivouac near I know not what village, when the battalion commander of the 4th invited a few officers, of whom I was one, to join him in eating a *pâté de foie gras* which he had just received from Strasbourg. We were standing round it, devouring it with our eyes, waiting to do so with our teeth, when a sinister cry was heard : " To arms ! to arms ! " This was from the vedettes of the guard of honour, who arrived at a rapid gallop, to warn us that the enemy was approaching. We ran to our companies, and the commandant, while calling for his horse, bade his servant " not to forget the *pâté !* " He told him this at least ten times over, which made us laugh, despite the vexation we felt at having to content ourselves with having seen it, for there was no longer any question of eating it " en famille," as the commandant said, to celebrate the New Year. They

were fine New Year's gifts, those of 1814 ! We continued
our retreat upon Worms.

On the 2nd January, on leaving Worms, we had to
repulse several charges of cavalry, which did us no harm,
but in which the enemy was rather severely punished.
Having marched all day we arrived in Mayence in the
middle of the night, with the Russian cavalry on our
heels.

Siege of Mayence.

The blockade began on the 4th January and ended only
on the 4th May.

The two battalions of the regiment were left in the
suburbs of Weisnau to defend and do duty in that part of
the town. This is a suburb on the Oppenheim road,
beside the Rhine, below a sort of entrenched camp which
was under our guard. Our duties were rigorous, especially
the night rounds, which were often repeated, on account
of the general desertions of Dutch, Belgian, Rhenian and
even Piedmontese soldiers. The frosts that year were
very hard ; the Rhine froze over completely, so that
carts could cross on the ice ; one could go on foot to the
fortress of Cassel. On this account the surveillance
of the outposts was made still more assiduous, for the
enemy might profit by the fact and complete the defection
already begun. During the two months that we spent in
this suburb we had some affairs with the blockading
troops, which were not very dangerous, for they were
mostly conscripts but newly raised, but we were so weak,
so crippled by typhus, that we were not much better than
the besiegers.

A great calamity had fallen on our unhappy garrison
and on the townsfolk. For more than two months the
fever had been raging among us with such violence that
we could not keep up with the work of removing the
victims of this horrible disease. The plagues of Asia, the

yellow fever of the colonies did not make such ravages as typhus in Mayence. It was estimated that 30,000 soldiers or townsfolk died. Trenches were dug containing as many as 1,500 corpses, which were burned with quicklime. We lost our three surgeons, three infantry officers, five or six others of the companies of the centre, and half our men. (Thus we were weaker on leaving Mayence than on crossing the Rhine after Leipzic, despite the numbers of recruits received before the blockade.) The prefect, the famous Jean Bon Saint-André, several generals, and many persons in high places succumbed.

When the warm weather returned we re-entered the city, which pleased us greatly, for we had had a very hard time during our two months in the ruined suburbs. With March, and the gentle warmth of spring, health, cheerfulness and deceitful hopes revived. An administrative Council for Convalescents was formed under the presidency of Colonel Follard, who had full powers as commander-in-chief to grant anything in the interest of the soldiers who were sent to the convalescent depot. I was the second member, and the most active, as I was entrusted with the execution of all measures discussed and adopted at the sittings of the Council, which met every morning. I had more than forty officers under my orders, one for each corps or portion of a corps. This Council began operations on the 1st March and did not finish until the end of April, when the sickness had quite disappeared. It met every day and often remained *en permanence*. Its action saved many sick men from certain death. My co-operation contributed a little to this result, for, as I have already stated, I was always there to see to the execution of the measures decided upon and to supplement them when needed.

There was not during the blockade any very great dearth of food. If we except butcher's meat, of which there was absolutely none after the first few days, bread, dried peas and beans, and salted meats were distributed with fair regularity and in sufficient quantities, according to the rules customary in besieged fortresses. Beef was replaced by horseflesh. One of my officers, entrusted with its distribution, saw that I did not go without. A little wine, brandy, salt cod, smoked herrings, etc., were distributed. Despite the privations, and the frightful mortality, the cafés, theatres, concerts and balls were copiously attended. The play was very good, despite the death of several of the actors. I often went to the theatre, in order to forget the preoccupations of the moment.

On the 11th April we learned of the events in Paris, and, in turn, of those that ensued. This staggering news was officially communicated to us by General Sémelé, who assembled the officers of his division in the Weisnau suburb, in order to inform them. All these officers almost shed tears of rage and grief at the reading of this crushing conclusion of our heroic struggle with all Europe. We withdrew in mournful silence, swallowing down the moral agony caused by events which, so it seemed to us, ought never to have occurred. Before returning to the city I was accosted by my battalion commander D——, who had not been able to get away from Mayence as he had intended.

" My God ! " I said to him, " what is going to become of France if she falls into the power of the Bourbons (who, I thought, were all dead, long ago) ? What will become of our institutions, of those who founded them, of those who bought national stock, and so forth ? "

" My dear captain," he replied emphatically, " you are like all the officers we have just seen and heard ; you imagine that the Bourbons, whom you know only by the horrible things that were said of them during the Revolution, are tyrants and imbeciles. Don't worry about the future of France. It will be happier under their paternal sceptre than under the rod of iron of this adventurer who is about to be turned out, if he hasn't been already."

I left him, furious, after saying : " You thought differently three months ago."

I was choking with grief and shame for my country.

On the 21st April we unfurled the white flag and took the cockade of the old monarchy. That same day the officers had individually to sign a statement of adhesion to the new order of things. From this moment communication with the outer world was permitted, and relations with our enemies, now called *our allies*, were authorized. Already a great many generals and officers of superior rank had left for Paris, to salute the new luminaries ; this haste was intensified after the ceremony of saluting the new flag. The tricolour cockade was sorrowfully relinquished and the white cockade displayed with a shrinking at the heart. On the day before the order to wear it was given I saw a second colonel of the guards of honour with a white cockade. I said aloud to the officers about me : " See there's a white cockade ! " The colonel angrily marched up to me, saying : " Well, sir, what have you to say about this cockade ? " I replied, coldly : " It is the first I have ever seen in my life." He retired without further words, but visibly annoyed by my exclamation. (He became a peer of France under the Restoration. He was the Marquis de Pange. I knew him well afterwards, when he was in command in the department of La Meurthe, and we used to laugh at the recollection of this incident.)

The order came to hand over the famous fortified city of Mayence, with its immense mass of material, to the Prince of Saxe-Coburg, who was commander of the blockading troops. We left it in virtue of the spoliating convention of the 23rd April, which confined France to her old frontiers. What loss we suffered in a single day ! What bitter regret this abandonment caused us !

The last days were somewhat disorderly. The soldiers,

glad to go and caring little for the preservation of things which they were compelled to surrender to foreigners, did a great deal of damage, removed what they could to sell it to the Jews, burned the powder of the batteries, pillaged the arsenal, etc. The officers could do nothing to check this disorder, as they shared the discontent of their men, who were indignant with the townsfolk, who were mutilating the eagles of the public buildings or openly manifesting their delight at seeing us depart. I had occasion to say to some townsfolk whom I knew : "You are glad to see us go. Before a month is out you will regret our power and our institutions."

THE FIRST RESTORATION

THE RETURN TO FRANCE.

AT last the day of our departure arrived, fixed for the 4th May. The 4th army corps, 15,000 strong, marched out in good order, with two guns per 1,000 men, and took the road to France. At Spire, on the 5th May, three captains and myself asked the major for leave to go ahead in order to visit Mannheim, and to travel independently until we were in garrison. We felt such a need of fresh air, liberty and independence, that we seemed to have nothing of them, even in the open. We hired a carriage and horse at the posting-station, and set off, happy to be our own masters. We visited in succession Franckhal, Mannheim and Ogersheim, changing our carriage at every relay.

At Landau, on the 7th, we found some of the agents of the new government, who had all the marks of the *ci-devant* nobles. This was the first time I saw the Cross of St. Louis. At Annweiler, a small town in the old duchy of Deux-Ponts, we rejoined the regiment. By the 7th June we had reached, by daily stages, a point between Verdun and Claremont. There, at the halt, a violent quarrel arose between our men and some Russian infantry-men who were in cantonments there. Without the active intervention of the officers a dangerous collision might have occurred and led to serious disorder. Our men teased these foreigners who were trampling on our country in a devilish manner. Already, since our departure from

Sarre, similar scenes had occurred. This one was more dangerous, as blood was shed.

On the 9th, at Châlons-sur-Marne, an old émigré, in whose house I was lodged, and whose sight was very feeble, took me for a Russian officer. He welcomed me in the most distinguished fashion. Nothing was good enough for me, nothing worthy of being offered to me. He made me some curious confidences. The boasting of this superannuated foot-soldier amused me greatly, and induced me to leave him in ignorance until my departure. When he was disillusioned his anger was comical. There were also quarrels between some non-commissioned officers of the corps and some Russian officers, complicated enough, which were, however, composed. For these reasons we were sent away from Châlons instead of staying there, and despatched to a village ruined by the invasion, on the road to Montmirail.

On the 12th June, an hour after our arrival at Montmirail, I set out, with three other officers, in a private carriage, for Paris. I was sent thither by the major to draw the pay of the officers and men for the month of May, which it had not been possible to obtain from the paymasters in the towns we had passed through, owing to the lack of funds. We spent the night at Tréport, a village on the left bank of the Marne. The inn at which we alighted was full of prostitutes from Paris, who had accompanied the retiring Russians as far as this village.

We came to Paris on the 13th, early in the afternoon, and it was all we could do to get settled by night. The restoration of the old monarchy had drawn to Paris so many nobles, émigrés, Vendéens, chouans, partisans of the Bourbons and victims of the Revolution, well-affected folk, and returned exiles, that the hotels were full to overflowing, the theatres too ; they were playing in them plays of the old repertoire, appropriate to the circumstances; I may mention among others the *Partie de chasse de Henri IV*, which was vigorously applauded. One might have thought that all Europe had met together in the garden of the Palais-Royal.

From the moment of my arrival I set about my errand, busily, but everywhere I was put off with excuses. I was sent to the Inspector of Revisions, to the Ministry for War, from him to the Ministry of Finance; with my papers all in order, I presented myself at the paymaster's, who had no money or would not give me any. I had again to begin running to and fro, to repeat my applications, to get my authorizations of payment renewed, and so forth. This went on for six days. At last, on the 20th, we were paid. During these interminable formalities the regiment, which I had left without money, made its poverty-stricken way towards Brittany, living almost on charity. I myself was not much happier during the last few days in Paris. Having shared what I had with my companions on this journey—and we were not sparing of these resources at the outset, since we counted on receiving our pay and travelling expenses—it came about that on the last day we should have had no breakfast had not a deputy friend of mine placed his purse at our disposal.

On the 21st June I was able to rejoin my comrades at Mortagne. I found them at table, eating their last coins. My arrival was greeted with transports of joy. With me their good spirits returned, for I brought the wherewithal to evoke and maintain them. The major confessed to me that they had that evening spent the last sou the battalions could produce. This state of affairs being intolerable, he had decided to halt at Alençon and beg the mayor to invite the townsfolk to feed the troops until they had received the money necessary to continue their march.

On the 6th July we arrived at Lorient, which was our destination.

During the month of September the commander of our battalion, D——, who had taken the title of count and remained in Paris since the time of our passing through, in order to obtain admission as an officer of the King's Household (Light Horse), having failed in his application, wrote to me asking whether he had any chance of being employed in the regiment. I replied that in virtue of his seniority he might still be employed, but that he must come quickly, as a great many officers of his rank were coming forward to compete. He came at once, thoroughly cured of his enthusiasm for the Bourbons, disgusted with the Court, and very wroth with the Duc de Berry, who had refused to admit his rights to the position for which he had applied.

I heard from him a great deal about the opposition which the new government was encountering, the blunders it was committing, the discontent which it was causing, and the acts of injustice of which it was accused. This talk astonished me, for, knowing nothing of Court intrigues or ministerial waiting-rooms, or of the credit of the protectors in favour, I had not understood that one needed to employ and did employ such means in order to gain promotion. But what amazed me most was to hear such things from the lips of a man who had taken me to task so sharply when I had cast a doubt on the merit of the Government which had just been imposed on us. During the month which he spent at Lorient we were nearly always together. Not having been appointed, he went to live on his half-pay in Paris. (On the occasion of the ceremony of the Champ de Mars in the following year he was one of the officers charged with ordering the troops in the Champ de Mars before the distribution of the eagles. This return to the "adventurer" resulted in his remaining without employ after the Hundred Days. But, thanks to the protection of his godfather, the Duc d'Orléans, to-day Louis-Philippe, he entered the royal bodyguard (infantry) and was successively lieutenant-general, director-general to the Minister for War, Councillor of State, etc.)

The obligation to attend Mass every Sunday greatly annoyed the officers and made them dislike the Bourbons ; still more did the certainty that an immense number of us would be put on half-pay. On the 1st October the organization of the 44th regiment of the line was effected in the colonel's office, in the presence of Inspector-General Comte de Clausel, but the results were kept secret. On the 3rd this operation was effected on the parade-ground of the polygon, in the presence of a large gathering of officers, who awaited with anxiety the result of the notes submitted in respect of each individual officer. The roll of the officers retained in active service was read, first for the superior officers, then for the paymasters, etc., and then for the field officers. Although I was more or less certain of the result it seemed a long time before I heard my name called. I was called last, for I was to command the 3rd regiment of foot.

Barrès, given six months' leave at the beginning of November 1814, retires to Auvergne, to his people.

23rd November.—At Blesle, where I had the pleasure of finding my mother and all my kinsfolk in good health.

The change of government had also caused a change in the spirit of society. There was no longer the animation of 1812. Politics had parted individuals and caused a coldness in families. The nobles had resumed their pride and no longer entertained with the same simplicity as before. In order not to witness their arrogance I did not often have anything to do with them ; I went out less and found the life rather tedious. However, there was one house illustrious in our province for its birth and its ancient pedigree, where I went, every Friday, with my brother, who was likewise on six months' leave, to spend twenty-four hours. This was the house of Comte Hippolyte d'Espinchal, squadron-leader of the 31st Chasseurs, living at Massiac, a small town a league from Blesle. My brother was serving in the same corps.

THE HUNDRED DAYS

IT was during the last of these visits, about the 9th March, 1815, that I learned, vaguely on the Friday night, but positively on the Saturday morning, by a number of letters from Paris, that Napoleon had landed in Provence on the 1st March, and was marching on Lyons. This stupendous piece of news greatly surprised and astonished me. Returning home, I restrained the joy I felt, without being able to define it, for I was as uneasy in respect of the results as I was pleased with the fact. I waited for a few days hoping that orders would reach me, but as I received none I went to Le Puy to learn what we were to do.

It was at this time that the courier who was carrying Government money was stopped between Le Puy and Yssengeaux by robbers. A general whom the Emperor had dismissed from the army and who was in command in the department infamously suspected the half-pay officers of this act of violence. He summoned them to his house directly he knew of the theft in order to make sure of their presence in the capital. When the officers understood the motive of this insulting summons they treated the general as he deserved, and when they learned that the Emperor was in Paris and that the King had left they went to him to warn him to leave Le Puy that very instant, since an hour later they would no longer answer for it that he would be alive. He left at once, very lucky to escape with no worse than threats.

On the day the news came that the Emperor had

arrived in Paris I went to the prefecture with my brother, to see our eldest brother, the secretary-general. We were both in uniform. When we had nearly reached the prefecture we were attacked by a crowd of ragged wretches, who fell on us shouting, "Long live the Emperor! Down with the white cockade!" and without giving us time to reply they jostled us, seized our shakoes, tore off our cockades and covered us with insults. My brother and I had drawn our swords to defend ourselves, but being at that moment seized from behind we could not use them. The prefecture guard came at once to our rescue and saved us from the hands of these criminals, who would have ended by hacking us to bits. My God, how angry I was! I wept with rage!

I took my route-papers next day, to rejoin the regiment at Brest. At Tours, in the hotel at which we alighted, we found several officers of the old army, who, having entered the King's bodyguard,[1] had accompanied him to the frontier. They complained bitterly of the bad behaviour of the troops sent in pursuit of the King, whom they encountered on their way back.

We bought a small boat or barge to descend the Loire as far as Nantes, and hired a man to steer it. We had to row long and often to overcome the resistance of the wind and avoid the waves, which were very high. I had more than twenty blisters on my hands when I left the boat. We sold it for more than it cost us, and the passage-money of three or four persons whom we picked up on the way covered all our expenses. The first two days of the voyage were delightful, and we were able to see, without exertion, and in detail, the far-famed banks of the majestic Loire.

At Quimper-Corentin my battalion commander, who was in garrison there, sought to quarrel with us because we were still wearing the *croix d'honneur* bearing the

---

[1] *Maison rouge.*—TR.

effigy of Henry IV ; this was the man who, a few months earlier, had wanted to put me under arrest because I had not replaced the effigy of Napoleon and the imperial eagle by the fleurs-de-lis of the old monarchy !

At Brest, where we arrived on the 18th March, our comrades welcomed us with that eagerness and cordiality which one seldom finds among those who are not soldiers. The colonel himself invited us to dinner, a thing he hardly ever did, and was extremely friendly. This was partly because, during our absence, he had been on the worst of terms with his officers. The latter, on the return of the Emperor, denounced him and demanded his discharge. A captain undertook to take the petition to Paris and hand it in person to the Emperor. This request, contrary to discipline and the rule of submission to one's superiors, was forwarded to the president of a commission entrusted with the purging of the army of all officers, émigrés and others, who had been introduced since the return of the Bourbons. This general, a friend of the colonel's, did not act in accordance with the denunciation, and sent the captain back to his regiment. He was placed under close arrest for absenting himself without leave. The captains who were the cause of his being punished united in demanding that he should be pardoned. This was audacious, but the effervescence of the times made many things lawful. The demand was refused ; they must wait their time ; but then such extraordinary things were said, such bitter reproaches uttered, such monstrous accusations, that most of the captains who heard them were alarmed. One captain accused the colonel, amongst a number of other things, of being a coward, a thief, a tiger : " You are a coward : I saw you run away at Wagram ; a thief, for you did the men out of such and such a sum of money ; a tiger, for you had negroes eaten by your dogs in San Domingo. You will not deny it ; I saw it. . . ." The colonel listened to all these accusations with great composure and dismissed us, saying : " This is what indiscipline leads to ; but I shall not lower myself by defending myself against such atrocious calumnies."

Brittany showed symptoms of insurrection in favour of the Bourbons, which necessitated sending troops into Morbihan. Two hundred men of the 3rd battalion were sent thither, under the command of the two senior captains. The general sent us to scour the department, to restrain the parties and watch the coast, and perhaps also to get rid of us, as he was already contriving the means of reconciliation with the Bourbons, of whose imminent return he must have known.

While we were at Morlaix several agents of the South American republics pressed us, in view of the unhappy conditions in France, to go and serve in their armies. These promises were advantageous, but they did not tempt any of us.

THE SECOND RESTORATION

A FEW days after our return to Brest, on the 8th July, we learned officially and in succession of the entry into Paris of France's enemies, the departure of Napoleon and the army for the left bank of the Loire, and the arrival of Louis XVIII with all his family in Paris. All these misfortunes, inevitable after the disaster of Waterloo, overwhelmed us with grief.

On the 19th July the general commanding us called together all the officers of the garrison to require us to accept the white cockade and sign the statement of adhesion to the new order of things. He demanded the sacrifice of our opinions in the interests of France, the country being in grave danger, as the enemy asked nothing better than disunion in the army, so that it might be broken into fragments and destroyed. The officers of the line bowed their heads, lamenting so many misfortunes ; but those of the battalions of the national guards of the Côtes-du-Nord refused with the greatest violence. At last, after a tumultuous dispute, a staff colonel said : " Come away and let us do our duty as good citizens, and submit to what we cannot prevent ! Leave this factious minority to its crazy dreams and its impotence ; let us rescue Brest from the Prussians, who are marching on Brittany, and from the English, who would like to see us in rebellion so that they might capture the town and destroy it."

The officers withdrew with their chiefs to deliberate anew. It was decided to agree with whatever the army of the Loire might do. Each of us entered into this engagement in writing and signed it individually. I was instructed to take these conditional pledges to the governor, who refused to accept them. " Go, my dear captain, and tell your comrades to be more responsible and to declare frankly for or against the government of the Bourbons. In an hour I shall announce by telegraph the entire submission of the garrison or the resistance of certain corps."

On returning to Major O'Neill, with whom the officers were awaiting me, I told them of the general's ultimatum. Thereupon were loud cries and a general uproar. . . . Having thoroughly explained the position of affairs to all my comrades, I took a sheet of paper, on which I wrote : " I recognize Louis XVIII as my lawful Sovereign and I swear faithfully to serve him " ; and having signed it I passed it round to several of those about me, who copied it. Half an hour later I gave the papers into the hands of the governor, who was very well satisfied. Major O'Neill, an excellent officer in every respect, had held aloof in order that he might not embarrass the officers in their decision.

On the 20th July, in the morning, the guns of the fortress, the marine forts, and the roadstead, saluted the new flag, and the white cockade was once more displayed. The excitement of the day before was over, and the national guards had orders to go home. The governor informed us that he counted on the valour and devotion of the troops of the garrison to save for France her richest stores of material.

The order of the 3rd August, disbanding the army, was not executed in Brittany until the beginning of October, owing to the fear inspired by the presence of the Prussians, who had penetrated as far as Morbihan.

Brigadier-General Fabre was ordered to disband us— a painful mission for a soldier who loved his comrades and his country.

On the 3rd October we were reviewed for the last time as the 47th. On the 4th the last remnants of this valiant army, which for twenty-four years had filled the world with its exploits and displayed its immortal colours in all the capitals of Europe, was scattered about the roads ; staff in hand, like so many pilgrims, begging assistance from the enemies we had so often defeated, more generous than our fellow-countrymen, who styled them noble veterans of glory, these victims of treachery, the brigands of the Loire.

There was in the port a lugger sailing for Bordeaux. That I might not have to meet on the road the oppressors of my country, the followers of those nobles who were avenging themselves for the twenty-five years of humiliation which the Revolution inflicted on them, I took passage on it with two officers.

The White Terror.

12*th October.*—On the day after I reached Bordeaux I went to see the few acquaintances I had in this city. In one house I was told : " We are good Royalists, but we wish harm to no one. You are probably Bonapartist ; we beg you to make sure that there is nothing seditious in your luggage, for they are quite capable of coming to search them while you are out; and don't go into the cafés, lest you should be insulted. Lastly, in your own interests and for your safety, we urge you to leave the town as soon as possible." It was a young woman of twenty who said this, with tears in her eyes.

In the evening I went to the theatre with my friends and a captain of the 86th of my acquaintance. Between the two plays they sang the famous cantata whose refrain is " *Vive le roi, vive le France,*" and the fashionable song " *Vive Henri Quatre.*" One had to stand up instantly and remain standing, and wave one's white handkerchief. If one had not done so, one would have been thrown from the boxes into the pit. I have never heard the words *Vive le roi* shouted, bawled, vociferated as on this infernal evening. It was not a theatre but a very pandemonium in which all the demons of both sexes, all ages and all conditions were assembled in order to express the most horrible sentiments. A few days earlier the two brothers Faucher, both brigadier-generals, were shot by the Bordeaux Royalists. The town accused the Bonapartists of having refused them the freedom of the port.

On the evening of the 14th I sent my trunk by the Clermont diligence and decided to make the journey on foot. My companions went in another direction. We had a farewell breakfast. In the course of this meal a commercial traveller, an old non-commissioned officer of the regiment, took the liberty of blaming us for our conduct in following the flag of a usurper. A violent quarrel ensued, which ended only with the departure of the man who provoked it. The landlord of the hotel, who had heard this discussion, said to us : " Go, quickly, in your own interests, and leave by the back door." We hastily said good-bye, and separated. Ten minutes later I had left Bordeaux, crossed the Garonne by boat, and was peacefully walking along the road to Brannes, where I spent the night.

At the inn I was taken for the son of the house, who was also in the army. At first I fell in with this amusing mistake, but when it became more serious I had to make a considerable effort to disabuse these worthy people, who would not believe me. To convince them I had to show them my route-papers and ask leave to go to my room. The old mother's tears wrung my heart.

On the 16th October I met at Bergerac, at the inn where I alighted, a captain of grenadiers of the 47th, one of my best friends. I remained at the inn, so as to spend a couple of days with him, in a delightful intimacy. This captain, an excellent officer and a brave soldier, was then enjoying a certain popularity in the part of France which the enemy had not invaded. His exploits and his praises were sung and he was applauded by all those Frenchmen who did not regard our enemies as *friends*. It was he who, being on guard at the entrance to the bridge at Tours, on the side of the town, on the birthday of the King of Prussia, forced all the ladies of Tours who had gone to celebrate this fête in the Prussian camps to sleep on the bridge. After the retreat the barriers at the two ends of the bridge were closed and all those who were at the time between the two barriers were compelled to remain there until the following morning. The ladies were made the subject of popular songs, and the captain was congratulated by all the generals for having done something to avenge the insult offered to France.

On the 20th October a poor fellow with whom I had travelled on the 17th, and whom I treated to a bottle of wine, knowing that I was to arrive that evening at Argentat, had the generosity to wait for me in the road in order to take me to the best inn. It was already dark and I was horribly tired when I entered. My fatigue, my despondent air and shabby uniform, doubtless made the people take me for one of the generals who had been proscribed during this time of vengeance, for directly I sat down near the fire someone left the inn to fetch the gendarmes to arrest me. I presented my route papers ; they would not look at them. They told me to follow them to the mayor ; I protested against their manner of doing their duty, but they persisted and I had to give way. The poor devil of whom I have spoken, who had not yet left me, said : " Don't lose your temper ; don't resist ; they would put you in prison." When they took me to the mayor the people shouted as I went by :

" Long live the King ! Down with the brigand of the Loire ! " Ten minutes later I was back at the inn, the mayor having found my papers in perfect order, apologizing profusely for having been obliged to observe this police measure. I went to bed without supper ; the day's march and my arrest in the evening had worn me out.

On the 21st, on leaving Argentat, I was caught in a heavy downpour, which accompanied me all the way to Pleau. Having only what I stood up in, I asked for some clothes, so that I could change while my own things were being dried, but I was staying at an inn where there were only women ; I had to content myself with one of their chemises and spend the rest of the day in bed, in a room that served as a dining-room. It was fair-day, and the weather was frightful : I had plenty of company.

In going through Pleau I had intended to cross the high Auvergne mountains in order to shorten my route, but I had to give up this plan, as all the mountain-folk assured me that at this time of year the mountains could not be crossed. I must therefore try to make for Aurillac, from which I had come away in coming to Pleau.

I reached Aurillac with my feet in too bad a state to walk any farther, and waited there for the diligence, to finish my journey in that.

On the 25th October I arrived at Blesle, very glad to be with my people again, and to have finished my journey. I had been twenty-two days on the road ; it had been a long and fatiguing experience. To travel afoot, alone, staff in hand, may be very pleasant in fine weather, for a lover of the picturesque, but for a soldier who has spent ten years of his life on the high-roads it has not the same attraction. I was disenchanted by my philosophic whim.

At my mother's I found a letter from Brigadier-General Romeuf, commanding the department of Haute-Loire, apprising me that I was appointed provisional commandant of the departmental legion, and was to report at Brioude, a town not in the occupation of our friends the enemy (they had not crossed the Allier), to take command of the nucleus there being formed. I needed rest, and took it, until the 4th November, flattered though I was by the preference shown me.

On the 4th November I went to Brioude, where I found a hundred men, and orders to take them to Craponne, where I should find instructions.

On the 6th I lost myself in the woods and the snows of the mountains of La Chaise-Dieu, which are both wild and lofty. Fortunately the mayor of La Chaise-Dieu had the bells rung, and the sound guided me.

On the 7th I reached Craponne from La Chaise-Dieu. It was believed that the prescribed generals had concealed themselves hereabouts. My mission was to inspect all the villages, disarm the inhabitants, beat the woods, search the mountains, and put myself in touch with the militia columns of the Loire and Le Puy-de-Dôme. I did this as my duty, without conviction ; somewhat ostensibly, so that my plans should be known beforehand. One day the little town of Craponne was like an army headquarters. The prefects of the three departments and General Comte de la Roche-Aymon, escorted by zealous Royalists on horseback and in sumptuous uniforms, met together to discuss the means of checking the revolutionary plans of the Bonapartists, the Liberals, and the brigands of the Loire. Fear made them see conspirators everywhere, but they did nothing to calm the irritated population.

On the 5th April, 1816, at Le Puy, some officers, at the hotel, proposed the King's health. Accused of not having responded to the invitation with sufficient eagerness, Barrès was denounced to the colonel, then to the general, then to the

*prefect, who decided to retain him in the legion, but to repri-
mand him. " It was necessary at that time," he wrote,
" to be a Royalist, even a hot and extravagant Royalist."*

My duties as town commandant subjected me to a great
many puerile occupations, to night journeys, preliminary
inquiries, and frequent summonses from the general
and the prefect. These gentlemen saw on every hand
plots, conspiracies, eagle buttons, tricolor cockades, signs
of rebellion. Each tried to outdo the other in zeal and
devotion to the good cause. One Sunday, in July 1816,
the prefect, in order to celebrate the anniversary of the
return of the Bourbons to Paris, gathered, in the largest
public square of Le Puy, all the stamped paper bearing the
Imperial effigy, the seals of the communes of the Republic
and the Empire, and a magnificent colossal bust, in
marble, of the Emperor Napoleon, a masterpiece of the
celebrated sculptor Julien, who had himself offered it
to his barbarous and ungrateful fellow-countrymen. All
these were burned, mutilated, shattered, in the presence
of the regular troops and the National Guard, standing
to arms, and the civil, military, and judicial authorities,
to the sound of artillery, and with savage cries of " Vive
le roi ! " This act of vandalism wrung my heart.[1]

On the 15th August, 1816, we received orders to proceed to Besançon. It was comical. General Romeuf
accompanied us to keep an eye on us during the march.
Behind us came the gendarmerie, to prevent the men
from deserting. At Yssingeaux the Comte de Moidière,
our lieutenant-colonel, seriously proposed to the company
commanders that they should take the men's breeches
away at night, to prevent their desertion, giving them

[1] M. Ulysse Rouchon informs me that the bust of Napoleon is still in
existence, in the town museum of Le Puy. Is it the same bust ? Was
J.-B. Barrès mistaken ?—M. B.

back next morning before they marched! Really, these people had lost their heads!

On reaching Besançon we saw the inspectors-general entrusted with completing our organization. One of them was a German general passed into the French service : Prince von Hohenlohe! Their first action was to order half the officers of all ranks to go on six months' compulsory leave. I was one of them. It may be imagined how this iniquitous measure displeased all those affected by it. For my own part it annoyed me greatly, since at the moment I was hardly in a position to bear the expenses of so unexpected a journey. I returned to Auvergne.

J.-B. Barrès, despite the accusation of having refused to drink the King's health, was appointed captain of Grenadiers of the 2nd battalion. In March 1817 he left Auvergne to rejoin the legion at Strasbourg, and in 1818 and 1819 was in garrison successively at Le Puy, Grenoble, and Montlouis, near the Spanish frontier.

BARRÈS IS PUT ON HALF-PAY.

Montlouis.—On the 15th October, 1820, the inspector-general, Brigadier-General Vautré, began his operations. They lasted a week. As in previous years, I was proposed for the post of battalion-leader and invited to dine with him. I was also proposed for the cross of St. Louis.

On the 17th December the same General Vautré returned. On his arrival he asked whether I still read *Le Constitutionnel.* The colonel, commandant of the fortress, replied " Yes." He lied. He should have said " No," and that the subscription to the paper had expired in September ; that would have been the truth. He knew this perfectly well, since we used to read it together (he, the colonel, a battalion-leader and ten captains) ;

but he was afraid, and was silent. On this assertion of his the General said : " Barrès will pay for the rest. I shall pass him into the 19th regiment of the line (legion of the Gironde). He will go on half-pay."

I knew nothing of this dialogue. All the officers were dejected, for they knew already the names of a number of us who were being changed to other corps or being sent on half-pay. I was among these. I was left a long time in ignorance, but was finally told of it. I was far from thinking that I should not be affected by such a measure. I had given such good service, my conduct, private and military, had been so blameless in all respects, that I was crushed and confounded.

Next day I went to see the general ; I was told to keep quiet, in my own interests. Thus I was condemned without being heard. I went to the colonel, who seemed to be very sorry for me. The lieutenant-colonel displayed more regret and indignation. But as I knew him to be deceitful and unreliable, I had no great illusions as to the sincerity of his demonstrations. (Here is a proof of the quality of that same sincerity : having told him that I greatly feared my brother, vicar-general of the arch-bishopric of Bordeaux, might think I had committed some action dishonouring to my military career, he wrote him a letter of four pages singing my praises. A fortnight later he withdrew this letter.) Fortunately I found some consolation for my profound unhappiness in the regret expressed by nearly all my comrades and in their kindly affection.

What afflicted me most in this cruel disgrace was to see that this colonel, who for five years had loaded me with kindness, had given me proofs of sincere attachment, including the command of two crack companies, had proposed me for the cross of St. Louis, and had selected me, from among all my comrades, for duty on court-martial, in the fortified towns and in the administration, was now sacrificing me to please a general who was himself anxious to give proof of his devotion to the Bourbons by sacrificing the career and future of officers who had been his companions under the Empire.

On the 25th December, in the morning, I bade farewell, with a heavy heart and eyes full of tears, to all the assembled officers. These last moments were very affecting. A number of my comrades accompanied me as far as Prades. At Perpignan, on the 27th, I found a number of my comrades of the 1st battalion, who had been a month in garrison at Collioure, had come to greet me. During the breakfast they gave me, General Vautré asked for me.

I found, in his company, Colonel O'Mahony, who seemed, I thought, greatly embarrassed. The general, coming up to me, said, in a rather casual tone :

" I have heard, to my surprise, my dear captain, that you were greatly annoyed by the measure I have taken with regard to you ; and that I have condemned you without having heard you ; which might make you suppose that I had acted with prejudice, and in accordance with reports that might have been aimed against you, with the desire to injure you. You are mistaken ; here is a Ministerial note in which your name figures with various others."

I looked at this document, emanating from the Ministry of War, which was headed : *Names of the officers as to whom inquiry is to be made.*

" Well, General, have you made inquiries with regard to me ? " He replied that he had. Then began a lively dialogue between us, in which I triumphantly refuted all the accusations which he brought against me.

" If I were alone with you, General, you might perhaps not believe me, but the colonel is here ; he hears me and can tell you whether I am lying."

At each reply of mine I said to the colonel : " Is that true ? " He was obliged to say " Yes." For the rest, the chief accusation of any weight was that I had subscribed to *Le Constitutionnel*. But when I explained that the colonel, a major and five or six other captains had also subscribed, this disconcerted him and greatly embarrassed the colonel. Then I said :

" If ever I am recalled to the army and am killed in the service of the King, will they ask, over my dead body, whether I used to read the *Constitutionnel* or the *Drapeau blanc ?* "

He replied, emphatically, as though moved by my apostrophe :

" I am convinced that the readers of the first will always do their duty better than the readers of the second."

At another juncture I said :

" How is it, General, that you proposed me as battalion commander two months ago and that to-day I am not even fit to serve in the army ? "

" That is true, but then I did not know that you were a Liberal."

He made me read the notes which he had made of me at that time, and said :

" You see that I was really thinking of you then and am now, for I give you my word of honour that before three weeks you will be replaced."

I went away content, less because I hoped to be restored to my command than because I had proved that I had been calumniated, misjudged and abandoned by my natural protector.

An hour later I got into a carriage for Montpellier. All the officers who had invited me to breakfast accompanied me as far as the posting-office. The captain, after enbracing me with all the impulsiveness of a warm and affectionate heart, as soon as I was out of sight, went to find the general. He found his aide de camp, who asked for me. He told him I had left.

" Good Lord, what a nuisance ; the general has just appointed him to the 15th regiment of light infantry ! "

" That's all right," said the effervescent Guinguené, " I'll bring him back to you within three hours."

He went to the posting-stables, got into the saddle and, sending a postilion ahead of him, said : " Hell for leather till we catch the carriage that has just left ! " Two hours later he was at the door of my carriage, saying : " Get out ; I've orders to fetch you back to Perpignan."

Absorbed in my dismal reflections, I thought I was dreaming when I saw him there. After some explanations I mounted behind the postilion and we galloped back to the town. The satisfaction I felt at this revulsion to a better appreciation of my military and private conduct was by no means equal to the pain I had suffered on learning of this deadly injustice, but I had a small sense of triumph over my cowardly accusers.

We were near Salus when I was asked to get out of the carriage. The weather was terrible ; the rain was falling in torrents, so that when we got to Perpignan we were horribly wet and encrusted with mud. Nevertheless, we alighted at the general's door and went up to him. On seeing me he came towards me, cordially pressed my hand, and said :

" You see, I don't always bear malice."

My only reply was to bow. He continued :

" You can leave when you will for Périgueux ; the 15th Light is there. I have already given notice of your appointment."

I said it would be disagreeable for me to go to the regiment before the organization was completed ; my presence would surely be painful to those who might find themselves in the position I had been in a few days earlier.

" Don't worry yourself," he said. " You won't displace anybody ; you will replace an officer who is asking leave to retire, and those who have to go have already left. For that matter, you can join up when you like ; I will give you an authorization to that effect."

At the Archbishop of Bordeaux'.

Barrès sets out for Périgueux, stopping on the way at Bordeaux, to see his brother.

At Agen three travellers got into the diligence ; one was greatly interested in magnetism, another deeply versed in English literature, an enthusiast as regards Lord Byron and Walter Scott, of whom I heard for the first time, and the third was editor-in-chief of a liberal Bordeaux newspaper, who had come to Agen to beg the prefect not to do him the honour of appointing a jury expressly for him, as he would be content with that entrusted with the trial of thieves and murderers. He was being prosecuted for an offence of the press ; for having demanded the demolition of the famous Column of the 12th March, which was an insult to France. The extremely witty conversation of these three men enabled me pleasantly to endure the tedium of a long journey in a lumbering diligence.

Having found a lodging, I went to the archbishop's palace to see my elder brother, the vicar-general. He had been successively a pupil at the École Normale and Professor of Literature at the École Centrale. Under the Empire he was twice a candidate for the Legislative Corps, and was a Chevalier of the Legion of Honour. In 1817, when he was secretary-general of the prefecture of Le Puy, he became disgusted with the world, took refuge in a seminary, for the purpose of taking orders.

He presented me to the archbishop. This good old man, as much to be respected for his virtues as for his great age, demanded of me, as a duty imposed on me, to dine at his table every day, as long as I remained in Bordeaux. I did so. At table he would not allow anyone to "talk shop," although there were commonly five or six priests present. One had to talk of war, battles, and so forth. He would allow none but himself to pour my wine. Finally, this holy man, as they called him in the household, made me promise, after he had given me his blessing, that in the warm spring weather I would come to see him again and stay in his beautiful country house, which was given him by the Emperor Napoleon. He told me that when he was made Chevalier of the Holy Ghost they wanted him to give up his officer's cross of the Legion of Honour, with which he was already decorated, but that he refused, saying that he who had given it him knew very well what he was doing.

During the four days which I spent in this city I went every night to the theatre, where I saw several new operas played, which gave me all the more pleasure in that I had for a long while been deprived of this distraction ; and they were very well produced. In the *Voitures versées*, with music by Boieldieu, there is a scene in which three young women in full toilette are on the stage together. Each had a crown : one was blue, one red, and one white, and they were placed in this order. When they appeared they were applauded. In 1815 the actresses and their admirers would have been torn to bits, literally ; I cannot recollect without a shudder the evening I spent there at that time. What a change in so few years ! After the play I went to spend the rest of my evening with some of the canons. They drank excellent Bordeaux, and the conversation was very cheerful and amusing.

I had the pleasure of inspecting all the details of a steamboat, the first I had seen, which was newly built.

From Grenoble, where he was present, on the 24th August,
1822, at a great military and civil ceremony, on the occasion

of moving the ashes of Bayard, Barrès returned, in 1823, to garrison in Paris.

On the 3rd July we were presented to Monsieur the Comte d'Artois—and Mme. la Duchesse de Berry, beside whom was the Duc de Bordeaux. On the following day, the 4th, the King received us. On the 15th August we lined the Quai de la Cité (Quai Napoléon) while the procession of Louis XIII's Vow went by, in which were Monsieur and the princesses of the royal family.

On the 25th August I was admitted Chevalier of St. Louis by Colonel Perrégaux, and immediately afterwards went to pay homage to Louis XVIII, on the occasion of his birthday. All the officers of the royal bodyguard, the garrison, and the national guards assembled in the great gallery of the Louvre, before marching past the throne. The King, weighed down by age and sickness, his head drooping over his knees, saw nothing, looked at no one. He was a corpse, before whom we passed without halting. He was surrounded by a splendid Court, notable for the richness of its costumes, the variety of colour displayed, the beauty of the embroideries, the number and brilliance of the decorations. We might have concluded that before many days had elapsed we should witness a royal funeral. However, it did not take place until the following year.

Barrès remains some time in the North, at Dunkirk, Lille, and Gravelines. In the camp of Saint-Omer large-scale manœuvres enabled Barrès to exhibit the training and bearing of his troops. A first attempt was made to establish direct communication between Dunkirk and the English coast by means of steamboats ; the venture failed for lack of passengers. A meeting with two English officers who had charge of Napoleon on St. Helena. " All they told me wrung my heart with grief, and drew me to them while I cursed them for having taken part in riveting his fetters." Barrès had occasion to go through Belgium, to Ypres, with his comrades, in uniform. " We were saluted with respect by all the inhabitants we met and asked to breakfast. They showed that they had not forgotten that they were once part of the great French nation." Thence he was sent to Nancy, where the event awaited him that was about to transform his life.

FROM SAINT-OMER TO NANCY. THE DANCES OF SAINT-MIHIEL.

The journey from Saint-Omer to Nancy was very pleasant. It was easy to see from the military bearing of our men and the smartness of their step that we had come from a perhaps rather hard school (the camp of Saint-Omer), but one favourable to discipline, good carriage, and the development of physical strength. Leaving Saint-Omer on the 28th September, we passed through Arras, Cambrai, Landrecies, Avesnes, Hirson, Charleville. At Sedan I dined at the house of the sister of one of my best friends, Mme. de Montagnac (the mother of the brave and unfortunate Montagnac who later on, in Africa, was the victim of an infamous act of treachery and perished with all the men of his command). On the 15th October, having passed Verdun, we came to Saint-Mihiel.

The evening of that day, which happened to be a Sunday, being very fine, with a wonderful moon, the entire dancing population of the town assembled in the squares and at the cross-roads, to dance the *ronde.* There was, in these improvised, open-air balls, such spirit and gaiety, and such melody in the airs which they sang, that I took an infinite pleasure in looking on. The joy of all this comely youth rejoiced my heart and made me remember that I too had been young. If I did not dance, at least I shared in the happiness of those who gave me such pleasant feelings. I did not withdraw until the singing was over.

Two days later, on the 17th October, we arrived at Nancy, through which I had passed once before, on the 5th February, 1806, on the way back from Austerlitz.

AT NANCY.

We were to remain eighteen months at Nancy. This is the pleasantest garrison in France, and one of the best. The women of Nancy are famed for their good taste, their skill in dress, and their art in wearing it.

Before proceeding to a personal detail I should mention at once that on the 9th November, 1827, the regiment paraded to witness the translation of the remains of the Dukes of Lorraine, whose numerous tombs had been isolated and scattered during the storms of the Revolution.

These dusty relics had been thrown into a pit in one of the city graveyards. They were carefully collected and borne to the cathedral, where they received the honours due to their rank and their record. A *chapelle ardente* was an impressive sight, as remarkable for its brilliance of colour and its lights as for its religious character. All the officers of the garrison, the general at their head, went to sprinkle holy water on the coffins and urns containing the ashes of these princes of Lorraine, some of whom had achieved such fame. On the following day was the translation; it was a solemn and majestic ceremony, both religious and military. The King of France and the Emperor of Austria were represented. The crowd was immense; wrapt in meditation. In the round or ducal chapel, arranged for the reception of these relics of so much greatness, were the hangings, sent from Paris, which were used at the obsequies of

Louis XVIII. I had never before seen anything to compare with the magnificence and majesty of these decorations.

This round chapel, repaired and beautified, is that of the ancient dukes, whose old palace is still standing, serving now as the barracks of the gendarmerie. A vault made expressly to receive all the remains and monuments erected to perpetuate the memory of the most illustrious princes of this famous House of Lorraine make the chapel, already remarkable for its architecture, a venerable spot. An address or sermon by the Bishop, Forbin-Janson, directed against the Revolution and philosophy, was a poor ending for the pomp of this ceremony. It was hotly censured, being unworthy of a Christian and a man reputed to possess both intelligence and judgment. It was largely responsible for the disgrace into which he fell after the July Revolution. Driven from his diocese by the people, he died without recovering it, prudence forbidding the government to restore him, for the hatred he had aroused was still unabated.

This was the fourth ceremony of the kind at which I had been present within a few years : two at Grenoble, in respect of the Constable de Lesdiguières, and Bayard, and a third at Cambrai, in respect of all the archbishops of that town, and in particular the precious remains of Fénelon, which were found under the parvise of the old cathedral when it was decided to turn it into a public square.

MY MARRIAGE.

On the very day of my arrival at Nancy I met one of my old Skirmisher comrades of Écouen, of whom I had seen nothing since I left the Imperial Guard at the beginning of 1808. He was an infantry captain, and was in charge of the recruiting in the department of La Meurthe. It was natural that two soldiers who for more than three years had lived the same life should give one another a joyous welcome.

Introduced, on the following day, to his young wife and his new family, I was made cordially welcome, and thereafter treated as a friend whom they were always glad to see. During the winter my friend proposed that in the spring I should go with him to Charmes, a little town in the Vosges, to make the acquaintance of his wife's grandmother.

I had no thought at the time that this little journey into a country as strange to me as the person I was going to see, a journey undertaken by complaisance as much as by choice, might give me a wife ; that my friend would become my cousin, his mother-in-law my aunt, and his grandmother mine by the same title as his own. Thus often do the most futile things become, by chance, the truly important things in life, and so do we enter upon actions which we should perhaps have avoided could we have foreseen their results.

14th April, 1827.—The day before Easter Day I arrived at the house of my future grandmother, who made me entirely welcome ; so did her children and grandchildren, who were living in the town ; that is, they received me politely, there being no reason why they should do more, since I was a stranger to them and in different circumstances. However, owing to a strange coincidence, I was considered more or less as one of the family ; namely, two brothers of the people I met had been Skirmishers.

The niece of one of these Skirmishers was a young woman whose charming manners, accomplishments, and age— this being not too far removed from my own—made an impression on me. A week spent in the town and daily intercourse led me to think of what had hitherto been far from my thoughts : namely, marriage. I spoke of it to my friend, who approved of my projected proposal, and then, on returning to Nancy, to his mother-in-law, who gave me hope that my prayers might be favourably received.

In short, when certain letters had been written, one by my excellent colonel, I was authorized to present myself.

I arrived on the 9th May and made my request on the 10th ; and thanks to those who interested themselves in my success all difficulties were smoothed away, arrangements were agreed upon and the day of the wedding fixed for the 3rd July.

From this moment I reflected seriously on the engagements into which I was about to enter, the obligations which my new situation would impose on me, and the steps to be taken to obtain all the documents which I should need. I made several trips to Charmes, to pay my court and make myself better known to her who was to become my life's companion. Once I went thither in order to bring her, with her mother, to Nancy, to make the usual purchases. Finally, on the 30th June, I left my messmates, never to dine with them again.

3rd July.—Celebration of my wedding with Marie-Reine Barbier.—I have never known the time to go so slowly as between the day on which I was permitted to present my respects and the day that sealed my happiness. To be the husband of the wife whom one has sought and wooed, to feel, for the first time, her hand trembling in yours, to reflect that you are for ever joined in sweet and sacred bonds ; when you feel that the chains imposed will be light to bear; this is a beautiful moment of one's life ; and I felt that I was going to be happy. The colonel and Captain Chardron were present at the wedding, which was celebrated with fitting dignity. On account of distance no member of my family was present.

On the 6th July we were *en famille* at the home of one of my wife's maternal uncles, an ironmaster, near

Rambervillers, who was afterwards deputy for the Vosges :
M. Gouvernel. On the 8th we returned ; on the 11th we
set out for Nancy, where, to our great satisfaction, we
entered into our little home. A few weeks later certain
hopeful symptoms told us that our union was prospering
and that a fresh pledge from the best of wives was
coming to bless the bonds that united us.

*Presently, as though to confirm his happiness, Barrès
received, at Nancy, the news of the promotion long awaited.*

On Sunday, the 18th November, just as the troops
were about to march past after a review by the brigadier-
general commanding the department, the colonel received
a letter from M. O'Neill announcing that I was appointed
battalion commander, from the 14th November, of the
3rd battalion, which was about to be organized. This
agreeable piece of news was divulged to me at once, and
also to my wife, who was in the Place Carrière, where the
troops were assembled. The compliments paid me on
this occasion and her delight doubled my own joy at
the news.

It was a great thing to be appointed major [1] and to
have been selected for the post ; for on the 1st January,
1827, I was the hundredth on the roll of infantry captains ;
and in my own regiment, so that I had not to make fresh
acquaintances, nor to change my uniform, nor, above all,
to go on a journey at a time when my wife could not do
so. Lastly, I should continue to serve under Colonel
Perrégaux, of whom I had had so much reason to think
highly ever since 1813, and I should not have to leave a
town I liked for its pleasant qualities and its nearness
to Charmes.

During the month of December I got my equipment
ready, received visits and serenades, and gave a big dinner

[1] Chef de bataillon.—Tr.

to the greater number of the officers. All this, including the purchase of a fine saddle-horse, cost me a good deal of money, but I did not regret it ; it seemed to me that I could not pay too dearly for the advantage and satisfaction of my new rank. What a change in my position, and what a difference in my duties !

However, on the 10th April, 1828, the regiment left for Lyons. Mme. Barrès, remaining at Charmes, brought into the world, on the 12th May, a son, who received the names of Joseph-Auguste. At the moment of his arrival Barrès found his wife dangerously ill with inflammation of the right kidney ; her life was saved, but she remained in a state of weakness that caused great anxiety.

The beginning of the year 1829 brought Barrès a fresh grief : he had the unhappiness to learn, on the 28th January, of the death of his mother, at Blesle, at the age of seventy-seven. He went to his people and spent some days with his sister, " to evoke the care-free times of childhood. The tomb is closed upon my worthy parents, and mine will be not near theirs. Other destinies, other duties have fixed my place elsewhere." In May 1829 the regiment was again sent to Paris.

It was not without the keenest and completest satisfaction that I found myself settled for at least a full year in Paris. I was beginning to weary of journeys and of the march, and I saw a possibility of taking my wife to Paris after she had taken the waters in the summer. It would give both of us a childlike joy to show her this beautiful Paris which she so greatly longed to know.

Charles X.

On the 31st May, 1828, I went to Saint-Cloud with all the officers of the superior ranks, to pay our court to the

King and the royal family. Presented first to Madame the Dauphine by the colonel, we were then presented to Monseigneur the Dauphin, who, on hearing my name, remembered that he had proposed me as battalion commander two years earlier, and spoke to me. I had not expected such an honour. Then, gathered together in the great gallery of the palace to await the King, we remained to hear Mass, or rather to chat, not having been able to get into the chapel, which is by no means capacious. After Mass the King walked to and fro in the gallery for a long time, speaking to all those who paid him homage, with a great deal of grace and amenity. This presentation gave me great pleasure; for a long time I had not seen so many dignitaries or famous personalities. There were the ministers, the marshals, peers, deputies, ambassadors and generals. The courtiers were numerous, and the assembly was glittering with gold embroidery, badges, sashes and diamonds. In this fine gallery we were all mixed together in a confused medley, each watching for a glance from the master, and trying to approach him in order to be seen or ask some favour. Standing in a corner, out of the whirlpool of the great and the impassioned admirers of sovereign power, I could observe at leisure this magnificent gathering of the great ones of the day, and endeavour to recognize all these illustrious figures, and obtain some idea of the brilliance of a Court. I could see nothing great or distinguished in the manners of the Duc d'Angoulême, nothing kindly in the eyes or features of Madame the Dauphine; as for Charles X, he gave me the impression of an old man still vigorous, who inspires respect, but whose face has something common about it.

This famous palace of Saint-Cloud reminded me that in other days I had mounted guard there, in the capacity of Skirmisher of the Chasseurs; that I had seen there a young, brilliant Court, full of hope and vigour. There were still plenty of men of that period in the Court of

Charles X, but they were no more than the shadows of those great characters, those valiant officers, so famed for their great feats of war. Glory had given place to devout hypocrisy, the famous men of the Empire to the little men of the emigration, and the great doings of Napoleon to the intrigues of an insecure government.

In the evening I went to the Théâtre-Français to see *Henri III*, a play in five acts by Alexandre Dumas. It was the play then in fashion, the triumph of the Romantics. Despite the fine talents of the actors, the luxury of the decorations and the accuracy of the costumes, I thought the play far inferior to its high reputation. At all events, I did not find in it the great emotions which I had felt formerly at the plays of Corneille and Racine. Mlle. Mars, as usual, electrified all the spectators.

7th June.—I went to the Tuileries to see the procession of the Chevaliers of the Holy Ghost, on Easter Day, the fête-day of the Order. The knights in mantles of green silk, richly embroidered, with hats *à la* Henri Quatre, tunics, breeches and stockings of white silk, the collar of the Order round their necks, came out of the great apartments two by two, on their way to the chapel, and in the same order returned to the throne room. The King came last. I could not go into the chapel to see their reception there, the doors being closed after the entry of the knights. When they came out, as I was in the first salon after that of the marshals, the King spoke to me concerning the stay of the regiment in Paris. This ceremonious procession, more curious than imposing, interested me because it gave me an opportunity of recognizing a host of great personages, as famed for their illustrious deeds as for their birth, their titles, their functions, and the services which they had rendered the State, and a great number of sometime émigrés. I saw there, for the first time, the whole family of the Duc d'Orléans.

A brief visit to Charmes, to his wife, whose state of health, after a passing improvement, had once more given rise to alarm, enabled Barrès to see his son, who was " beginning to prattle and walk." But the charm of the child hardly sufficed to call a truce to his increasing anxieties. He returned to Paris in July, after three weeks' absence.

8th *August.*—Murmuring and uneasiness in Paris over the announcement that a change of ministry would take place during the day, and that Prince de Polignac would be appointed President of Council. This news of a Clerical and counter-Revolutionary ministry filled all lovers of our constitutional institutions with consternation.

Headed by Comte Coutard, commanding the 1st division, all the officers of the garrison paid an official visit to the Minister of War, Lieutenant-General Comte de Bourmont. I found the Minister embarrassed and perhaps ashamed to find himself the leader of a French army—he who a few days before the disastrous battle of Waterloo had deserted the army defeated on that dreadful day, to the sorrow and misfortune of France. The burden of this treachery must have oppressed his heart with remorse, if, as was said in the salons of the ministry, some of the generals refused to take the hand he offered them.

15th *August.*—I took command of 280 picked men of the regiment to line the route along part of the Quai de la Cité, as far as the doors of the Métropole, on the occasion of the procession of the Vow of Louis XIII. At four o'clock the King, the Dauphin, the Dauphine and the Court passed on foot through our ranks, escorted by the foot bodyguard of the King (the Hundred Swiss). The procession was splendid, though simple. No cries of joy and homage were heard as the King went by. All hearts were chilled, all faces cold and dejected, since the advent of the Polignac ministry.

A Session of the French Academy.

25th August.—Public and ceremonial session of the Académie française. Before going thither I went to Saint-Germain-l'Auxerrois to hear the panegyric on St. Louis, pronounced before the members of the Academy, in accordance with the ancient custom. There were few Immortals [1] and hardly any audience. Neither the eulogy nor the orator was effective.

At one o'clock I entered the public sessions hall of the Institute. As I was one of the first three, I was able to choose my seat. The hall, which was not very large, seemed to me well arranged and decorated with taste and simplicity. Admission is only by tickets, which have to be applied for several days beforehand. The audience commonly consists of the pick of the "great world," French and foreign scholars, and a few diligent students. In the numerous rooms preceding the hall are the marble statues of our great poets and prose-writers, historians and philosophers, orators, scholars and scientists. I noted that of La Fontaine, the work of Julien of Le Puy, my compatriot and a friend of my brother's. At two o'clock the hall and the tribunes were full; there was no room for the late arrivals.

At half-past two M. Cuvier, the acting director, opened the session. The first address was by M. Andrieux, permanent secretary, and the speech on the occasion of the distribution of the prizes for merit by the president, Baron Cuvier. The verses which were the prize were read by M. Lemercier, with a spirit and warmth which doubled the merit of the composition. The subject for competition was the discovery of printing. Many lines

[1] The forty members of the Académie Française.—Tr.

were vigorously applauded, above all those that treated of the liberty of the Press, and the dangers to which it might be subjected under a Government inimical to enlightenment. When the poet laureate, M. Legouvé, son of the deceased Academician, author of *La Mort d'Abel* and *Le Mérite des femmes*, presented himself at the desk to receive the gold medal his name was greeted with applause. I noticed, on the desks intended for the members of the Institute, MM. de Lally-Tollendal, Barbé-Marbois, Chaptal, Arago, de Ségur, Casimir Delavigne, etc., and in the hall or the tribunes the last president of the Consistory, M. Marron, Mlle. Léontine Fay, etc. I regretted that I was not sitting next to someone who was well acquainted with the Academicians and the distinguished personalities present at this assembly, who could tell me their names. At half-past four they left. I had spent part of my day in this famous building in a very interesting fashion.

30th August.—I went this afternoon to the Faubourg Saint-Antoine to visit the owner of the house in which I was living. There I met a young Russian, a captain of the mounted grenadiers of the Royal Guard, by name Espinay Saint-Luc, and a few others. The conversation turned on the crossing of the Balkans by the Russians and their triumphant march upon Constantinople. The young Russian, full of enthusiasm, warmly extolled the valour of his countrymen. The captain defended the Turks and bitterly deplored the unhappy position in which the Sultan Mahmud would find himself. He was finally asked what was his interest in this monarch, that he commiserated him so keenly. He replied, with tears in his eyes: " Mahmud is my first cousin. His mother and mine were sisters." After this extraordinary confidence, which surprised us all, we were silent.

The Sultan's mother was in fact a demoiselle d'Espinay

Saint-Luc. She was captured by Algerian corsairs about 1786, being then three years of age.

31*st* *August.*—I went to the Opéra-Comique, in the Salle Ventadour, newly built, which I had not yet seen. A superb hall. They played *La Dame Blanche* and *Marie,* operas which I had already seen in the country, but which I heard again with pleasure. This was the last time I went to the theatre : I had no desire, afterwards, to go there, nor could I take pleasure in any amusement of this kind.

At this period Barrès was to experience the great sorrow of his life ; his wife, who, after her cure at Plombières, had come to rejoin him in Paris, underwent a serious operation, on the 4th October, at the hands of Dr. Piollet, on the advice of Dupuytren. The slight improvement that followed gave a momentary hope of her recovery. Barrès was able to return to duty.

In the Plaine de Grenelle.

29*th October.*—Review by the King of the troops of the garrison and district of Paris, in the Plaine de Grenelle.

The whole of the troops of the line was placed in the front line, the infantry of the Guard in the second. The whole of the cavalry, both line and Guard, was likewise in two lines behind the infantry. Lastly, the fine artillery of the Guard was on the flanks, in the intervals and in reserve. Our first battalion, as skirmishers, covered the front of the battle, which faced toward the Seine. My battalion was in its battle position on the left of the front line. In all there were sixteen battalions of infantry and five regiments of cavalry. The emplacement and order of battle being determined, we awaited in this position for the arrival of the King.

At one o'clock the guns, the bands, the trumpets and

the drums announced his approach. He passed in succession before the battle front of the four lines, preceded and followed by an innumerable staff, brilliant with gold embroidery and decorations. In a calèche, following the King, were the Dauphine, the Duchesse de Berry, Mlle. de Berry and the Duc de Bordeaux. In another, closely following the first, were the princesses of Orléans. The Duc d'Orléans, in the uniform of a general of Hussars, and his two elder sons, the Ducs de Chartres and de Nemours, surrounded the Dauphin, the chief of staff. After some evolutions of the lines of battle, with firing, advancing and retreating, we prepared to execute the famous manœuvre of Wagram, where the army of Italy, under the command of Prince Eugène and Macdonald, then a mere general of division, drove in the centre of the Austrian Army and decided the victory. This great strategic movement completed, we marched past, the left at the head. By my rank in order of battle I marched in front of all and opened the march past.

The crowd of sightseers was prodigious; one could see nothing but heads in this vast Plaine de Grenelle. Everything there was beautiful, superb, majestic, as was the weather, which contributed to the brilliance of the review. The rarity of the shouts of " Vive le roi ! " must have made Charles X conscious that the Polignac ministry was odious to the nation.

Marshal Macdonald, Duke of Taranto, major-general of the Guard, commanded and directed the various movements, which were all executed with precision and uniformity.

Mme. Barrès died on the 25th November, in the prime of her youth, watched by her husband until the latest moment. The obsequies were celebrated at Saint-Jacques-du-Haut-Pas. Barrès' only consolation was his love for the young son in whom he was assured of one day finding " a friend to recall

16

to him the worth of her who would remain for ever beloved by him." After forty days at Charmes he returned to Paris in January 1830.

31*st May.*—I went to the Palais-Royal to see the illumination of the palace and garden, in preparation for the fête given by the Duc d'Orléans to the King of Naples, his brother-in-law, and to the Court of France. The superior officers of the regiment were invited ; a few went, but I refrained, firstly because of my position and secondly because one had to wear white breeches, silk stockings, and gold buckles, an expense which I did not care to incur for the one or two Court balls I might have been able to attend. As soon as night fell the garden and the great courtyard of the palace were full of sightseers, in such numbers that one could hardly move, yet in spite of this the crowd was visibly increasing. I thought that if I did not leave early I should no longer be able to get away without very great difficulty. This crowd of men of all ranks, but above all of young people and working men, the tumultuous excitement, the uneasiness visible on many faces, above all on those of the salesmen in the galleries, who hastily shut their shops ; in short, all these symptoms of riot and disorder decided me to leave a spot kindling with all the fires of discord. I left shortly after nine o'clock, as Charles X arrived on the scene, in great splendour, with some difficulty, but without incident.

When I heard next day that there had been a riot, and that the people had burned all the chairs in the garden, destroyed the railings of the flower-beds, and trampled the flowers under foot, shouting " Down with Polignac ! Down with the ministers ! Long live the Duc d'Orléans ! " I congratulated myself sincerely that I had not been in this tempestuous crush.

27*th June.*—A Sunday. I went to Saint-Cloud in the colonel's calèche to pay our court to the King and the members of the royal family. The Comtesse de Bourmont, the wife of the commander-in-chief of the Algerian expedition, received the compliments of the King and the royal family on her husband's success and the fortunate opening of the campaign. She thereupon became the object of assiduous attention.

11*th July.*—A solemn *Te Deum* was sung at Nôtre-Dame in the presence of the King, the Court and all the high officers of the Crown and the kingdom, as an act of thanksgiving for the capture of Algiers, which took place on the 5th, the news having reached Paris during the course of the previous day. As I was not on duty to line the streets as His Majesty went by, I went to the cathedral. In less than twenty-four hours it had been magnificently decorated with hangings. The ceremony was majestic, the music and singing very pleasing. There were many present ; entrance was only by ticket or to those in uniform. —Well, despite the importance of the victory, despite the laurels just won by our fine, valiant African army, there were no shouts of rejoicing. Neither when the King went by, nor amidst the crowd in the parvise of the cathedral, nor in the streets traversed by the glittering escort, were there any signs of enthusiasm or sympathy. The King was received at the door of the cathedral by the archbishop, who preached a sermon bitterly censured on the following day by the entire Liberal press. This sermon resulted in the sack of the archiepiscopal palace less than three weeks later. Charles X, placed under a canopy, was led to his seat by the whole chapter ; around him were the princes of the House of Orléans, the ministers, the marshals, and the high officers of the Court.

While they were singing the hymn by which they thanked Heaven for the triumph just achieved in Algeria I recalled, as a splendid memory of my own, that I had seen, in this same sacred edifice, a ceremony even more stately, majestic and sublime—the coronation of the Emperor Napoleon by a Pope, surrounded by the flower of the French nation; twenty-six years had elapsed since that great Imperial epoch. The master of the world, the man of destiny, the conqueror of kings, had been twice dethroned in a reign of only ten years, and had died in exile, on a frightful rock in the midst of the ocean. Who could have told me that the venerable sovereign before my eyes, kneeling at no more than ten paces from me, at the foot of the altar, intoxicated with homage and surrounded by the profoundest respect, who appeared so powerful and mighty, should within three weeks be driven from his palace, and forced for the third time to leave France, the country that one of his armies had just made illustrious, and once more to tread the path of exile! O human vicissitudes, how unforeseen are your blows, and how hard they fall!

The prayers ended, the King was led back with the same ceremonial, and the Orléans family, having accompanied him to the door, went out by another exit, in order to re-enter their carriages. When the grand master of ceremonies, the Marquis de Dreux-Brézé, whom I knew slightly, said to me, touching me on the shoulder with his ebony staff: "My dear Commandant, make way for Monsieur le Duc d'Orléans," whom he was escorting back to his carriage, he thought no more than I did that it was for his future sovereign that he asked me to make way.

21st July.—I went to the Royal Observatory to be present at the beginning of the lectures on astronomy given by M. Arago. His brother, an artillery captain of my acquaintance, was anxious to take me. These public lectures, intended for a fashionable audience, promised to be of great interest. I proposed to follow very closely the great astronomer's lessons, in order to gratify in this way a very pronounced taste for this difficult and sublime science, but the political events which occurred some days later checked at the outset both the good intentions of the professor and those of one of his most zealous listeners.

25th July.—All the superior officers of the regiment went to Saint-Cloud to see the Dauphin, of whom the colonel had a favour to ask, on behalf of the widow of a captain in the regiment ; she had been refused a pension because she could not prove that she was legally married, the marriage having taken place in a foreign country. Our interview ended, we went into the Apollo gallery to await the King and hear Mass. Remaining in the gallery, I conversed with several generals and other officers of my acquaintance. No one showed any signs of excitement or uneasiness, although the news from the departments was unfavourable to the ministry. While the faces of the courtiers were gloomy, if many isolated groups appeared to be preoccupied, the King's countenance was remarkably placid. He conversed as usual with the persons presented to him, nothing in his calm expression betraying that he had formed a great resolution. He had a conversation of some length with the Hospodar of Moldavia, who, it was said, expressed the desire that he would be able to overcome the resistance offered to his conciliatory intentions, to which the King replied : " The matter has been considered." Nevertheless, it was on returning to his closet after this reception that the fatal Ordinances of July were signed : fatal especially to him and his family.

This was the last Mass I heard in Paris and the last visit I paid to the Bourbons of the elder branch.

THE REVOLUTION OF 1830

THE ORDINANCES OF JULY.

26th July.—Early on the morning of this great day the regiment paraded for the administrative review by M. le Baron Joinville, military intendant of the first division, and for this purpose proceeded to the enclosure of Henri IV's college, behind the Panthéon. By ten o'clock the troops had returned to their quarters and the officers to their lodgings, and not a word had reached our ears as to what was already astir in Paris. At eleven o'clock I was completely ignorant of the fact that the capital was in an uproar and that I was on a volcano which was to overturn a throne, or that I should be called upon to become one of its defenders. A violent ring of the bell roused me from this tranquillity of mind. It was my colonel, who had come to inform me of the stunning news published in the *Moniteur officiel:* the publication of a number of ordinances destroying the liberty of the press, cancelling various articles of the Constitutional Charter, the Civil Code and the Criminal Code, annulling the electoral laws voted by the legislative powers, suppressing the guarantees of personal liberty and dissolving the Chamber of Deputies.

I was frozen with horror at the enumeration of these odious measures and the thought of the misery about to descend upon our France. So painful was the impression made upon me that I seemed already to foresee the greater part of the sinister events that were about to follow.

The colonel said to me on leaving : " There will be an uproar in Paris to-day. To-morrow there will be shots fired, to protest against this *coup d'état* and if possible to undo it."

I went out to try to get a *Moniteur ;* I could not manage to obtain a copy ; there was such a run on it that the people were soon waiting in queues to take their turn at it in the reading-room. Numerous groups, in the streets, were talking excitedly ; the public places were full of young men talking loudly and already conspiring to resist the threatening tyranny. Their faces were solemn and intent ; great excitement was manifest when acquaintances came together. After spending some time in scouring the streets of various quarters of the city, in order to study public opinion, and after I had dined, I went for a walk in the garden of the Luxembourg. There were a great many more people there than usual. The event of the day was the sole subject of conversation. I heard some priests saying, speaking of Charles X : " Now he is the master, the absolute monarch ! God has inspired him ! " The madmen ! I was indignant. I went home early, my heart wrung, a prey to painful reflections.

The Three Glorious Days :—27th July.

On waking I learned that the night before there had been, at the Palais-Royal and the surrounding streets, a great tumult and considerable rioting ; this was the prelude. At half-past three I got into the saddle to go to the Champ de Mars, where the regiment was to drill as part of its ordinary instruction.

At the first interval of rest the colonel assembled the officers round him to speak to them of what was so vividly preoccupying our minds. He told them that it might be possible that the regiment would be called out on active service during the day, to maintain order and disperse assemblies. " If this happens I recommend everyone, officers and men, to be extremely prudent, cool, and indifferent to the provocations, insults and threats you may receive. Do not in any case take the initiative ; wait for the attack before countering ; but then—and only then—you will defend yourselves."

Before the completion of the drill the fortress command ordered out a picket of 200 men and warned the officers not to leave their quarters. The revolutionary storm was beginning to mutter. Everything foretold that it would break that night. The officers were thoughtful ; they dared hardly speak to one another of the uneasiness they felt, so great was the anxiety caused by what was passing. A very small number approved of the ordinances, the great majority condemned them ; yet in a few hours' time we were to take arms to support them, to make them valid and legal ! A cruel and distressing position !

A little before five o'clock in the afternoon the order was given to turn out, at six o'clock, the 1st battalion, with Commandant Barthélemy and the staff, on the Pont-Neuf, facing the Rue de la Monnaie ; the 3rd, Commandant Maillart, successor to battalion-commander Garcias, on the Quai aux Fleurs, guarding the Pont-au-Change, etc. ; and the 2nd (mine) on the Place du Panthéon, with a strong detachment on the Place de l'École-de-Médecine. I, with part of my battalion (they had taken two of my companies to reinforce the two other battalions), was to maintain order in this populous quarter (the districts of Saint-Jacques and Saint-Marceau), contain the Polytechnique and the Schools of Law and Medicine, guard the military prison of Montaigne, La Dette and Sainte-Pélagie, and protect the military hospital of Val-de-Grâce. My instructions were that I must, by means of strong and frequent patrols, maintain my communications with all the establishments of which I have spoken, with the barracks of the Rue de Tournon, and with the two battalions on the Seine.

This was a great deal more than I could have done, even with ten times the force ; moreover, after several rounds through the interior of the area I was guarding, I was compelled gradually to concentrate my forces and to confine my defence to the streets round the Place du Panthéon, in order not to risk, uselessly, the lives of my men in case of an unforeseen surprise attack prepared under the appearance of a friendly attitude. Sixty cartridges were served to each man. In distributing them, as in sending out the patrols, I gave careful commands and explained to the patrol-leaders the use they were to make of them, and how they were to behave in the critical position in which they might frequently find themselves.

Early in the night, about ten o'clock, numerous gatherings of men of all ranks and ages appeared at the entrance to the Place du Panthéon, shouting " Up, the Charter ! Up, the Army ! " [1] but always without hostile intentions, or, at least, without any appearance of such, for they saw very plainly that I was inexpugnable in the position I was occupying on the parvise of the building. In a number of the groups they were carrying dead bodies brought from the Rue Richelieu, the Rue Saint-Honoré, etc. The men who were carrying and accompanying them were shouting, in strident voices : " To arms ! They are killing your brothers, your friends ! Polignac wants to make you slaves," etc. Some men and women went down into the street, right under the eyes of the patrols, to soak their kerchiefs in the blood of these first victims of a revolution beginning under these sinister auspices. The excitement was intense ; shouts of indignation and vengeance were heard on every hand ; but the presence of the

---

[1] I use this modern expression as a more faithful translation, in spirit, of the French *Vive* than the usual " *Long live !* "—TR.

troops still restrained the violence of the masses, or rather their moment for vigorous action had not yet arrived.

In this remote quarter silence fell early. The shops were shut long before dark ; the arms of France and the names of the King and the royal family had been effaced from the shop-signs, and the escutcheons with the Bourbon lilies torn down and shattered. But more serious events were passing elsewhere. We heard musket-shots and volleys of musketry following one another in rapid succession. The civil war had begun ; the troops were at grips with an immense population, ardent, young, brave, indignant. What a constriction of the heart I felt as I heard the first shots ! My God, how they tortured me ! It was war between Frenchmen, in the heart of the kingdom ; there might be great massacres and the loss of all our civil and political rights. The position of those officers who did not share the opinions of the ultra-monarchists, émigrés and priests was truly pitiable. To kill or be killed, for an anti-national cause, which they were defending with regret, was horrible, yet duty demanded it.

After ten o'clock all the lanterns round about were broken, only those on the Place du Panthéon remaining intact. At eleven all was quiet. I stopped the patrols and called off the detachments stationed at different points. Part of my communications were interrupted ; to re-establish them I must have employed force ; I was opposed to doing so. My aim and my instructions were to maintain order and not to irritate that part of the population which had so far displayed a great deal of prudence and moderation.

Shortly before two o'clock I received the order to withdraw my troops to the Mouffetard barracks. The men were dreadfully exhausted. Thus closed the evening of this first day, which, if it was tempestuous, was at least not bloody.

28TH JULY.

At eight o'clock in the morning the order came to take arms and reoccupy the positions of the day before. At nine o'clock I took up my position on the peristyle of the Panthéon, and sent outposts to all the openings debouching on the Place. I wished also to extend my influence to other remote points, but the insurrection was making such progress and the hostile feeling was increasing so that I had, in order not to expose, uselessly, the lives of my men, to restrict my defensive action to the ground I occupied.

A few hours later the insurrectionary bands became more numerous, more arrogant, more hideous, in a certain sense, in their monstrous composition. They were all armed with infantry muskets or shot-guns which had been taken from the depots of the National Guard, the *mairies*, or the houses of the sergeant-majors, who had retained them on disbanding in 1827 ; others came from the troops who had been disarmed at their guard-houses, or were obtained by pillaging the armourers' shops of Paris. Those who had no muskets were armed with pistols, sabres, foils with the buttons off, hatchets, scythes, pitchforks or iron-bound cudgels. Flags, black or tricoloured, with incendiary inscriptions, made their appearance. Excited shouts, provocations, threats and sinister outcries were heard in all directions, but always at a respectful distance from the troops. Calm and inspiring in their restrained strength, they watched unmoved the passage of the surging populace, who shouted continually : " Down with the Guard ! Down with the gendarmes ! Down with the King ! Down with the Bourbons ! Down with the Ministers ! " and then : " Up the Charter, up the Republic, up the Army ! " accordingly as they were led by men of more or less anarchical leanings, or those who were more or less civilized. At the same time the general was being beaten in all the streets, the tocsin sounding in all the churches, while the great bell of the cathedral made its mighty voice heard, and all together sounded the call to arms. The paving of the streets was being torn up, and they were being barricaded, while paving-stones were being accumulated in the upper storeys of the houses in order to stop the progress of the troops and crush the soldiers. In the centre of Paris there was fighting to the death ; all those who sought to defend themselves or offered resistance were being massacred, hacked to pieces. From the position I occupied I could distinctly hear the constant firing and the long whistle of the bullets, many of which flew over us, fired from the Place de Grève to bring down the tricolour that floated from one of the towers of Nôtre-Dame. It was a grand and terrible spectacle ; that of a nation awaking to shatter its fetters, and demand an accounting for the blood it had been made to shed. While I was the adversary of a revolutionary uprising, which I had to oppose, I could not refrain from admiring the energy of these effeminate Parisians, who defended their rights with a courage worthy of this great cause.

My position was momently becoming more difficult. I was surrounded by enemies who still passed me, or were heedful of me. My position, entirely correct in the military sense, almost unassailable, gave them food for reflection. On my side, I did not deceive myself ; if violently attacked I should in no short time succumb, owing to the fewness of my men and the great numbers of combatants I should have had against me, at the first shot fired, without hope of succour or retreat, and with no chance of success, whether for the triumph of the cause I was bound to defend, or the honour of our arms. I tried therefore to act with prudence, to avoid anything that might disturb the sort of neutrality which had naturally established itself between the two parties. I urged

the people to withdraw, or at least to keep to the other
end of the Place, in the Rue Saint-Jacques, and not to
seek to seduce my men from their duty, so as to refrain
from forcing me to the harsh necessity of resorting to
arms. I was often given a hearing and obeyed, but often,
too, we had to march on them with crossed bayonets, to
force them to make room.

At every moment street-corner orators, mandatories
of the people, came up to speak to me, to harangue my
troops at long range, the soldiers laughing at their grotesque appearance and the originality of their language,
which strongly resembled that of their predecessor,
the sans-culotte Père Duchesne of bloody memory.
At other times it was the leaders of passing mobs
who wanted to know my opinions, my feelings ; who
came to sound me, hoping to draw me into their
rebellion. Many of them—these were the better educated
—begged me not to shed French blood and the blood
of my fellow-citizens and subordinates, and made other
requests equally wise and humane, though often deficient
in common sense. I replied to them, time and time
again, that I most certainly should not begin, but that
I should defend myself vigorously if attacked ; that I
wished to have the Place entirely at my disposal, and that
whatever happened I should never abandon my post ;
that if need be I should take refuge in the church and so
entrench myself as to defy all the efforts of the mob.
Several times I was personally threatened ; I had pistols
or daggers held against my chest, to intimidate me, but
this violence did not impress me. I replied peaceably that
they might kill me, but that I had behind me avengers
who would see that the assassins repented of their action.
The sensible men retired, shouting " Up, the major ! "
the hot-headed and ultra-revolutionary with angry threats.
These popular and demagogic incidents were constantly
repeated ; every minute I had to hurry to the head of

these bands, nearly always hideous in appearance, to prevent them from approaching my men, and to listen to their harangues. I had to reply to them and often to handle them most carefully, in order to prevent the misfortune I hoped to avoid, even at the risk of compromising myself in the eyes of the authorities.

My position, already delicate, was aggravated by the vicinity of the military prison of Montaigne, where 400 bandits had been in violent insurrection since the morning, seeking to escape and join the Parisian mob. I had detached a hundred men to contain them. This was a great loss to me, who had only a hundred and fifty men left under my direct command. I once more ran the risk of seeing my detachment carried away or massacred. I was in great perplexity; to leave the prisoners to themselves was to send them to the banks of the Seine, where the question of the divine right of kings or the sovereignty of the people was being decided; it was to send the Parisians a strong reinforcement. I resolved, in the interest of the citizens themselves, not to allow their victory to be dishonoured by auxiliaries so criminal as bad soldiers, but to keep them, at any cost, where they were. Before night they had broken several of the doors and reached that of the courtyard, which they were about to cross, when the captain in command of the detachment warned them that if at the third demand they had not returned to their dormitories he would fire on them. This threat did not stop them; they continued to demolish the building with greater fury than before. Finally, after the third reading of the martial law, in the presence of a commissary of police, the captain gave the order to fire. One man was killed and five fell wounded at the first volley aimed toward the door. The men at once entered the building with crossed bayonets and all was quiet for the rest of the night.

The heat all day was excessive. The men stationed

on the peristyle of the Panthéon, exposed for eight hours to the scorching rays of the sun, were affected by a thirst which greatly exhausted them.   I was careful to give them water acidulated with vinegar, the better to quench their thirst and to prevent illness.   A few townsfolk brought them wine ;   I should have received it with gratitude under any other circumstances, but as things were I feared the intoxication, the mental excitement and disorders to which it might lead.

Through the medium of some peaceable townsfolk who were loyal to me I had kept more or less in touch with the barracks of Mouffetard, where the stores of clothing, provisions, arms and munitions of war were kept, and the records of the corps, etc.   These means of communication eventually broke down, so that I no longer knew what was happening outside the area which I occupied.   I saw no agent of the authorities, received no advice, no instructions to guide me ;   I was left entirely to my own resources :   on which, as a matter of fact, I congratulated myself, as I was able to act on my own inspiration.

Mine was the only body under arms in all this part of Paris.   But for the Place du Panthéon and a few regimental depots, well barricaded, the population was master of the entire left bank of the Seine.   It was in the Paris of the right bank that the fighting was going on.   All those outposts which, stupidly, were not ordered to rejoin their corps had been swept away, disarmed, massacred as long ago as the morning.   The powder-magazine of Deux-Moulins had been captured and the stores of arms at the *mairies* pillaged, so that the rebellion had acquired, by the evening, an incontestable superiority over the defenders of a throne which, by nightfall, was irrevocably lost.

About ten o'clock I learned from men on whom I could rely that an attack was to be attempted on my barracks, to carry off the arms and powder stored there ;   and that the troops stationed there were to retire on the Tuileries when the rioting was less violent. All seemed fairly quiet around me and in front. The distressing scenes of the day were over ; but this might well be a deceptive calm, the precursor of a storm that might break upon me at any moment. Some formidable barricades had been raised between me and my barracks, and in all the streets that led to the outer boulevard. My presence where I was becoming useless, I decided, after all I had learned, to get out of this rat-trap as quickly as I could and retire to my barracks at Mouffetard and Lourcine, either to protect them or to await there the climax of events.

Before beginning my movement of retreat I sent men to occupy the principal turnings into the streets I should have to traverse and stop the building of the barricades, so that I could effect this voluntary withdrawal in order. As guard at the military prison of Montaigne I left my company and a section of light infantry. All was done in the profoundest silence, with the regularity of a strategical retreat. We were everywhere respected and even welcomed as we passed. The inhabitants of these quarters, less excited than in the centre of Paris, were interested in treating us carefully ; only the hot-heads and ex-convicts who abound in the Faubourg Saint-Marceau, and the drunkards, were likely to oppose our return to barracks in order to cause a disturbance and, as regards some of them, to profit by it. By eleven o'clock at night I was back in barracks. Similarly, the companies from the Lourcine barracks at once returned thither. I organized my means of defence and distributed officers and men over all the necessary points, to avoid any surprise or to repel any open attack in strength. I expressly forbade them to fire first and to do nothing without sending to me for orders.

In the course of the night I had news of the two other

battalions and some details as to their operations during
the day. In the case of the first there had been some
bloodshed despite all the measures taken to avoid this
misfortune. It cost them so much to fire on their fellow-
citizens, and to defend by such cruel means a cause of
which all men who loved their country disapproved,
that it would have required a very weighty motive to
lead Colonel Perrégaux, one of the most humane soldiers
I have ever known, to depart from the moderate line of
conduct which he had laid down for himself. This is
how the thing came about :

The 1st battalion had been some hours at the entrance
of the Rue de la Monnaie, on the continuation of the
Pont-Neuf, guarding the quays and this street, when it
received orders to extricate a battalion of the Royal
Guard and two guns which were blocked in the market
of Les Innocents. It marched in column along the Rue
de la Monnaie and the Rue du Roule, meeting with no
resistance, crossing the barricades without opposition, the
inhabitants readily giving way to the colonel's entreaties
and the force of the reasons which he gave for fulfilling
his mission, without shedding blood. " Fall back ! " he
cried to them ; " I shall not fire on you ; I shall never
give such an order as that." They replied : " Up, the
colonel ! long live the god of prudence ! " But when
the battalion came to the Rue Saint-Honoré things were
no longer the same ; in vain did the officers parley ; they
could not make themselves heard. In the heat of the
discussion an officer of the gendarmerie came on the scene
with some gendarmes, who, being between the 1st and
2nd half-companies, opened fire with their pistols on the
defenders of the barricades at the points of intersection
of the cross-roads. From that moment all was lost ;
a brisk fusillade began on either side ; the barricades were
carried with the bayonet, and the battalion presently found
itself in the market-place of the Rue des Prouvaires.

There the resistance was so vigorous that in spite of the good behaviour and extreme bravery of the troops they were forced to retake by fighting the position from which they had started. This affair cost the life of a lieutenant (Mari) and eight soldiers; two officers and twenty soldiers were seriously wounded. A sergeant was killed by a pistol-bullet fired by a virago who came out of an alley where she was in ambush. The colonel was for a long time the target of concealed marksmen, but his lucky star saved him from being hit in the body; only his clothes were perforated. His horse received six bullets and fell with its rider as it was crossing a barricade in front of the carabiniers.

Meanwhile the 3rd battalion, stationed at the flower-market, remained there all day in a position as critical as those of the other two, but without any armed enemies before it. Commandant Maillart was three times ordered by General Taton in person to open fire on the snarling crowd surrounding them. He firmly refused, stating that he would not do so until he was fired on. The general withdrew, furious, threats on his lips and vengeance in his heart. Thanks to the prudence and great coolness of the commandant this same general and the battalions of the Guard who occupied the Hotel de Ville and the Place de Grève were able to retire in safety during the night. If the commandant had obeyed the general's thoughtless orders he would infallibly have lost the position; there were armed men at all the windows in the market-place, who would have fired with deadly effect; the battalion would have been decimated, the position lost, and communications between La Grève and the Tuileries intercepted.

At two o'clock in the morning the two battalions were able to bivouac in the garden of the Tuileries. At this hour the tricolour flag was floating over nine-tenths of Paris.

29TH JULY.

Daylight found me ready to defend myself if I were suddenly attacked, as the success of the previous day made me fear might happen, but I decided by all means possible to avoid the disaster on the point of befalling us and all the townsfolk round about us. So far I had no plan of conduct but that which honour bade me follow: to defend myself and die. However, when I had secret warning that my barracks were mined; that petards had been prepared to blow up the gates and a wall separating us from the adjacent gardens; that some of the troops of the garrison (two regiments, the 5th and 53rd of the line) were wearing the tricolour cockade; that the Royal Guard itself refused to fight any longer; that all were retreating toward Saint-Cloud and that the evacuation of Paris would in a few hours be complete, if it was not so already, I understood, after due reflection, that my position was neither reasonable nor tenable. To accept battle would have been to doom to certain death the fifteen officers and two hundred men, sick and whole, whom I had with me; to doom to destruction the barracks, the valuable stores and the neighbouring houses. Torrents of blood would flow; my memory would be held responsible for all these calamities; and for whom? For a perjured king, for an inept Government imposed on France by foreign bayonets. Until then I had served faithfully and conscientiously; I had nothing with which to reproach myself as regards the Bourbons; but as this wretched, ill-advised sovereign had broken his oaths, had he not freed me from mine?

Another motive, no less powerful, ought also to guide me. However excellent my defence I must in the end succumb, for I could not look to anyone for succour and all paths of retreat were cut off. How could I retreat in the midst of an infuriated populace, through barricaded streets, struggling with forces ten times as great as my own, or perhaps more numerous still ? To begin hostilities and then to surrender if fortune were unfavourable would be to get ourselves slaughtered without mercy, for we could expect no generosity from those that we ourselves had just been trying to kill. . . . I reflected thus walking to and fro in the courtyard ; I was calm and gave my orders very coolly, but inwardly I experienced an uneasiness more readily understood than defined.

Before ten o'clock I was warned by all the assembled officers that numerous bands were moving on all the barracks about Paris to disarm the troops shut up in them and seize the weapons in the stores. Nowhere had any resistance been offered ; the troops had submitted to the right of might, to the law of reason. The officers told me it would be insane to behave otherwise, and that for their part they were resolved to give way if proposals were made which one could accept without dishonour. I replied that I was certainly of the same opinion, and sent them to their several posts.

After ten o'clock several bodies of the populace, more or less numerous, presented themselves in front of the barracks (Rue Neuve-Sainte-Geneviève). Their voices, gestures, costumes and general aspect were horrifying. The greater number of these heroes of the faubourgs and suburbs were armed. At their head we noted well-dressed men of good manners, wearing decorations ; leaders, in short, with whom one might open negotiations. From the window of the first floor, where I was stationed, I made a sign that I wished to speak. At first they were silent, but when they heard me speak of conditions and stipulations, of neutrality to be observed, shouts of " Throw down your weapons ! To the assault !" from energumens, drunk with success, drowned my voice. All their muskets were pointed at me ; a few soldiers standing about me seized me, saying : " Come back, commandant, they will kill you!" The excitement was intense; already they were climbing up the lamp-posts. This was, in every sense of the words, one of the hideous scenes of 1793.

Still remaining at my post, I succeeded in making them understand that I wished to speak with two or three of their leaders. This proposal accepted, I had the gate opened for the three deputed persons who were there : a pupil of the Polytechnique, a law student of my acquaintance, and a man wearing decorations, probably a half-pay officer, which did not please me at all. After a rather lengthy discussion, it was agreed, at this diplomatic and military conference, which took place in the guard-house, that no one should enter the barracks, that I should hand over only a certain number of muskets, which would be passed through the windows, and that the student of the École Polytechnique, who was rather unwell, should remain with me as hostage for the guarantee of the agreed conditions. All, on both sides, was done in good faith. When I had declared, several times, that I had no more weapons to give they retired well satisfied, shouting "Long live the commandant and the 15th Light Infantry!" As for me, I cordially consigned them to the devil. I re-armed those of the men who were no longer armed and sent them all back to their appointed posts.

I could but congratulate myself on the leaders with whom I negotiated. They were full of delicacy and good feeling. In order to make the affair less painful to me they complimented me with much goodwill on the manner in which I had conducted the affair to its termination, my success in saving the stores, my prudent and able conduct the previous day, in the Place du Panthéon, etc. Despite all these laudatory and generous expressions the idea of having surrendered arms without fighting obsessed me like a disgrace. It seemed to me that I had tarnished my twenty-six years' service by a shameful weakness.

For that matter, I saw no sign whatever, in the looks of
the officers, of blame or displeasure ; on the contrary,
they all assured me of their profound gratitude and their
satisfaction at having been honourably extricated from
a pretty ticklish position.   To prove this to me they all
embraced me.   This opening of hearts, after such a crisis,
was in some sense salutary for us.   If this did not justify
me, I had at least the approval of all.

The Lourcine and Le Foin barracks were pillaged, but
the soldiers in occupation were respected.   The same fate
befell the barracks of the Bodyguard, the Guard, and
other regiments of the garrison.   The Babylon barracks,
occupied by the Swiss of the Guard, was first of all defended
and then abandoned, after several of the Swiss had fallen
under the fire of an ordered attack by a mass of insurgents.
Fortunately the defenders were able to gain the boulevards
not far away, for they would all have been massacred.
After they had pillaged the barracks the insurgents set
fire to them.

Shortly after I had given up part of my arms other
bands of insurgents presented themselves.   We had to
give still more ;   other bodies followed, with the same
demands.   In vain did I tell them I had no more ;   they
absolutely insisted.   They demanded leave to inspect
the barracks, which I absolutely refused.   To avoid
this misfortune and contact with these tatterdemalion
hordes, I had a few muskets brought up from the magazine,
where there were more than five hundred, with several
thousand ball cartridges.   These bands kept on arriving,
so that I found my position becoming complicated and
alarming.   To save my men, who very soon would be
unable to defend themselves if the plan of entering the
barracks was persisted in, I left the building to invite
a captain of the National Guard, whom I saw in uniform
at the end of the street, to set a post of armed National
Guards to guard and protect it, I ceasing to do so any

longer. I gave him the keys of the magazines and offices, making him responsible for all their contents. He accepted the charge and saved everything except articles of armament and general equipment, which he had brought out in order to organize the companies of his legion.

It was to me a great satisfaction to have no further dealings with all these evil-visaged mobs, most of whom came to obtain muskets in order to sell them to the National Guard, which was hastily organizing itself to save Paris from pillage. I knew the regiment had left Paris, and had no longer any fear that the weapons I was giving up would be employed against it. This is what made me so insistent on retaining them. On his part, the captain whom I installed in the guardroom would no longer give them to all who applied. To obtain weapons one had to belong to the ward and be known to a respectable citizen. I said to him repeatedly : " Don't arm the proletariat now that all is over. They might continue the revolution on their own account, and sacrifice us all to demagogic anarchy." My relations with this captain and several other officers who came to support him were most amicable.

During this upheaval the detachment left the day before as guard over the prison of Montaigne returned in good order, but disarmed. In vain did Captain Chardron, who was in command, tell the insurgents that his duty was to prevent the malefactors confined there from scattering through Paris and committing offences and perhaps crimes. There was one of these later gatherings, less prudent than many others that had preceded it, which could not or would not understand his reasons for retaining his arms. They would not listen to him : he had to give way. To resist would have been folly, when all were submitting all round him. However, he did so only at my request. Once he had left, the prisoners came out and soon spread consternation through the streets. The first use they made of their liberty was to call on the captain who had ordered his men to fire on them, that they might kill him. Fortunately he was able to escape by the back door of his apartment and take refuge in a house which no one saw him enter.

At the barracks I had remained, the sole officer, to keep the soldiers true to their duty, protect them, and acquaint them with the new position in which they were about to find themselves. I thought I had convinced them, but the demon of discord and insubordination rose up to destroy the effect of my fatherly advice. " We have no longer any weapons ; we have no flag, no government ; we are therefore freed from the army and masters of our actions ! Hurrah for liberty ! To the devil with discipline and obedience ! " And that very moment they rushed to the door, in order to leave. In vain did I oppose their departure ; the bonds of submission to the laws were shattered ; my voice and my rank were disregarded. I had to give way to this fresh rebellion. At six o'clock I left the barracks. All that had been happening during the last three days had broken my heart ; I still found it difficult to believe, after leaving the barracks in which my power had been so great a few hours earlier, that a throne set so high in the opinion of the nations had just collapsed ; that a king so powerful was cast aside, his crown shattered, while he himself perhaps had fled, to avoid the anger of a great and wrathful nation. When I thought of all this I felt dizzy and a prey to a sort of consuming fever.

My brother-in-law, M. Kellermann, librarian at the École des Ponts et Chaussées, came to the barracks for me shortly before I left. His presence did me good. I had need of sympathy and consolation, of proofs of friendship that might drive from my mind the impressions of the day. They were painful ones. I could not be otherwise than pleased to see France recovering her political power, but the shock had been too violent, too extraordinary, not to shake my reason; so that I could not at first sight appreciate all the advantages that such an upheaval might bring about. I was afraid of civil war, the triumph of the proletarians, the institution of a republic, war with our neighbours; in short, all the ills engendered by anarchy and the triumph of extremists.

My brother-in-law dined with me at my lodgings in a private boarding-house which provided us with all we needed. He gave me the details of what had happened during the last few days, of which I was completely ignorant. During dinner a lady, young and comely, but whom I did not know well enough to hope for such a great proof of interest, came to see me with her husband, to express her joy in finding me safe and sound. I was very greatly touched by this kindly attention; a mother, a wife, a sister, could not have expressed her delight more fully, nor her natural affection. This unexpected visit made me forget many bitter reflections.

In the course of this day, the 29th, the two battalions of the regiment which were on the other bank of the Seine, after passing the part of the night and the early part of the day in the garden of the Tuileries, went to take up their position in the Champs-Élysées. This was the moment when the Parisians attacked the King's palace and, a little later, the Louvre. The palace taken, all the troops retired in disorder on Saint-Cloud, by all the roads that led thither. Our 15th, still rallied and self-possessed, formed the rear-guard supporting the retreat. It withdrew along the riverside quays. Unfortunately the Les Bonshommes or Passy barrier was closed and defended by the National Guards of Auteuil, Boulogne, Passy, etc. The situation was critical; attacked in the rear and on the flank, placed between

the Seine and the hill of Chaillot, which was covered
with bold and skilful sharpshooters, they found themselves in a trap, unable to make any movement, unless
to retrace their steps, march over the dead bodies of the
Parisians, and capture the Pont d'Iéna. Captain Bidou,
who was in command of the first company of carabineers,
had the happy idea of ordering his company to hold the
butt-ends of their muskets in the air. This pacific signal
was understood, and the barrier was opened to give passage
to the one regiment that was not demoralized. Although
it did not return their fire, some marksmen ensconced
on the hill, and hidden behind walls, still continued to
fire on it, and, unhappily, with cruel accuracy. A
captain was killed, as well as several men, while two
officers and a number of men were wounded. They fell
victims to the deadly skill of a few individuals, who,
doubtless, thought to win distinction by murdering,
in cold blood and without danger to themselves, fellow-
countrymen, truer Frenchmen and better citizens than
themselves, since they did not reply to their attacks,
but withdrew without fighting. This barbarous action
was indeed a crime which one cannot too violently
reprobate.

Having passed the barrier, the regiment proceeded
to rest in the shade of the Bois de Boulogne, where the
people of Auteuil, at the request of the colonel, eagerly
brought them food. The heat was excessive ; they were
worn out with fatigue, exasperation and dismal fore-
bodings. It was early afternoon. The Dauphin came
to see the regiment. He was welcomed coldly. Prestige
had flown ; misfortune had fallen on all the heads that
a few days earlier had been so proud and erect. They
saw a man, of less than average merit, who came forward
when the danger was passed, who had the grace neither
to thank nor to encourage them. The defection of the
troops began after this review. They began to march

towards Vaucresson, passing by Saint-Cloud, where they deliberated for some time, to decide whether they should take the liberty of crossing the park, in order to shorten the distance. The regiment passed under the King's windows ; he was then at dinner, which was doubtless why he did not trouble himself to look out and seize the opportunity to utter such words as might have repaid the troops a little for the fatigue and danger they had incurred. This uncouth indifference keenly wounded the officers, who greatly regretted having left Paris, and having risked their lives for a prince who held them of no account.

ADHESION TO THE NEW GOVERNMENT.

30th July.—Early in the morning the greater number of the officers of the regiment who were in Paris assembled at my rooms to form, in concert, a decision as to the line of conduct we should follow. It was unanimously resolved that I should, during the forenoon, call on the lieutenant-general, Comte Gérard, a member of the Provisional Government, and at the house of M. Laffitte, banker and deputy, to give our adhesion to the new order of things, and to receive orders in our singular position.

Being in command of the corps in the absence of the colonel, who was with the two battalions, and the lieutenant-colonel, who was on leave at Lyons, I had, to begin with, to consider the means of subsistence of the troops, who for two days had been without bread ; and also to make the men plainly understand that they must not imitate the conduct of their comrades, who had left their companies, and before long would be arrested, either in Paris or on the highways, if they should attempt to go to their homes. I advised them, above all, to retain their kit, and in good condition, if they left their quarters, and to refrain from going to drink in the cabarets, for fear of quarrels with the heroes of the day, who were extremely insolent. This advice was largely wasted. The work of several years disappeared completely in a day. No more respect, submission, discipline or soldierly bearing; the anarchy and disorder were almost complete. By the evening the men's kits were sold, torn up, covered with mud and grease. They were no longer soldiers.

After my visit to the barracks I proceeded to the seat of the Provisional Government, Rue d'Artois (now Rue Laffitte) to fulfil my mission. General Gérard was not there, so I addressed myself to General Pajol, second in command of the armed forces of Paris. My welcome left nothing to be desired, and I obtained all I asked for the well-being of my subordinates. After a long talk with him concerning our position and the part we had played in the recent events, I withdrew, very well satisfied, more so than I had dared to hope, for I had feared lest the violent articles published in the newspapers, attacking the regiment, might have prejudiced him against us.

I then went to the Hôtel de Ville to see General La Fayette, to inform him of our intentions. He did not keep me long, being very busy receiving reports and giving instructions. I was horribly tired when I reached home again.

This necessary walk through Paris, this long journey in civilian clothes, on foot, on account of the barricades, and in an overwhelming heat, showed me the stupendous effects and frightful ravages of three days' civil war. In all the streets, on all the quays, on the boulevards and the bridges, barricades had been established every sixty paces, four to five feet in height, built of stagecoaches, omnibuses, private carriages, carts, lorries, barrels, boxes or planks. On the boulevards the trees were felled and thrown across the road; the streets were partly torn up and littered with broken bottle-glass to hold up the cavalry. Paris was like a city taken by assault. Its aspect was stern and melancholy. There was little movement in the streets ; numbers of ill-dressed men grouped at different points ; no well-dressed women, no carriages, no open shops ; but there were funeral processions, women busied in making lint, improvised guard-houses at all the street corners, broken windows, broken street lanterns, walls covered with proclamations calling the people to arms, and orderlies on horseback going in all directions. This sad and striking spectacle proved how fierce the storm of revolution had been. Almost all the barriers and the guard-houses of the garrison had been burned. Many works of art were mutilated, broken, stolen, in the galleries of the Louvre and the apartments of the palace ; the artillery museum, the archbishop's palace and the cathedral had likewise been sacked and devastated. Often enough the victors gave proof of generosity, humanity and a disinterested spirit. But there were also those who mercilessly killed unarmed men, threw them alive into the Seine or slew them from behind. Four men of the regiment, a captain of the Royal Guard, a friend, with whom I had dined on Sunday, the 25th, some of the men of the Royal Guard, some of the Swiss, and some gendarmes had suffered this fate. The total losses of the regiment were a captain, a lieutenant and sixteen sergeants, corporals or men killed ; four officers and thirty-nine non-commissioned officers and men wounded. The regiment was one of those which behaved with the greatest prudence and fired the fewest shots, and was none the less vituperated by the Liberal press as parricidal and an enemy to liberty.

On returning to the Hôtel de Ville I learned that two of our officers (a captain, loaded with debt, and the standard-bearer, a man of very dubious reputation, both in debt to the colonel) who had deserted their comrades and their flag the previous day, in the Bois de

Boulogne, had called at the Hôtel de Ville to offer their services to the Provisional Government and to parade a patriotic devotion of which they knew nothing two days earlier. By dint of lies and calumnies they induced General Dubourg to believe that if he gave them full powers they would organize a model and reliable battalion, which it would not be if it were left in the hands of the present officers, all inspired, especially their commander (myself), with a very bad spirit. They obtained without difficulty the powers they asked for and at once got to work. The captain appointed himself battalion commander, and made all the sergeants-major sub-lieutenants, until he could entice over to his side a few officers, whom he could make captains and lieutenants. I reached home just as he was thus revolutionizing the three barracks. I found there all the officers of my battalion, who were impatiently awaiting me, furious with indignation against the audacity of these officers, whose behaviour in this matter was on a par with their habitual cowardice. Having heard their reports and entreaties and received proof of their esteem and affection, I wrote to General La Fayette to advise him of what was happening, of the surprise which had been sprung on General Dubourg, and of the honourable conduct of all the officers of my battalion during the three critical days, and to prove to him that we were calumniated by two intriguers without influence over the spirit of the troops, who had basely deserted their flag in order to go begging to Paris for promotion which they did not deserve.

An officer took my letter, and half an hour later I received orders to retain the command, and likewise all the officers who were with me. I immediately inserted this reply in the order of the day in each of the three barracks and gave orders for the arrest of the two officers and their removal to the Abbaye prison.

31*st July.*—In the forenoon I called on Lieutenant-
General Comte Roguet, appointed commandant of the
troops in Paris, to take his orders and report as to what
had happened in the corps. The act of indiscipline of
the two officers greatly displeased him. He ordered me
to have them arrested. He requested me to send him
that evening a very circumstantial report as to the spirit
and situation of that portion of the corps which I commanded, the regimental stores, the losses experienced,
and the means employed to assure the subsistence of
the troops since the recent events.

At three o'clock, when the report was completed, the
lieutenant-colonel arrived from Lyons. I presented it
to him to sign and convey to its destination in his quality
of corps commander. Out of modesty he refused both
proposals, but then, on reflection, foreseeing that this
visit might be useful to him later, he accompanied me to
headquarters, in the Place Vendôme, where the Comte
Roguet was lodging. What was my surprise, in our
interview with the general on the efforts we should have
to make to restore discipline, to hear this officer say,
with great sufficiency, that he greatly regretted having
been absent from the regiment during the recent events ;
that his presence in the corps, and the influence which
he exerted there, would have prevented the 15th from
taking part in this conflict, and that on the very first day
he would have induced it to take the side of the people !
This impudence disgusted me, and evoked the perfectly
simple and natural retort : " And duty, and your oaths ? "
The general nodded approval of my remark, and
dismissed us.

Out of doors we had a lively altercation, in which I
reproached him for seeming to endeavour to cast blame
on those who had merely put into practice what he himself had so often recommended in his addresses to the
assembled troops, when he could not find words to express

his fidelity and devotion to the King and his love for the royal family. Such is indeed the spirit of many men I have known ! When the idol is erect they burn incense before it ; when it lies prostrate they kick it.

This same day the Duc d'Orléans was recognized as lieutenant-general of the kingdom, having accepted the offer made him by the Chamber of Deputies to place himself at the head of the Provisional Government. His arrival in Paris and his presentation to the people by General La Fayette in the Place de Grève produced a good effect on all who loved their country. They no longer despaired of the salvation of the motherland.

1st August.—In the forenoon the lieutenant-colonel, to whom I had just restored the command of the regiment, assembled all the men in the courtyard of the Lourcine barracks to address them. He told us very solemnly that he had faithfully served the Republic, the Consulate, the Emperor Napoleon, Louis XVIII and Charles X, and that he would similarly serve the sovereign whom the Chambers might call to the throne. The officers smiled, knowing him for the veteran weathercock of the regiment. As a matter of fact, it was neither his fault nor ours if events had forced us to serve so many different governments, but he might have dispensed with making a parade of our shameful palinodes, of the frequency with which we had solemnly taken our oaths, which often were so lightly held. His expenditure of eloquence did little to move the soldiers, who regarded themselves as released from all kinds of discipline since the 29th July.

2nd August.—On this day the remnants of the 1st and 3rd battalions returned to us. The colonel sent them back to us without accompanying them.

This is their history : I have said that the two battalions arrived in Vaucresson on the 29th July. Very uncomfortable in their bivouac and uneasy as to the consequences which their departure from Paris might have for the officers, the latter began to grumble. By the 30th the ambitious officers, and those who were married men, began furtively to slip away. Their defection, and the desertion of the soldiers, became more ostensible on the 31st. Indeed, on that day, Colonel Perrégaux gave orders to move towards Rambouillet, whither the Court had retired. The colonel, who had bitterly censured the ordinances of the 25th July, did not wish to involve his regiment in continuing a defence which was in accordance neither with its principles nor with its interests, but it was distasteful to him to desert an unlucky cause without having received official notice that his services were no longer necessary. This was why he thought it necessary to approach Rambouillet, where the King had already been abandoned by the greater part of his bodyguard and by his courtiers. This advance singularly thinned the ranks; by night practically none were left but those loyal and devoted men who, whatever may befall, are always found at their posts. Consequently, the colonel invited the two battalion commanders to march their men to Paris, taking suitable measures to ensure their return in a lawful fashion. He had the flag saluted with military honours and set out for Rambouillet accompanied by an officer and a detachment of sergeants and corporals who offered of their own accord to escort the flag. On his arrival at the château he returned the flag of the 15th regiment to the King, saying: " Sire, you entrusted it to me; I return it to you, since I can no longer defend it." The King thanked him earnestly and appointed him Commander of the Legion of Honour, thinking still further to reward his loyalty to misfortune, but the sovereign power was shattered in his hands since his departure from Saint-Cloud. It was a dead letter.

We, then, the remnants of our 1st and 3rd battalions,

arrived in Paris during the forenoon of the 2nd August, under the command of the officers, drums beating and bayonets fixed. This was the first body of armed troops of the line seen in our quarter since the Revolution, and they appeared in this martial fashion by virtue of a convention made with the commissaries sent to receive their adhesion. Honest folks saw with pleasure that the regular and disciplined armed forces were about to resume their duties in the capital.

Thanks to the arrival of these two battalions, the regiment was once more united. But it was no longer the same regiment. What divisions among the officers! Ambitions were betrayed that had but little to justify them ; hatred was manifested whenever we met together. The 15th had ceased to be the model of the other corps. Of the 1,500 men who stood to attention at the review of the 26th not 400 were left. More than 1,000 men had deserted. As for its smart bearing and appearance, they no longer existed. Most of the soldiers sold at night the equipment which had been served out to them in the morning.

THE JULY MONARCHY

9th August, 1830.—Louis-Philippe, King of the French, accepted the new Charter and took the oath before the deputies assembled in the palace of the Chamber. . . .

As for me, at half-past two in the morning I took command of a numerous fatigue party which I was to lead to Vincennes, there to receive 600 muskets. I returned at two o'clock in the afternoon, greatly displeased with the men, and with their officers, who no longer dared to give them orders. This day left me with painful memories of the disastrous effect of indiscipline. What a difference from the soldiers of before the Revolution! What a profound change in their characters in so few days! One thing that was very largely responsible for the numerous acts of disobedience of which the men were guilty was hunger. Remaining at Vincennes longer than was expected, nine other regiments were there at the same time; the hour of breakfast had long gone by when our turn came to go on duty, which exasperated the men, who were very easily irritated at this time of social dissolution. The greatest difficulty was to prevent them from entering Paris by the Rue du Faubourg-Saint-Antoine, which I did not wish them to pass through lest the people, greedy for weapons, should disarm them; to which my insubordinate fellows would readily have lent themselves, in order to save themselves the trouble of carrying arms. Finally, almost single-handed, I managed to overcome all resistance and reached our quarters without losing a single musket, despite all the temptations for the men to sell them that occurred during this long march, round the enclosure walls, from the barrier of La Rapée to the barracks. If the men were at that date bad soldiers, they were at least honest fellows.

THE ROYAL FAMILY.

On the evening of the 9th August I went, with the other field officers of the regiment, to pay my respects to our new King and the royal family. I was greatly surprised by the remarkable simplicity and kindliness of this fine and interesting family, which was there amidst us all to save us from anarchy. After conversing a few minutes with the King we were presented to the Queen, and to Mme. Adélaïde, the young princesses, the Duc de Chartres and the Duc de Nemours. There were many present, notably the marshals : the Duke of Dalmatia (Soult), the Duke of Treviso (Mortier), the Duke of Taranto (Macdonald), the Duke of Reggio (Oudinarde), Comte Jourdan, and Comte Molitor, all in full uniform as dignitaries of the kingdom, amidst a great number of general officers. We were in the glazed gallery of the Palais-Royal, as much to enjoy the freshness of the evening as to see the crowd of sightseers in the great courtyard and the garden. The whole place was full. Shouts of " Long live the King ! " and patriotic airs played by different bands were continually audible, until the rain came to interrupt this admirable universality of satisfaction. We passed into the salons. The Queen, the princesses and a few ladies took their places by a round table, at which they were working ; the men moved slowly through the salons, conversing. The King, M. Laffitte and other political personages, whom the Revolution had just raised to the highest offices, were conversing together in the embrasure of a window ; the princes were receiving fresh arrivals and especially their fellow-disciples of Henri IV's College. In short, everything about this first royal assembly charmed one by its simplicity. It was a family picture, full of pleasant feeling and hopes of happiness.

REVIEW OF THE NATIONAL GUARD.

On the 28th August the regiment changed its barracks. It was sent to the École Militaire. On the 29th, in the Champ de Mars, there was a great review of the National Guard, held for the purpose of distributing flags to the battalions of the twelve legions.

This ceremony filled all those who witnessed it with admiration. It was difficult to realize that in the space of a month 45,000 men could have been clothed, armed and equipped, and have acquired sufficient training to execute passably well the different movements of their drill and of marching in column. The Champ de Mars was almost filled by these citizen-soldiers, who, drawn up in several lines, offered a spectacle calculated to inspire a justifiable pride.

The arrival of the " king of the barricades," as the Parisians called him, was announced less loudly by the salvoes of artillery at the Invalides than by the enthusiastic cheers of 300,000 people, gathered on the sloping sides and the benches of this vast forum. This immense population, eager to see the sovereign it had just set over itself, crowded round him, seized his hands, and lavished on him all manner of expressions of its homage. He was a father amidst his children, a crowned citizen amidst his equals. No guards, no gold-laced courtiers, but many officers of all ranks who formed his retinue. As the legions were not yet all assembled, he entered the palace, going up into the apartments of honour, where the Queen was in the midst of her little family, to wait until all was ready. He then repaired on foot to an enormous tent, erected on a tall staging opposite the palace of the École Militaire. Some of the marshals of France, some generals, and a numerous staff accompanied him. General Lafayette, commander-in-chief of the National Guards of France, suffering from gout, was leaning on the arm of the Duc d'Orléans. After the distribution of the colours and the administration of the oath, the King, mounted on horseback, passed along the front of all the legions, and then took his place under the balcony of the palace of the École Militaire, to watch them march past in column.

The officers of the regiment, as the hosts of the École Militaire, stood at the foot of the great staircase to receive the Queen, who came through the courtyard of the barracks in an ordinary open carriage. Some deputations of young ladies offered her flowers, having first congratulated her. She kissed them all with much feeling. Twelve young ladies who represented the twelve wards of Paris were remarkable for their beauty and graceful elegance. I followed the Queen into the large apartments, where I remained for some time to enjoy the magnificent view of the Champ de Mars at this stage of the proceedings.

On the 13th September the new oath was administered, taken individually by all the officers, non-commissioned officers and men, in front of the tricolour flag, in the courtyard of the barracks. On the 26th there was a review by the King.

The King, passing before the front of each regiment, made a prodigious number of promotions to fill the vacancies and attach the army to the new institutions. One would have thought there had been a battle of Wagram or Moscow. But is not a great political revolution, which overturns all acquired positions and has to satisfy many new demands, likewise a great and victorious battle, with victors and devoted combatants to be rewarded ? It was 1815 over again ; the same claims, the same ridiculous features, the same apostasies.

The Duc d'Aumale at Eight Years of Age.

A few days later, on the 28th September, Barrès dined at the Palais-Royal.

I sat at the King's table. We were sixty-three. Placed at one end of the table, beside the aide de camp on duty, Brigadier-General Comte de Rumigny, I was able from this point to observe all the guests, whose names I obtained from the aide de camp. The beauty and symmetry of the table appointments, the delicacy of the dishes, many of which were new to me, the luxury of the decorations and the resplendent accessories, such as one could hardly find save on a royal table, enlightened me in the most attractive fashion as to the advantages of wealth and the delights of the great world.

At this table were the King, the Queen, Madame Adélaïde, and the eldest daughter of the King. The Duc d'Orléans and his brother, the Duc de Nemours, sat at the head of another table, where all the younger guests were placed. Coffee was served in the great reception-rooms, where I was accosted by the Duc d'Aumale, a child of eight, who charmed me by his amiable babble and by knowledge that astonished me, although I did not take it to be greater than it really was because of his rank. He knew that the regiment was going to Strasbourg and I to Wissemburg. Surprised by his remarks, I asked him how he could know this.

" It is very simple," he said. " Your captain of carabineers is a friend of my tutor. It was from him I heard all I know about where you are going, and when you go."

This charming child did not leave me all the evening, explaining to me all the pictures of the gallery, the names of the painters and the beauties of each. All this was said with delightful grace and ease of manner.

STROLLS IN PARIS.

Not content with noting from day to day the many important events which he witnessed, Barrès, with that unsleeping curiosity which was one of his characteristics, was careful to note in his diary all the novelties which impressed him in Paris during his seven years' residence (1823-1830). Public buildings, plays, public vehicles—Favorites, Dames Blanches, Batignollaises, etc.—everything interested him, and he did not fail to remark on the increasing difficulties of vehicular traffic and foot-passengers in the streets.

My favourite promenade was the garden of the Luxembourg ; but after my wife's death I went there less frequently, the neighbourhood recalling too many painful memories. I inspected with pleasure its superb collection of rose-bushes, as well as the nursery in the enclosure of the Chartreuse. I went often to the galleries of the Luxembourg Palace, to admire the fine modern paintings assembled there. They are not there permanently ; when the painter who has produced them dies his works are taken to the Louvre, and replaced by those which the Government has bought from the public exhibitions. Thus the museum of the Luxembourg is the museum of the living painters : the Louvre that of the dead painters. Generally speaking, the sight of pictures of the modern school gives greater pleasure to those who are not connoisseurs than the majority of the pictures in the Louvre. But artists and cultivated amateurs judge otherwise.

Another public promenade which I greatly liked was the Jardin des Plantes. There, in the fine weather, I spent many charming mornings and evenings. How I delighted to inspect in detail the Botanic Garden, to go through the hothouses and the numerous galleries of the Museum! For the rest, the whole of Paris drew me into all its corners. There is not a quarter of the city, old or new, not a newly opened street, a public building, a passage-way, a bazaar, a bridge, a fountain that I have not visited ; above all, those built or improved since 1823. I will suppress a host of facts and comments noted in my old travelling-diary, which have little interest for me now that I am growing old ; but here are some that still give me food for reflection :

On the public place where the unfortunate Louis XVI was guillotined on the 21st January, 1793—a place which has necessarily borne the names of Louis XV (before 1789) ; de la Revolution (until 1802) ; de la Concorde (until 1814) ; de Louis XVI (until 1830)—and which is now until further notice once more known as the Place de la Concorde. On this public square, where one beholds a palace without a king—the Tuileries ; a temple without dedication —the Madeleine ; and a triumphal arch without consecration—the Arc de l'Étoile—a monument was being erected to Louis XVI. The pedestal only was completed when the revolution of 1830 broke forth.

During my residence in Paris the colossal statues were placed on the balustrades of the handsome bridge that bore the name of Louis XVI : white marble statues of Condé, Turenne, Du Guesclin, Bayard, Suger, Sully, Richelieu, Colbert, Tourville, Duquesne, Duguay-Trouin and Suffren ; these have disappeared. At the central point of the Champs-Élysée a monument to Louis XV was being erected, still far from completion ; I think recent events will prevent further work upon it. The superb Arc de Triomphe at the barrier of l'Étoile or Neuilly was nearing completion. I saw the first stone of it laid in

1806 ; it was then dedicated to the French armies of the Republic and the Empire ; under the Bourbons of the elder branch it was to be dedicated to the Duc d'Angoulême, for his glorious campaign in Spain. Another statue that was commenced was one of Louis XVIII, author of the Charter and founder of representative government in France, on the Place du Palais-Bourbon, facing the Chamber of Deputies ; it was not completed on the downfall of Charles X. What has become of it ?

I often went to the church of Sainte-Geneviève, to make myself thoroughly acquainted with its beautiful architecture and to study the fresco painted by Baron Gros, in the second cupola. One group in this fresco was to have represented Napoleon with Marie-Louise, the King of Rome, and the leading soldiers ; but the invasions of 1814 and 1815 led to the substitution of Louis XVIII and the Charter. The Revolution, France, the Duc de Bordeaux, the Spanish War and the Dauphin surround the King, in the place of the personages who should have figured round about Napoleon. This curious fact is one more detail of the history of the changes which the church of Sainte-Geneviève has undergone ; a church once more destined to perpetuate the memory of the great.

Whenever I caught sight of the triumphal column of the Place Vendôme I stood contemplating it as long as though I had been regarding it for the first time. Its bas-reliefs recalled glorious and honourable memories. Time has not dimmed the vivid impressions of the famous campaign of Austerlitz. The revolution of July swept away the white flag that was unfurled there and restored the tricolour under which we vanquished the Austrians, on that immortal day of 1805.

I had planned, before my arrival in Paris, to attend the lectures of the most illustrious professors at the Collège de France and the Jardin d'Histoire Naturelle. I counted on my own eagerness to do so, but it was something wanting, and all sorts of disturbing factors, inspections, and twenty other obstacles combined to prevent me. I did not very punctually attend any course but that in chemistry : M. Thénard's, at the Sorbonne. I reproach myself now for this indifference in so far as it was not involuntary.

One man had at this time a sort of celebrity which few would have envied ; but people were eager to see him, and I myself gazed at him every time I went to stroll about the galleries of the Palais-Royal : this was the Diogenes of that brilliant bazaar, the famous Chodruc Duclos of Bordeaux. This man, who was once in enjoyment of a tidy fortune, the ornament of society, riding excellent horses, remarkable for his good form, his luxury of dress, his frequent duels and numerous mistresses, now displayed his cynicism, his poverty and his rags on that spot which of all Paris was most frequented by foreigners, provincials, and the idle. People gazed at him with astonishment, admiring his fine figure, his expressive face, his flashing eyes, but at once looked away, so afflicting were the abjectness and misfortune of this still proud individual. He had been the friend, it was said, of Comte du Peyronnet, who was twice minister, and signed the ordinances of July.

Thus, during the first few months I ran about a good deal, seeing everything, but later, as much by reason of my grief as from weariness and lassitude, I was less eager ; my curiosity being less intense, or satisfied, I became more indifferent, and thus it was that I left Paris without being present at a single session of the Chamber of Deputies.

I had seen a great revolution take place in those days ; a throne overturned and another set up by the nation's will ; a mighty king who fled with all his family to a foreign country, closely watched along his path of exile lest he should depart from the route laid down for him. I had seen the white flag forced on France by foreigners hauled down and the glorious tricolour cockade reappear after fifteen years of proscription. I had seen a superb Royal Guard, splendid in bearing, finely disciplined, generously treated and full of devotion, crumble, melt away and disappear even before its royal master had released it from its oaths. I had seen insubordination almost encouraged in the troops, the officers and men denouncing their superiors ; I had seen mediocrity and inferiority vaunting themselves because they were not employed under the Restoration, claiming office and high promotion and reward above those who for fifteen years had devoted themselves to the service of their country and preserved the good traditions of the Empire, meriting the praise of all good citizens for their perfect discipline. I had seen the mother of my beloved son laid in the tomb. When I said to Colonel Perrégaux and other officers with whom I was conversing before our departure from Lyons : " Since we are going to Paris I should like to see something important happen there," I did not think my wish would be granted in so grievous a fashion. What an unreflecting thirst for emotion and novelty, and how fatally gratified, with what hurt to my happiness !

The soldiers learned with pleasure that they were going to leave this brilliant Paris, which for them was only a place of intense weariness and painful vigils. Personally, I was very glad to go. I had been too unhappy there ; I had known too much disgust and weariness to regard as other than a great favour the order that bade us go into garrison in another part of France. A village, at that period, seemed to me preferable to the capital of the civilized world.

AT THE DUC DE DOUDEAUVILLE'S.

In 1830 *Barrès, by right of seniority, became the senior commandant of the* 15th. *His battalion was the first to leave for Alsace on the 1st October. On the way thither, at Mont-mirail, through which he had already passed in 1808, 1814 and 1829, his billet-paper made him a guest of the Duc de Doudeauville, peer of France and ex-minister of Charles X, " in the beautiful castle in which Cardinal de Retz was born."*

3rd October 1830.—Billeted in the household of the noble duke, I received, soon after I had gone to the room intended for me, a visit from a *valet-de-chambre*, who came to announce a visit from his master and at the same time brought me some refreshments and seven or eight newspapers of various political colours. Having dressed myself, I said I was ready to receive the honour the Duke proposed to pay me. M. de Doudeauville came to pay his respects and invited me to dine with him at six o'clock. Later I returned his visit, and then went for a walk in the great park of the château, notable for its fine position on the slope of the Petit Morin and its fine viewpoints. The château is an old building modernized, flanked by square towers, on one of which floated an immense tricolour flag.

Dinner brought together the Duke and Duchess, M. and Mme. Sosthène de Rochefoucauld, he having been aide de camp of Charles X, Director of Fine Arts in the King's Household, a man noted for his high breeding, and for having lengthened the skirts of the young ladies of the Opera, in the interests of morality ; the Duchesse Mathieu de Montmorency, widow of the Saintly Duke (as the devout called him at the time of his sudden death at St. Thomas d'Acquin), a sometime minister of Charles X ; the Marquis Chapt de Rastignac, a peer deprived by the July revolution ; and a number of other persons, who were, as far as I could judge, of less aristocratic origin. There was little said. M. de La Rochefoucauld and I were almost the only ones to exchange a few words in a low voice. For the rest, I could only feel gratified by the courtesy and attention shown me.

In the salon the company was more expansive. There was a great deal of talk of politics, of the July revolution and the misfortunes of the Royal family. " Unhappy king ! " said M. de Doudeauville, " he had no lack of good advice, but more influential men circumvented it and brought about his fall." All these people had left Paris only a few days earlier ; they had come to this ancient house to console themselves for the fall of the King, and to forget, if possible, their lost greatness. M. de Doudeauville was a small, wiry man, already aged ; his wife was almost blind ; their son, a handsome man with the grand manner ; their daughter-in-law, still young, but not especially remarkable, although her figure was well enough. As for M. de Rastignac, I thought him a theatrical figure, like the marquis in a play of Marivaux'. The ladies did not speak ; they would have compromised themselves before a plebeian in the service of a usurper. But although I was a stranger to this high society, I held my own in it and was received in a perfectly satisfactory manner.[1]

From Metz to Wissembourg.

On the 11th October Barrès arrived at Metz, which he saw for the third time.

At the gate of the town, where I had to halt, form half companies, and dress the ranks before entering, I saw coming towards me my son, led by his grandfather, his grandmother and his aunt Élisa Belfoy. With what joy I embraced all four, and tenderly pressed my little Augusta

---

[1] I cannot resist the pleasure of comparing this visit of my grandfather's to the visit which I paid to the same château the very day after the battle of the Marne (19th September, 1914 ; p. 233 of the *Chronique de la Grande Guerre*, vol. i).—M. B.

to my heart ! This new testimony of the affection in which my good kinsfolk held me touched me deeply. To make a journey of fifty leagues in order to give me the pleasure of embracing my child was to give me a very great proof of their attachment and to offer me a delightful distraction from the tedium of a long route-march. I found my son strong, frolicsome and overflowing with health. The forty-eight hours I spent with my family seemed short indeed to me.

18th October.—Some leagues beyond Bitche, marching through the mist along an indistinct sandy track, the battalion left the road and wandered to the left, toward Rhenian Bavaria. When we had almost reached the frontier a peasant came hurrying up, all out of breath, to warn us of our mistake, and to guide us back into the direction we had to follow. I thanked him suitably for the service he had rendered me, for, in our circumstances, a violation of this territory might have seemed intentional and given rise to more or less absurd commentaries. At this period all Europe was in an excited state. The kings were making ready for war, either to restrain the peoples, whom the revolution of July had set in commotion, or to resist France, whom they believed was induced to carry her principles into Germany and undertake an armed propaganda. What an effect might have been produced by the apparition of the tricolour flag in an old French province, and the unexpected arrival of a battalion which would have been taken for the vanguard of an invading army ! The alarm would have spread swiftly ; joy or fear would have exaggerated the event.

Shortly after this, at half a league from Lembach, I saw coming along the road towards me some sort of armed body marching in column, drums beating and flag flying. Arrived within the range of the voice these troops halted and their leader cried : " Who goes there ? " After the customary replies he approached, saluted me with his sword, and told me that the citizens of Lembach would with pleasure welcome the soldiers of the valiant 15th light infantry. This captain was an urchin of fifteen, very well built and displaying much coolness and assurance. He commanded a company of more than a hundred boys, from twelve to fourteen years of age, well organized, having all officers, sergeants and corporals, drummers, standard-bearer, and a canteen-keeper. Nothing was lacking, not even training and silence in the ranks. Having conversed for some minutes with this interesting youth, I told him to take the head of the column and lead us to the place where we were to halt. At our halting-place I invited him to dine with me, which he did with great pleasure. I learned that it was a retired captain who had had the patience to organize and drill these children with such success. It was a pleasure to see them. They had for arms large wooden sabres, which the officers, decorated with epaulettes or chevrons according to their rank, often used on the backs of their subordinates. We were in Alsace.

To sum up : the nineteen days' march from Paris to Wissembourg was made under the pleasantest conditions. All along this route, particularly in Champagne and the Loire, the people of the towns came to meet us, shouting " Long live the King ! Long live the Great Days ! " [1] All the houses were decorated with tricolour flags, and everywhere the soldiers were kindly welcomed and made much of. On leaving Paris I thought this march might be tedious and unpleasant, that the men would behave foolishly, fail to answer the roll, or fall to the rear. Nothing of the kind occurred. When we reached Wissembourg they were so little fatigued and their appearance was so smart that the inhabitants might have thought we had come in from a morning march of a few leagues only.

[1] The three " days of July."—Tr.

Having taken possession of the barracks and installed his battalion, Barrès presently obtained leave to go to Charmes ; but his stay there was cut short by a letter of recall from the colonel, who believed that a declaration of war was imminent. What follows is a humbler episode, characteristic of the Alsatian mind.

SCHOLASTIC DIFFICULTIES IN ALSACE.

On the 9th March, 1831, I received orders from General Fehrmann to repair with the whole of my battalion to the village of Ober-Belschdorf, four leagues distant, to take part in repressing resistance to the decisions of the higher administration. This semi-insurrection was caused by the appointment of a schoolmaster whom the inhabitants did not want. In vain were they told that the man they preferred was an ignorant fellow and had failed in all his examinations. They insisted, because he was the son-in-law of the forest guard, and the latter had warned them that if they took another he would report them whenever they went to fetch wood in the beautiful forest of Haguenau. The rebellion was manifest ; the gendarmerie had been driven out of the village on several occasions when it attempted to take possession of the school-house ; some of the men had built barricades, and, armed with muskets, had entrenched themselves in the school. The authorities temporized, hoping that reflection and lassitude would make them more reasonable. This patience made them bolder. The gendarmerie was driven back a third time and the sub-prefect of Wissembourg scoffed at. In this state of affairs force had to intervene to make the law respected.

On my arrival on the 10th March I found the barricades evacuated, but the school-house was still occupied. Having taken certain precautions and called upon the rebels to withdraw, I sent against them my company of light

19

infantry. On its approach they ran away by the back door, which, expressly, had been left unguarded, and got themselves into the forest at the top of their speed. The schoolmaster appointed by the administration was immediately installed in the presence of M. Matter, school-inspector, the sub-prefect, the justice of the peace of Soultz-sous-Forêt, the mayor, and all the officers. All the children had been warned and compelled to attend and witness the ceremony, which would have seemed ridiculous under any other circumstances, but was now both impressive and painful, all these wretched children imagining that their throats would be cut without mercy. They shrieked in such a way as to alarm the hearers. After speeches had been delivered, advice given and the parents exhorted, the children were dismissed. The commune having resumed its usual calm, and the children displaying no further fear, I returned to garrison on the 13th, leaving two companies to keep them in this salutary frame of mind.

These two companies returned a fortnight later, when the gendarmerie had arrested most of the principal mutineers. This prudent expedition, which caused no tears but those of the children, had a very good result, since it taught the population that the authorities were strong enough to turn back those who strayed from the path of duty. Since 1830 the communes had been in a state of unrest and commotion, and the inhabitants were inclined to take advantage of the kind of power which the July revolution had given them. They wasted the State forests in broad daylight, drove out the forest guards, threatened the mayors and brought to the market the products of their theft without blushing for their actions. I was often obliged, during the winter, to send companies to garrison the villages on the eastern slope of the Vosges, to put an end to this scandalous brigandage.

ALSACE ACCLAIMS THE CITIZEN-KING.

I was officially advised some days beforehand of the coming arrival of the King in Alsace, and of my departure for Strasbourg, so that I might be present with the whole regiment at his entry into the capital of the province and the reviews that would follow. The political object of this journey was to make known to the population of the East, and to the army, the monarch whom the France of July had chosen. It was important to give the King a good impression of the regiment, and likewise to give Germany, who would be watching us, a similar opinion of our young army, which had to some extent been re-created. I took all measures to ensure by frequent reviews that my battalion should be as smart and in as great strength as possible. My success was complete.

18th June.—The garrison, the troops that had arrived for review by the King, and the National Guards of the wards of Strasbourg and Wissembourg, took arms to line the highway from the White or National Gate to the royal palace. The King made his solemn entry on horseback, having beside him his two sons, the Ducs d'Orléans and de Nemours, accompanied by the marshals Soult and Gérard, the Minister of Commerce, Comte d'Argout, and an immense staff. He was preceded and followed by twelve regiments of cavalry and some hundreds of Alsatian carriages adorned with foliage and ribbons and tricoloured flags and filled with young, fresh peasant-girls, wearing the costumes of the country. This entry into a famous warlike city was magnificently impressive. An immense concourse of citizens, and also strangers to Alsace, a general gaiety, and lively shouts spontaneously uttered as the King went by, proved that he had the assent of the whole population. The public spirit was still good, and demagogic tendencies had not yet perverted the masses or changed into culpable indifference the testimonies of affection which the King had hitherto received.

When he had gone by and the ranks were broken the officers reassembled to go to the palace, where they were presented by General Brayer, commanding the division. We found there the Grand Duke of Baden and a numerous suite, the envoys of the German sovereigns, and the French ambassadors or agents attached to their Courts.

19th June.—We took arms early in the morning, parading at an early hour on the polygon. This vast manœuvring-ground was presently filled with troops of all arms and a crowd of French and German spectators. Independently of the National Guards, horse and foot, there were three regiments of infantry (59th of the line, 5th and 15th Light), twelve regiments of cavalry, two of artillery, and more than five hundred guns, caissons, baggage-waggons, bridge equipments, etc., with their teams. The foreigners, like the French, were amazed to see that we had been able, in so few months, to reorganize the army, triple its effective, mount the cavalry and create an immense amount of campaigning material. Thanks to Marshal Soult France had already 400,000 men on a war footing, 600 guns with teams, and all the other military services, brought up to a strength and a degree of training that seemed almost miraculous.

The arrival of the King was saluted by the deafening acclamations of an immense population, by a general discharge of all the guns, and by the trumpets, drums and bands of all the corps in battle formation in several ranks. When the sovereign had taken his place on a wide railed platform built on one side of this vast square, the colonels or corps commanders went up to him to receive from his hands the flags and standards of their regiments, which were then recognized and saluted by their subordinates. The cries of "Long live the King!" and the loud rolling of the drums announced that the soldiers were saluting with enthusiasm the national symbol which was to guide them and lead them to victory.

This recognition accomplished, the King passed in succession along the front of all the corps. On reaching the centre of the regiment he sent for me, gave me the officer's cross of the Legion of Honour, and told me that he thought himself most happy to be able to reward, by a new distinction, my long and loyal services. This promotion in the Order pleased me greatly, though I did not feel as flattered as when I was appointed a simple legionary in 1813. General Schramm was kind enough to warn me beforehand and to compliment me on my appointment before I was decorated by His Majesty himself.

During the day I received my third decoration and took my oath to serve a sixth flag. The first, with an eagle, on the Champ de Mars, under the Empire; the second in 1814, with the fleurs de lis, on the first restoration of the Bourbons; the third, the tricolour, with the eagle, during the Hundred Days; the fourth, the white flag, on the second return of the Bourbons, given to the departmental legions in 1816; the fifth in 1821, when the regiments were re-established; and the sixth, and I trust the last, the tricolour with the Gaulish cock. As for the decoration of the Legion of Honour, that too had had its vicissitudes. In 1814 the effigy of Napoleon and the Imperial eagle were replaced by the effigy of Henri IV and the arms of France with three fleurs de lis; 1815 restored the decoration to its original form; the catastrophe of Waterloo restored the Bourbons and with them the changes of the previous year; lastly, the revolution of July substituted for the fleurs de lis of the monarchy by divine right the tricolour flag of the representative, regenerated monarchy. Thus the escutcheons are now, on one side the head of Henri IV, and on the other, two crossed flags with the fundamental device : *Honneur et Patrie*. The Cross of Saint-Louis, without being forbidden, is no longer worn. . . .

The review over, we marched past quickly, at the double once we had passed the King, in order to leave the ground free for the cavalry and material. It was nearly night when ranks were broken, on the Place du Temple Neuf. We had been more than fourteen hours under arms.

Having repaired the disorder of my uniform, I went to the château to mount guard, as superior officer of the day and the senior battalion commander. These two titles gave me the right to sit at the King's table. I took my place there as the officer on duty and did great honour to the royal banquet. There were two tables in the same hall, each with forty-five to fifty covers : the Grand Duke of Baden, his brother, his brother-in-law, and the notables of his court, the envoys of Bavaria, Wurtemburg, Hesse-Darmstadt, Frankfort, etc., a number of generals, in active service or reserve, the commandants of the National Guard, and several corps commanders. Nearly all the members of the Duke of Baden's military suite were decorated with the Legion of Honour. They were officers who had formerly fought in our ranks. I talked for some time with several of them of our past wars and our hope that the peace would not be broken. The review, and the smart appearance and bearing and the level of training which our young army had already achieved had struck them greatly. " Only the French," they said, " could have done such great things in so short a time."

After dinner the King went to the theatre, where the city was giving a ball. This building, magnificently decorated, though very spacious, was so full, and the heat was so stifling, that it took a certain courage to endure such paralysing conditions with no other motive than curiosity; the place was really unbearable. I remained there as a matter of duty, and to see whether I might not meet someone whom I had courted in 1817–18, and whom I should probably have married had I not left before the final matrimonial negotiations. After eighteen or twenty months of correspondence all relations had ceased. My search amidst these hundreds of women was not in vain. Although each of us had changed a good deal we recognized one another at first sight. She received my renewed attentions becomingly, told me that she was married and the mother of a family, and would be glad to receive me if I would give her the pleasure of calling on her. When I saw her again the following day I willingly forgave her for her kindly reproaches. Time had assuaged their bitterness if ever they were serious.

The King returned to the palace at an early hour. My duty compelled me to follow him. I passed the night on a chair, in the courtyard of the château, or strolling to and fro with the officers of the guard of three arms which I had under my orders, infantry, cavalry and National Guards. The night was as cool and peaceful as the day had been hot and bustling. I breakfasted there the following day and dined again in the evening, having received an individual invitation, at the same table as the night before. The fare was pretty good and the guests men of good family, so that one had no fear of compromising oneself.

The departure of the King for Colmar was followed by a great inspection by Lieutenant-General Baron Sémélé, under whom Barrès had served at Mayence. The general " was more than astonished to find the regiment so far advanced in its training." All had worked night and day to achieve this result, " as Marshal Soult intended to have 500,000 men under arms, equipped and drilled, to confront the Northern powers during the summer if they persisted in their intention

*to attack us." Barrès played a great part in these activities,
and his battalion, as his colonel admitted, was " more advanced
than the others."*

INSURRECTIONS AT STRASBOURG AND LYONS.

*On the 13th September, 1831, Barrès obtained a month's
leave to go to Charmes, to see his son and his family ; but
serious incidents at Strasbourg necessitated his immediate
return.*

The colonel wrote to me requesting me to return at once
to my garrison, my presence being rendered necessary by
a sort of insurrection on the part of the National Guard
against one of the laws of the State : an insurrection which
had been suppressed, but which might be renewed, so
that every man must needs be at his post. This was on
the 6th ; an hour later I was on the way to Lunéville,
where I took the Paris diligence to Strasbourg.

7th October.—The attempted insurrection was on the part
of the Republican portion of the National Guard, under the
pretext of enfranchising foreign cattle from the customs
tariff at the frontier, but in reality to try its strength and
to open the gates of this outer defence of France to a
member of the Napoleonic Imperial family, if it was
impossible to proclaim a Republic. To this end 400 to 500
National Guards took arms during the night of the 4th
October, without being authorized by their officers, and
marched upon the Little Rhine, forcing the guard at the
Austerlitz gate to let them pass, so that they might burn
the customs-house and let in the foreign cattle without
paying the dues imposed by the law.

The military authorities were warned in time by a
sergeant of the regiment. They marched my battalion
in the night, under the command of the lieutenant-colonel,

across country, to lend assistance to the customs officials. Shortly after daybreak, when the National Guards arrived on the Little Rhine, they found, to their great surprise, that their road was barred; they disbanded and were driven back to the town at the point of the bayonet, though no actual use was made of that weapon. Once back in the town they combined with such of the malcontents as had remained, but these, restrained by the garrison, which had been under arms since daybreak, had been no happier in their attempts at disorder. They were about to withdraw to eat their sauerkraut when the prefect, out of fear or weakness, took it upon himself to reduce the dues by half. This cowardly submission would have spoiled everything; fortunately during the day a telegraphic despatch announced the cancellation of the prefect's decree, and the dismissal of this magistrate, who received orders to repair to Paris then and there, to give an account of his conduct.

When I arrived in haste from Charmes quiet was almost re-established, and the troops called in from outside were on the point of returning to their cantonments.

I learned many years afterwards that a distinguished soldier with whom I had frequent relations both before and after this event, was not entirely a stranger to this Bonapartist enterprise. This was Commandant Parquin, chief of a squadron of gendarmerie at Strasbourg, the companion of Prince Louis-Napoléon at the time of his insurrectional attempts at Strasbourg in 1837 and Boulogne in 1840. He died recently at Ham, a prisoner of State.

November.—The insurrection at Lyons very nearly drew us into the movement of the troops which were at this time ordered to retake the city, whence the rising had just driven the authorities. The Minister for War, Marshal Soult, before leaving for Lyons with the Prince Royal, had given orders that troops summoned from all parts of

France should assemble, moving by forced marches, under
the walls of Lyons. The regiment was to form part of
them, but for some reason that no one has been able to
explain, the telegraphic despatch did not arrive. It had
probably evaporated into the air! Nothing was known
of the order until a courier from Lyons ordered the colonel
to return to Strasbourg, the co-operation of his regiment
no longer being necessary; the city of Lyons had been
evacuated by the insurgents and the King's government
established in the fulness of its powers. The courier, not
encountering the 15th Light on the road, pushed on to
Strasbourg and there found, lying snug in his bed, the
colonel whom he should have met floundering in the mud
of Franche-Comté. The colonel was greatly surprised to
receive a countermand of an order which he had not
executed. This blunder or negligence on the part of the
administration saved us from a hasty departure, sixteen days of forced marches through the mud, rain
and snow, and great fatigue, which would have been
wholly wasted.

THE CHOLERA OF 1832.

In April, 1832, *Barrès received a visit from his late wife's
parents and sister-in-law, who brought him his young son;
he had the pleasure of keeping them beside him for some days,
and of showing the Rhine to his boy. But a terrible scourge
was about to add to his sorrows.*

May and June, 1832.—A few days after my visitors
had left they wrote me that the cholera, which was working havoc in Paris and the adjacent parts, had broken
out in Charmes with great violence. This sinister news
paralysed me with terror. How was it possible that this
terrible malady had invaded a wholesome, clean, airy
town when it had not made its way into Lorraine, and was

apparently more than forty leagues from the point where it had thus shown itself ? How was it that it had passed over larger towns, mountains and rivers and left no traces of its gigantic stride ? I had cruel apprehensions to endure.

They were realized only too soon. My brother-in-law, a notary at Charmes, less than thirty years of age, hale and hearty, was struck down by this horrible malady on the 24th June, and a few hours later was a corpse. His young daughter, the elder of his two children, followed him closely. At the same time one of my sisters-in-law, Mme. Élisa Belfoy, was dying of a decline, and succumbed on the 5th December. So many afflictions befalling the family in so short a time broke my heart.

A DAY OF REVOLUTION.

9th June.—The revolutionary and republican risings of the 5th–6th June in Paris, of bloody memory, had a repercussion in Strasbourg, where the revolutionaries of the capital had some fanatical adepts. We were on the *qui vive* until the 9th; on that day the " brothers and friends," ashamed of their inertia, informed the prefect that as the Republic was proclaimed in Paris, so, they intended, it should be in Strasbourg. They said that the fact was attested by all correspondence from Paris, and that the discarded Government, on leaving the capital, had had the line of semaphores broken so that this great change should not be known in the country. To seek to convince them that they were spreading lies would have been waste of time ; they wanted to create a sensation, show their sympathy for the revolutionists in Paris, and prove that they were worthy to imitate them. To reassure the population the garrison took arms, and its battalions proceeded to different points of the town.

My battalion was posted on the Place d'Armes, where

it remained from three in the afternoon until one in the morning. During the daytime no one appeared on the Place but children, who whistled, shouted insults, or threw missiles, which did not greatly endanger the officers or the men. But at nightfall the agitators took a hand; the troops of malcontents became considerable and their anarchical shouts resounded. To have done with this snarling scum, General Brayer gave me the order to charge with fixed bayonets and clear the Place. This was done without either casualties or resistance. Later on he ordered me to have the martial law read by a police commissary in the Rue des Arcades, where the mob was thickest. I went thither at the head of my men, with a drummer to beat the rolls, and with flaming torches to give more circumstance to this serious mission. Before beginning to read I gave the crowd to understand that when I had finished I should three times request the public to withdraw, and that I should then give the order to fire. I had beside me Generals Brayer, commanding the division; Tririon, commanding the depot of the Lower Rhine; Lallemand, commanding the cavalry stationed in Alsace; and Marion, of the School of Artillery. There was something fine about this display of force, which explains before it strikes. At the first summons the crowd began to thin; at the second it disappeared almost entirely; at the third the long street was empty, and by eleven o'clock the whole town was profoundly quiet.

Such was the part which the Strasbourg party, in response to the pledges it had made the party in Paris, played during the days of revolution in June. While they were not extremely bellicose, it was an unpleasant business, by reason of the grave insults addressed to the generals present and the bruises received in the dark by some of the officers and men from the stones thrown into their ranks. Not a single townsman was hurt, but it needed all the officers' prudence, and their disdain of the insults offered, to prevent the soldiers from avenging themselves for such numerous provocations and acts of violence.

LIFE AT STRASBOURG.

Recommended for promotion to the rank of lieutenant-colonel, Barrès shortly afterwards changed his garrison. His battalion was despatched to Haguenau. Before leaving Strasbourg, on the 5th October, he records a few more recollections of a sojourn whose termination was not unregretted.

The garrison was more than a little fatigued with constant duties, and was often obliged to take arms or to remain shut up in the barracks to be ready for unforeseen political events. This year 1832 was so disturbed, so stormy for the new Government, that its only declared defenders had their full share of its bad times.

Almost every Sunday, when the weather was not too bad, there was a great parade on the Place d'Armes. It is probable that this was due more to necessity than to the wish of General Drayer, the divisional commander. This excellent and charmingly agreeable man loved the regiment, and had great confidence in it. The malcontents, who did not forget their abortive raid to the Rhine and the martial law of the 9th June, used to call us " Brayer's bodyguard." Brayer was their compatriot, a self-made man, who had been condemned to death in 1815 ; he defeated the Chouans at La Roche-Servière and (during banishment) the Spaniards in South America ; but he spared Strasbourg the horrors of Paris and Lyons, and for this he was not forgiven. We often dined with him and he was sometimes an honoured guest at our mess. His daughter, distinguished for her extreme courtesy, had married M. Marchand, *valet-de-chambre* to Napoleon at St. Helena. Marchand was full of modesty and urbanity, and very reserved in respect of his illustrious and unfortunate master's captivity. The Emperor, in his last testament, made him a count and bade him marry the daughter of a soldier who had suffered in his cause. He chose Mlle. Brayer.

The defenders of unhappy Poland, escaping *en masse* from their enslaved country, were arriving in Strasbourg by all the German highways. Warmly welcomed and fêted by the inhabitants, they were treated by the officers of the garrison as comrades in misfortune, as ancient companions in glory, persecuted by proscription after a glorious defeat. But the ridiculous entry of the emergency generals, Romarino and Langerman, and several instances of bad behaviour on the part of some Polish officers, inspired us with a certain coolness ; and we saw that the *Boussingots* of Strasbourg were trying to profit by their arrival by making partisans of them and causing trouble for the Government.

In November, 1832, the colonel, Major Aguilloni and I made arrangements for the winter. We ate together and commonly spent our evenings at the same house, the guests of ladies who were patterns of grace and amenity, in whose homes assembled all the most distinguished society of the city. There was music, dancing and card-playing. I should have been very happy to pass the winter in this charming and delightful idleness. My lodgings were pleasant ; our duties in the cold weather were by no means onerous ; the boisterous wind and the pelting rain meant nothing to me, for I hoped to be sheltered from such inclemencies. In short, I had surrendered myself, with the good Dr. Margaillant,[1] who had the room neighbouring mine, to the delights of peace and the charms of the fireside, when I was suddenly awakened, on the night of the 9th November, by my adjutant, who came to

---

[1] Presumably the same person as Major (Surgeon) Aguilloni. M. Aguilloni or M. Arguilloni might easily be misread as Margaillant.—TR.

inform me, without consideration for my delicious dreams, of our departure for Belgium.

A fresh campaign was announced. Two war battalions and two picked companies were hastily formed by incessant labour. On the 12th November, on the road to Mezières, Barrès halted at Niederbronn, where he was lodged in the house of M. Dietrich, ex-mayor of Strasbourg. On reaching Mezierès the regiment was told off to form part of the reserve force being formed on the Meuse to prevent the Prussians from interfering with the reign of Antwerp. This soon ended in the Dutch being driven out. The object of the expedition to Belgium having been thus achieved, Barrès received, at Charleville, orders to proceed to Sedan to make room for the troops returning from the siege. He remained there a fortnight and then proceeded to other cantonments. In February, 1833, he at last received orders to return to his garrison in Alsace, after four months of an " armed chase," which the rain and the frost made an exhausting one.

Attacked by rheumatism of the head, Barrès shortly afterwards obtained convalescent leave, which he spent at Charmes. But the insurrection at Lyons forced him to leave on the 16th April. On reaching Lyons he found the city had been quiet for three days, after sanguinary fighting in which more than 300 men of the garrison had been put out of action.

The 8th July 1834 marked, for Barrès, his fiftieth year and his thirty years of service.

AFTER THIRTY YEARS' SERVICE.

This day, so long desired, found me inclined to take advantage of the opportunity it gave me to terminate my military career in an honourable manner and apply for my pension. For some years I had been feeling the need of rest, of living a little for myself, and to enjoy that complete independence which one finds only in civil life, and most conveniently in one's own home.

While I did not feel quite decided, while I was not absolutely weary of the noble profession of arms, I was led to this resolution by the desire to be nearer my child, to watch over his education, to guide him, as far as my poor capacities would permit, along the right path, and to warn him in due season of the dangers that must be avoided if one would not lose oneself at the very outset of life. I was easily alarmed if they forgot to give me news of him; I was desperately anxious during such moments of suspense, which made my life painful to me and myself dejected and morose. Both my families pressed me to leave the service, to preserve, for my child, a life that was so often endangered, and had been so fortunately protected against all the perils of a long career that had been full of vicissitudes. Despite myself, with the best will in the world, I had lost the fiery energy of my first and best years, the activity so necessary in the service, if one is to do one's duty conscientiously, when one's self-respect urges one to do at least as well as others and to set a good example to one's subordinates. Large-scale manœuvres, days in the saddle and my increasing flesh fatigued me so that I became discouraged. On the other hand, it was with regret that I saw myself compelled to retire with the rank I then held, so certain was I of promotion to that of lieutenant-colonel before a year had passed, and of obtaining my pension two years after such promotion. I cheerfully renounced an honourable and comfortable life amidst the society and the pleasures of the fashionable world, the delights and amusements of great cities, to go and live in a little town that offered no resources, far from my own countryside, which was still dear to me, although thirty years had effaced my most vivid memories.

Having reflected at length on the advantages and dis-

advantages of the resolution I was about to take, I
determined, at the end of the month, to put my application
in writing and address it to the colonel. When it reached
the hands of Lieutenant-General Aymard, our inspector-
general for 1834, he would not accept it until he had seen
me and learned from me in person that it was not a
question of my giving way to any sort of displeasure or
discontent. He showed me a letter from the Minister
for War, which advised him that Commandant Barrès,
having been recommended at the previous general
inspections for the rank of lieutenant-colonel, must by
right be placed on the list of promotions for that year.
" You are," he said, " the senior battalion-commander
in my district, and recommended for higher rank ; you
will be named first in my report and will infallibly be
appointed within a year. There is everything to induce
you to withdraw your application." Despite the efforts
of the colonel, who was present at this interview, and who
added his arguments to the general's, I resisted these
kindly marks of affection and interest. The only favour
I asked was three months' leave to visit my father's
family and bid farewell to my relatives, and lay some
flowers on the graves of my father and mother.

This the general readily granted me, adding that he
regretted that I did not pay more deference to his desire
and the arguments of my comrades.

Believing that on returning from leave I should be
ordered to wait at Charmes for my discharge, I sold my
horse for a pretty good price after riding him for some
years, which is very rare among infantry officers, who
are more often than not mounted on screws. The good
service I had had from him made me regret him. Although
but a very middling horseman, I had not once the painful
experience of being thrown.

I left on the 10th August and made the first part of
my journey by the railway from Lyons to Saint-Étienne.

20

This was the first time I had made use of this mode of travel. I found it pleasant, and above all most convenient, although it was far from being as rapid as it has become with steam. The carriages were well sprung and very comfortable, each being drawn by two powerful horses, which went at a gallop, making a pace of three and a half leagues an hour.[1] From Saint-Étienne to Givors the carriages went without the assistance of the horses, the gentle slope between these two points being sufficient to give them a speed of six to seven leagues an hour.

By way of Monistrol, Issengeaux, Le Puy and Brioude, I came to Blesle on the 13th August, after an absence of more than thirty years ! My younger brother, a soldier like myself, had retired less than a year previously and was living with my sister. As my visit was made especially to see them it was of course at their house that I alighted. For me they were the successors of my father and mother, the representatives of the family.

So long an absence, the death of the authors of my being, and of many of my contemporaries, might have weakened my feeling for my native soil and my pious recollections. But in spite of so many causes of indifference and oblivion, it was with ineffable delight that I returned to the beloved scenes of my first youth. The three months I was to pass in this humble valley, so peaceful and picturesque, with my own kind and the friends that heaven had spared me, could but offer me smiling images and delicious distractions, according to the point of view from which I regarded them. I felt the need of enjoying the singular favour that had been granted me, after so many dangers, fatigues and vicissitudes, of finding myself once more amidst the scene I had left at the age of twenty without greatly thinking of what I might become. I had come in search of intimate joys ; I was happy enough

---

[1] About nine miles ; downhill they made fifteen to eighteen miles an hour.—Tr.

to find them and to appreciate them with the eager fealty of a man who regrets that he has for years been deprived of them.

My arrival was the occasion of numerous and frequent gatherings at the houses of my relatives and friends, or in my own quarters. In response to so many marks of affectionate freindship I gave a dinner almost every Monday to ten or twelve persons, to relatives, good friends and old acquaintances, whose presence recalled a little the days we loved to remember. If the fare at these banquets reflected the poor resources of the country, I had at least the satisfaction of offering some excellent wines—Bordeaux, Burgundy and Champagne—which I had brought with me.

The fine vintages of that year gave occasion for numerous vineyard parties, which were as merry as they were delightful. This was almost a novelty for me, who had not enjoyed these rustic functions since the year 1803.

After several excursions into the country round about and a visit to my worthy kinsfolk at Brioude, the hour for packing arrived. Although the fine days and the season of pleasures were gone, I saw with regret the approach of the moment when I must embrace, perhaps for the last time, my brothers, my friends, and above all my sister, whom I found it difficult to leave behind me. She accompanied me on the 6th November as far as Lempde, where we slept, because she wanted to see me into the diligence. Our parting on the 7th was sad indeed.

At Lyons Barrès learned that he could not be finally released until his retirement on pension was announced in the Bulletin des Lois. *After weeks of uncertainty he decided to appeal to General Aymard for further leave and to await the good pleasure of the official* Bulletin *at Charmes.*

On the 19th January, 1835, I arrived at Charmes during the forenoon, when I had the pleasure of find-

ing my son and my father-in-law's family in perfect
health.

Although I could not yet regard myself as entirely
released from service, I none the less busied myself about
my future establishment with all the activity that we
display in the things we do with pleasure. A few days
after my arrival I set about finding a suitable lodging,
and having found it, in supervising the work of arranging
and embellishing it, and buying the furniture and other
household articles, which I had to get from Nancy,
Lunéville, Épinal or Charmes, according to the advantages
to be obtained by procuring them in one or other of these
towns.

Thus ended a career which, if it was not very brilliant,
was at least useful to France and honourable to myself.
I say, with pride, *honourable*, for during thirty-one years
I always conscientiously did my duty, on all occasions
and wherever I went; I had no bad actions with which
to reproach myself, and I had always deserved the esteem
and confidence of my superiors and subordinates, as well
as the friendship of my comrades and the corps in which
I had served. That this career was not more brilliant in
the matter of activities and promotion was due to the
fact that it is not given to all soldiers to find themselves
in favourable situations, at propitious moments, that result
in the citing of their names with favourable mention;
such occasions are rare, above all in the infantry, whose
merits and services are not strong enough to win eulogists.
In respect of advancement I might and should have hoped
to be more favoured if circumstances had served me better;
if I had had more ambition, more talent for intrigue, and
if, like so many others, I had sought to exploit my services.
But such means, though in very general employ, are
scarcely legitimate and have always repelled me. I may
say with sincerity that I have never written to anyone
to recommend myself, nor have I once entered the Ministry

for War to introduce myself to the dispensers of gifts and favours ; I have been content with the protection of my immediate or superior chiefs. Nevertheless, I ought to congratulate myself that my fortune has not been too adverse, and to be grateful to Providence, since I have had the satisfaction of retiring from the service with no infirmities or serious wounds, which is a great compensation and an inestimable blessing for my old age.[1]

[1] J.-B. Barrès died at Charmes fourteen years later, in January, 1849, having had the satisfaction of seeing his son, as he desired, enter the École Centrale.—M. B.

INDEX

Abrantès, Duc and Duchesse d', 136, 138, 142
Abrantès, siege of, 149, 152
Academy, the French, 238
Alarms, false, 68
Alexander I at Tilsit, 113
Albion, la perfide, 55
Algiers, capture of, 243
Almeida, siege of and explosion at, 142 ; Barrès sick at, 156
Alsace, insubordination in, 289–91
Ampère, 22
Amstetten, battle of, 71
Angoulême, Duc d', 235
Arago, 244
Arc de Triomphe, 120
Argentat, a misunderstanding at, 216–17
Artillery fire, 77, 100, 101, 109, 161, 178
Artois, Comte d', 227
Astorga, siege of, 137–9
Augsburg, 60, 67
Aumale, Duc d', 279–80
Aurillac, 217
Austerlitz, the eve of, 17 ; battle of, 18, 74–9
Austria, war with, 55, 58 *et seq.*
Auttemberg, 59
Aymard, General, 305, 307

Bamberg, 84–5 ; family, the, 12–13
Barrès, Jean-Baptiste, 9 *et seq.* ; joins Consular Guard, 29–30 ; promotion, 123–4; is put on half-pay, 220 ; reinstated, 224 ; his marriage, 231–3 ; promoted, 233 ; retires, 301–4
Barrès, Joseph-Auguste, 234
Barrès, Madame, 231 ; death of, 241–2
Barrès, Maurice, 9–15, 21–3
Barrès, Pierre-Maurice, 25–7
Bautzen, battles of, 164–7
Bayard, Chevalier, 48
Bearskins of the Guard, 15, 42, 123
Beauharnais, Eugène, 46, 50, 241
Beauharnais, Josephine, *see* Josephine
Belle-Ile, Barrès on, 127–33
Bernadotte, 09, 75
Berry, Duc de, 205
Berry, Duchesse de, 227, 241
Bessières, Marshal, 58, 65, 102, 119, 160
Berlin, the French enter, 89–93 ; fire in, 91
Bidassoa, 158
Bigarré, Colonel, 48, 133
Blesle, 206, 217
Blücher, 195
Bonaparte, First Consul, 29–30
Bonaparte, Joseph, 48
Bonaparte, Louis, 50
Bordeaux, Archbishop of, 225–6
Bordeaux, Duc de, 227
Bordeaux, the White Terror in, 214–15 ; royalism of, 226
Borna, 163
Boudinhox, Colonel, 118, 177

Boulogne, troops at, 35, 54–5
Bourbons, distrust of, 199 ; res-
    toration of, 200, 202 ; disliked
    by officers, 206
Bourmont, Comte de, 237, 243
Brera library, 51
Brest, regiment at, 210 ;   Bour-
    bons accepted at, 213
Brittany, poverty of regiment in,
    204
Bug, crossing the,
Buglers, wounded, 162
Burgos, 135–6

Campaigning, miseries of, 61
Campaigns, Austrian, 58 ;   1813
    and 1814, 159–
Champs-de-Mars, fêtes in,123, 205
Charles X, 164, 235–6, 241, 242,
    243, 247, 273
Charmes, 10–15 ;   Barrès visits,
    231, 237 ;   retires, to, 305
Chasseurs of the Guard, 9, 15, 43,
    46, 67, 79, 83, 110
Chasseur Skirmishers, 33, 35
Cholera, 298–9
Ciudad-Rodrigo, 141, 154–5
Closler-Brach, 84
Coimbra, 144
Coloun, capture of, 67
Compans, General, 165, 170, 184
Conscripts, refractory, 134–5 ;
    excellent conduct of young,
    162
Constitutionnel, etc., 223
Copenhagen, news of, 118
Cossacks, engagements with,
    177–80
Coswick, battle of, 179
Court, the Bourbon, 227, 235,
    242, 245 ; the Orléans, 276–7
Croats, treachery of, 180–1
Cuvier, 239

Danube, the, 50, 61, 79
Dauphin, the, 235, 237, 241, 245,
    266

Dauphine, the, 235, 237, 241
Davoust, Marshal, 76
Depradt, Abbé, 51
De Vigny, 20
Disbanding of Grand Army, 213–
    14
Donawerth, 59
Doudeauville, Duc d', 285–6
Dresden, battle of, 173–4
Duclos, Chodruc, 283
Duel to the death, a, 37
Dumas, Alexandre, 236
Duroc, Duc de Friuli, 167

Eagles,   distribution   of,   40 ;
    wreaths voted for, 118–19,
    122
Écouen, 35, 36
Elchingen, battle of, 63–5
Electoral Guard, 68
Émigrés, return of, 16
Emperor, the, see Alexandre,
    Napoleon
England, intended descent on,
    54–5
English in Portugal, 146–8
Espinchal, Comte H. d', 207
Essonnes, 43, 45
Ettlingen, 58
Execution, a painful, 171 ;   an
    unjust, 188
Explosion, an, averted, 139
Eylau, battle of, 98–103 ; cour-
    age at, 102 ;   battlefield of,
    109–10

Fabre, Major, 168, 183, 191, 213
Finckenstein, 106
Forbin-Janson, Bishop, 230
Foy, General, 150, 151, 153
Friedland, 109–11

Garnerin (aeronaut), 50
Geltkendorf, 97
Genoa, Doge of, 51
Gérard, Comte, 267
Girls' school, a deserted, 89

Gradefès, 136
Grand Army, the, 19; disbanded, 213–14
Grenadiers of the Guard, 29, 76, 79
Grenadier Skirmishers, 32, 33
Guard, Barrès mounts, 68, 81
Guard, the Consular, 29, 34
Guard, the Imperial, 18–19, 33, 57, 60; acclaims Napoleon at Austerlitz, 24–5; reviewed, 82, 113–14; triumphal entry into Paris, 119–23
Guard, the Italian Royal, 76
Guard, the Royal, 269
Guard, the Russian Imperial, 76, 77
Guards, Chasseurs, Grenadiers, Skirmishers of the, *see under those terms*
Guards, the, 17–18
Guards, the Horse, 76
Guerillas, 157
Guntzburg, 61, 63

Haff, 98
Halle, action in, 185–6
Hanau, 191–2
Hanover, 117–19
Hats of the Chasseurs, 97; thrown away, 110
Heilsberg battle, a, 107–9
Höchst, 191
Hohenlohe, Prince, 220
Holy Ghost, Chevaliers of the, 236
Hospital, Barrès in, 154–6
Hugo, Victor, 21
Hundred Days, the, 208

Ice, Russians fall through, 77; bivouac fire disappears through, 98
Imperial Guard, *see* Guard, Imperial
Infantry, 47th, Barrès appointed to, 159

Inovraslov, 105
Issoire, 30–1
Istria, Marshal the Duc d', 157–8, 160
Italy, departure for, 42–3

Jeannin, General, 139
Jena, battle of, 86–9
Josephine, Empress, 50, 122
Joubert, General, 167, 170, 192
Jourdan, 49
July Monarchy, the, 275
July, the Ordinances of, 246–7
July, the Three Days of, 247–60

Katsbach, crossing the, 168
Kinzig, crossing the, 189–90
Klein-Possna, 181–2
Königsberg, 115–17

La Coste, General, 123
La Fayette, 268, 270, 272
Lannes, Marshal, 59
Larrey, Surgeon-in-Chief, 171
Las-Cases, Comte de, 158
Lefèvre, Marshal, 86
Legion of Honour, the, 35, 46, 163; Barrès receives, 164, 171, 226, 273
Leon, 137
Lembach, amusing incident near, 287–8
Le Palais, 127, 132
Le Puy, 25–6, 30; robbery near, 208–9; Barrès denounced at, 219
Leipzic, disaster of, 180–7
Les Sablons, review at, 83
Liebstadt, 103
Ligurian Republic, 51
Löplitz, 174
Loire, a journey on the, 209
Lorraine, Dukes of, 229
Louis XIII, the vow of, 237
Louis XVIII recognized by army, 213, 227

314 MEMOIRS OF A NAPOLEONIC OFFICER

Louis-Philippe, 205, 244, 272, 275, 277–8 ; visits Alsace, 291–5
Ludwig of Prussia, Prince, 85
Lutzen, battle of, 160, 187
Luxembourg Palace, 280

Macdonald, Marshal, 241
Mack, General, 66
Maggiore, Lake, 52
Mahmud, Sultan, 239
Maillard, Commandant, 258
Mamelukes, 43
Mannheim, 195 ; Prussians take redoubt at, 196
Marlborough, H.M.S., 131
Marmont, Marshal, 184
Mayence, 159, 187, 194, 195, 196; siege of, 197–201 ; surrender of, 200
Masséna, 140, 142–3
Meissen, 178
Metz, 286
Milan, 48 ; Napoleon's entry and coronation, 49–52
Moniteur, Le, 246–7
Montaigne, prison of, in July revolution, 254, 256, 263–5
Mont Cenis, 47, 53
Morbihan, Prussians in, 213
Moreau, General, death of, 174
Moulins, 31
Munich, 67–70
Murat, 50, 59

Nancy, in garrison at, 229
Napoleon, 18–19 ; proclaimed Emperor, 30, 35–6 ; coronation of, 38–40, 43 ; coronation as King of Italy, 46, 49–50, 51 ; at Strasbourg, 56–8 ; in the field, 64–7 ; before Vienna, 71 ; at Austerlitz, 74–9 ; at Jena, 87–8 ; at Berlin, 89, 92–3 ; at Warsaw, 96, 97 ; at Eylau, 102–3, 106–7 ; tastes Barrès' bread, 106–

7 ; at Heilsberg, 108–9 ; at Tilsit, 113–15 ; at Bautzen, 166 ; at Leipzic, 186 ; news of his abdication, 199 ; on St. Helena, 227–8, 244
Napoléon, Prince Louis-, 297
National Guards in July revolution, 202, 263 ; reviewed by Louis-Philippe, 277–8
Nemours, 32
Neudorf, 169–70
Neuf-Brisach, 126
Neufchâtel, Prince of, 97, 194
Ney, Marshal, 63, 184
Nobles, arrogance of, in 1815, 16
Nordlingen, 59

O'Mahony, Colonel, 222
O'Neill, Major, 213, 233
Oppenheim, 194
Orléans family, the, on accession of Louis-Philippe, 276
Osterode, 104–5

Pailhès, Abbé, 27
Palais-Royal, the, 41, 204, 242, 247
Panthéon, Place du, Barrès holds the, 249
Paravagna, 31
Parquin, Commandant, 297
Paris, Barrès arrives in, 32–3 ; leaves, 42 ; returns to, 53 ; leaves for German campaign, 55 ; return of army to, 119 ; army fêted, 121–3 ; an errand in, 159 ; Barrès returns to, 204 ; in July 1830, 268–9 ; strolls in, 280–4
Pavette, Colonel, 141
Pegau, 163
Peninsular campaign, *see* Spain, Portugal
Perregaux, Colonel, 233, 273, 284
Pig, incident of a, 86
Plaine de Grenelle, review in, 240–1

Poiret, 158
Poland, French enter, 93
Polignac ministry, 237, 241–2, 249
Polish campaign, 93
Ponte de Mugen, 148
Port, salvage of, 131–2
Portugal, campaign in, 142–58
Posen, 93
Promotions in the army, 82, 117, 118 ; Barrès promoted, 123–4
Provisional Government of July, 268
Prussia, campaign against, 83
Purging of army, 206, 210, 212–13

Quentin, General, 128, 132–3
Quiberon, 127

Ragusa, Duc de, 172
Regnier, Comte, 146
Rennes, 126–7
Restoration, the first, 202
Restoration, the second, 212
Revolution of 1830, 246
Revolution of 1832, 299–300
Rhine, the, 55, 192, 193
Roguet, Comte, 271
Romana, Marquis de la, 118
Rome, King of, news of birth of, 156
Romeuf, General, absurd behaviour of, 219–20
Rouchon, Ulysse, 27
Roulland, General, 129
Rousset, General, 108
Rueil, 80–3
Russian infantrymen, quarrel with, 202
Russians on the Danube, 70 ; disaster to, at Austerlitz, 77 ; campaign against, 93

Saale, crossing the, 187
Saalfeld, battle of, 85

Saint-Cloud, 81, 235
Saint-Luc, d'Espinay, 239–40
Saint-Mihiel, Dances of, 228–9
Saint-Omer, 227
Salamanca, 140
Saxons desert the French, 183–4
Schildeck, 104
Schleitz, 85
Schönbrunn, 72, 80
Sémélé, General, 199, 295
Sens, 45
Sentries, behaviour of, 62
Septembriseur, a, 130
Serdao, Pass of, 143–4
Simplon, the, 53
Sgaisgirren, 111
Skirmishers of the Guard, 29, 34–5, 44, 45, 57, 118
Soulis, General, 54, 108, 124–5
Soult, Marshal, 43, 76, 295, 297
Spain, departure for, 134
Steamboats run to English coast, 227
Stendhal, 20
Stockerau, 73
Storm, a great, 130–1
Strasbourg, 56–8 ; Louis-Philippe ordained in, 291–3 ; insurrection in, 296–8, 301–2
Strasiedel, battle of, 161
Suicide before action, 160 ; a painful, 188
Swiss Guard, 262

Tagus, banks of the, 145
Tancos, 149, 150
Taya, crossing the, 73
Terror, the white, 214–18
Tilsit, negotiations, etc., at, 111–15
Torgau, blockade of, 178–9
Tour d'Auvergne, La, " the first Grenadier," 60
Tournilhac, 38
Treasury of army, 80 ; of Guard, captured, 192

Tricolour relinquished, 200 ; restored, 259
Tuileries, reviews at, 43
Turin, 48
Typhus in Mayence, 197–8

Ulm, 39, 63, 64, 66

Vandamme, General, 176
Vélites, see Skirmishers
Vendôme column, 282
Vermin, 135
Vienna, entry into, 71–3, 79 ; frozen, 96

Villafranca, 145–8
Vistula, the, 93 ; crossing the, 94

War, Barrès' opinion of, 55, 62
Warsaw, capture of, 93–6
Warsaw, Bishop of, 96
Wellington, Duke of, 143
Wine, effects of, 73
Wounded, after Jena, 89 ; at Haff, 98 ; at Friedland, 110

Zezer, crossing the, 150
Zinnwald, battle of, 174

PRINTED BY UNWIN BROTHERS, LIMITED, LONDON AND WOKING, GREAT BRITAIN

Redwood Library

SELECTIONS FROM THE RULES

1. Three volumes may be taken at a time and only three on one share. Two unbound numbers of a monthly and three numbers of a weekly publication are counted as a volume.

2. Books other than 7-day and 14-day ones may be kept out 28 days. **Books cannot be renewed or transferred.**

3. Books overdue are subject to a fine of one cent a day for fourteen days, **and five cents a day for each day thereafter.**

4. Neglect to pay the fine will debar from the use of the Library.

5. No book is to be lent out of the house of the person to whom it is charged.

6. Any person who shall soil (deface) or damage or lose a book belonging to the Library shall be liable to such fine as the Directors may impose; or shall pay the value of the book or of the set, if it be a part of a set, as the Directors may elect. All scribbling or any marking or writing whatever, folding or turning down the leaves, as well as cutting or tearing any matter from a book belonging to the Library, will be considered defacement and damage.